Studies in Indian Public Finance

Endorsement

Prof. Govinda Rao has produced a truly comprehensive book on India's Public Finance. It covers every aspect of Public Finance from taxation to expenditure, and to fiscal deficit, sustainable debt and fiscal federalism. Rigorous Analysis supported by relevant data is the hallmark of the book. For policymakers at all levels, this must be a compulsory reading.

Dr. C. Rangarajan
Former Chairman, Economic Advisory Council to the Prime Minister &
Former Governor, RBI
Chairman, Madras School of Economics

Studies in Indian Public Finance is a comprehensive, contemporary and insightful account of theory and global practices with focus on Indian fiscal issues in a broader political economy perspective. Undoubtedly a reference book for scholars, financial market participants and policy practitioners.

Dr. Y. Venugopal Reddy.
Former Governor, Reserve Bank of India &
Chairman, Fourteenth Finance Commission

Arguably, Govinda Rao is the foremost living expert on India's public finances. Few economists can match his ability to combine theory and practice of public finance as applied to India. In this comprehensive text, he offers a definitive treatment of India's tax and expenditure policies and their implications for growth, stability and equity. It promises to become the 'go to' text for commentators, policy makers, researchers and students of Indian public finance for many years to come.

Dr. Arvind Panagariya,
Professor of Economics and the
Jagdish Bhagwati Professor of Indian Political Economy
Columbia University, New York. U. S. A.

Studies in Indian Public Finance

M. GOVINDA RAO

OXFORD
UNIVERSITY PRESS

OXFORD
UNIVERSITY PRESS

Great Clarendon Street, Oxford, ox2 6dp,
United Kingdom

Oxford University Press is a department of the University of Oxford.
It furthers the University's objective of excellence in research, scholarship,
and education by publishing worldwide. Oxford is a registered trade mark of
Oxford University Press in the UK and in certain other countries

First Edition published in 2022

Published in the United States of America by Oxford University Press
198 Madison Avenue, New York, NY 10016, United States of America

British Library Cataloguing in Publication Data

Data available

Library of Congress Control Number: 2022931293

ISBN 978–0–19–284960–1

DOI: 10.1093/oso/9780192849601.001.0001

Dedicated to the memory of my mother Krishnaveni, who was not fortunate to be schooled but wanted her children to study and achieve.

Preface

The issues in public finance have dominated the discussion in Indian policy space and yet, it is hard to find a book critically reviewing Indian experience in tax policy and reforms, public spending, deficits and debt, and intergovernmental finance. During the seven and a half decades following independence of the country, the instruments of public finance have evolved to serve changing economic strategy and environment. During the first four decades, tax and expenditure policies were designed to mobilize resources for public sector dominated, heavy industry based import-substituting development strategy. Besides, rising inequalities arising from oligopolistic market structure (partly due to the licence–permit raj) was to be corrected through extortionary taxation. Drawing up investment plans beyond the availability of resources to finance them meant financing the large public investments through borrowing and as the availability of savings was limited, through monetization. Besides raising questions about sustainability, this posed risks to macroeconomic stability and episodes of inflation from time to time.

While liberalizing economic reforms have tried to break away from the autarchic economic regime, the problems of low revenue productivity of the tax system and rising expenditures on wages and salaries, interest payments and subsidies, and transfers have continued to plague. These have resulted in spiking deficits and accumulation of debt to unsustainable levels. The problem has continued largely because of the legacy of thinking that the government is a social guardian who can do no wrong and hence should foray into even activities in which it has no expertise to undertake, and the markets are cruel Shylocks whose activities should be closely monitored. Unfortunately, the experience has shown that the government is not a benevolent entity and the agents of the government focus on maximizing their own welfare rather than the welfare of the people. The actions are dictated by getting re-elected.

Of course, governments are necessary to intervene when the markets fail and not to replace the markets. The nature of intervention should depend upon the nature of market failure. It is in the provision of public services (which Richard Musgrave calls 'social goods') that governments will have important roles and the subject of public finance assumes relevance. In the case of market failures due to asymmetric information or oligopolistic markets, the role of the governments is to ensure free flow of information or regulating the markets and not getting involved in the production, or prevent predatory competition and promote fair competition. Unfortunately, even after the liberalizing reforms, the assumption that the government is the saviour for all our problems continues and often this can lead to Government failures.

This book analyses the experience of calibrating public finance policies in India. It begins with the role of the State, goes on to analyse public expenditures keeping in view the demographic trends and examines the sources of financing the expenditures—taxes, user charges, and borrowing. The problem of intergenerational equity due to unsustainable deficits and debt and the mechanisms to enforce discipline by ensuring comprehensiveness and accountable systems of rule-based fiscal policy calibration are analysed. This is followed by the analysis of the complexities in providing public services in India's multilevel fiscal system. These are issues in public finances during normal times. The COVID-19 pandemic has thrown formidable new challenges. Meeting these challenges and preparing the ground for recovery too need a detailed analysis. The pandemic is still unfolding, and public finance instruments will have to be deployed not only to protect the lives and livelihoods and to revive the economy but also to chart a sustainable fiscal strategy for development in the short and medium term.

I have been planning to write this book for long. My greatest debt of gratitude goes to late Shibshankar Prasad Gupta, my teacher who introduced me to the rigours of modern public finance. After I joined the National Institute of Public Finance and Policy, Raja Chelliah was my mentor in every sense of the term; he taught me not only to understand the practical issues relevant to policy reform but also to express them in a manner intelligible to general readers. Others from whom I learnt a great deal through constant interactions on various topics include Richard Bird, Albert Breton, Wallace Oates and Mancur Olson on various topics in tax policy, public choice and fiscal federalism.

After I assumed charge as the Director in NIPFP, I introduced one month-long refresher Course every year in 'Public Finance: Theory and Practice', to the teachers from colleges and universities from all parts of India during summer vacations. The objective was to expose them to practical aspects of public finance and trigger their interest on the subject, help them improve teaching and research on the subject. They were also empowered to make critical analysis of State budgets. The programme was conducted for 8 years, and I personally took interest in interacting with the teachers. Many of them have continued to interact with me. I would like to thank them for their continued interest.

During the last 5 years, I have been invited to deliver lectures on various topics in public finance at the Centre for Public Policy, IIM Bangalore, and Takshashila Institution. Thanks are due to Arnab Mukherji and M. S Sriram from IIM Bangalore and Mr. Nitin Pai from Takshashila Institution. Professor K. L. Krishna invited me to deliver the Foundation Day Lecture at the Madras Institute of Development Studies where he was the Chairman and I delivered a lecture on 'Public Finance in India: Equity, Efficiency and Political Economy'. This provided me an opportunity to structure my thinking on the book. The first I. S. Gulati Memorial Lecture at the Gulati Institute of Finance and Taxation at Trivandrum on 'Goods and Services Tax: Is it a Gorilla, Chimpanzee or a Genus Like Primate', helped me to explore the subject from the perspective of international experiences. I am grateful to Thomas Isaac, the former Finance Minister of Kerala for the invitation. The invitation by Deepak and Neera Raj Centre in Indian Economic Policies, School of International and Public Affairs, Columbia University to write and present the paper on 'Goods and Services Tax in India: Progress, Performance and Prospects' in the Indian Economic Summit in 2019 provided me an opportunity to explore the GST implementation issues in greater detail which forms a separate chapter in the book. Grateful thanks are due to Arvind Panagariya for the invitation. The chapter on intergovernmental transfers in the book also draws from the report prepared for the NITI Aayog on 'Central Transfers to States in India: Rewarding Performance While Ensuring Equity'. Some of the issues discussed in the book have been developed from the ideas first presented in the monthly columns in Business Standard (2006–2010) and

Financial Express (2010–2012 and 2014–2020) and thanks are due to T. N. Ninan and Sunil Jain, the editors of the two newspapers.

I have had wide ranging discussions on the public finance issues with a number of friends and some have gone through various chapters. These include C. Rangarajan, Viral Acharya, Arvind Panagariya, Y. V. Reddy, and Pinaki Chakraborty. I have also used my young colleagues at the Taskshashila Institution as sounding boards on a number of issues discussed in the book. I am grateful particularly to Nitin Pai and Pranay Kotasthane for allowing me to bother them from time to time. H. K. Amar Nath of NIPFP helped me with some of the data used in the book.

It is not the person who works on the book who bears the burden, but the members of family who have to put up with the elusiveness and eccentricities of the writer. I am grateful to my wife, Devaki, and children, Sunil and Sneha, and their respective spouses, Parul Mehta and Venkatesh Kulkarni and even more, my grandchildren, Sahana, Samhita, and Zara for their forbearance. Of course, when you come to the end of a venture, you feel that much more remains to be done and I alone am responsible for this feeling and for other shortcomings.

—M. Govinda Rao

Contents

Figures

Tables

Abbreviations

ASER	Annual Status of Education Report
AWP&B	Annual Work Programme and Budget
BSNL	Bharat Sanchar Nigam Limited
C&AG	Comptroller and Auditor General
CBDT	Central Board of Direct Taxes
CBEC	Central Board of Excise and Customs
CBIT	Central Board of Indirect Taxes
CENVAT	Central Value Added Tax
CGA	Controller General of Accounts
CGST	Central Goods and Services Tax
COVID-19	Coronavirus Disease 2019
DPEP	District Primary Education Programme
EAG	Empowered Action Group
EU	European Union
EWS	Economically Weaker Section
FCI	Food Corporation of India
FRBM	Fiscal Responsibility and Budget Management
GCS	General Category States
GDP	Gross Domestic Product
GNP	Gross National Product
GSDP	Gross State Domestic Product
GST	Goods and Services Tax
GSTN	Goods and Services Tax Network
GVA	Gross Value Added
HSN	Harmonized System of Nomenclature
HST	Harmonized Sales Tax
IFI	Independent Fiscal Institution
IGST	Inter-state GST
IL&FS	Infrastructure Leasing and Finance Limited
IMF	International Monetary Fund
IMR	Infant Mortality Rate
IRFC	Indian Railway Finance Corporation
IT	Income Tax
ITC	Input Tax credit
LIC	Life Insurance Corporation
LTIF	Long Term Irrigation Fund

MAT	Minimum Alternative Tax
MGNREGA	Mahatma Gandhi National Rural Employment Guarantee
MINL	Mahanagar Telephone Nigam Limited
MIS	Management Information System
MPF	Market Promoting Federalism
MTFP	Medium Term Fiscal Plan
NABARD	National Bank for Agriculture and Rural Development
NBFC	Non-Banking Finance Company
NFHS	National Family Health Survey
NHM	National Health Mission
NIPFP	National Institute of Public Finance and Policy
NOFSA	No one size fits all
NPCC	National Programme Coordination Committee
NRHM	National Rural Health Mission
OBB	Operation Black Board
OECD	Organisation of Economic Co-operation and Development
PFC	Power Finance Corporation
PIP	Programme Implementation Plans
PPP	Purchasing Power Parity
PSB	Public Sector Banks
RBI	Reserve Bank of India
RCEP	Regional Cooperation and Economic Partnership
REC	Rural Electrification Corporation
RTE	Right to Education
SC	Scheduled Caste
SCS	Special category states
SGRY	Sampoorna Grameen Rozgar Yojana
SGST	State Goods and Services Tax
SKP	Shiksha Karmi Project
SSA	Sarva Shiksha Abhiyan
ST	Scheduled Tribe
TIN	Tax Information Network
TRU	Tax Research Unit
UDAY	Ujwala Discom Assurance Yojana
UK	United Kingdom
UN	United Nations
USA	United States of America
UTGST	Union Territory Goods and Services Tax
VAT	Value Added Tax
WTO	World Trade Organization

1

Studies in Indian Public Finance

An Overview

A wise and frugal Government which shall restrain men from injuring one another, which shall leave them otherwise free to regulate their own pursuits of industry and improvement, and shall not take from the mouth of labor the bread it has earned. This is the sum of good government, and this is necessary to close the circle of our own felicities.

—Thomas Jefferson, 1st Inaugural, 1801,
Memorial Edition; 3:320

1.1. Introduction

The subject of public finance deals with public spending and its financing. It begins with the question of the role of the State, what it should do, how its functions should be financed and what are its effects on efficiency, growth, stability, and equity. The State exists to further the common interests of its citizens. The pursuit of common economic interest of the citizens requires an organization which has the powers to provide, regulate, and coerce. The subject has been studied for long. Even in *Arthashastra*, a treatise believed to have been written over 2300 years ago, Kautilya devoted a chapter on, 'treasury, sources of revenue, accounts and audit'. Governments do exist, whether they are considered as omniscient, selfless, benevolent social guardians armed with perfect information and knowledge to maximize the welfare of the people or malevolent institutions furthering the interest of its own agents and special interest groups constraining the freedom of the individuals is a debate that remains yet to

Studies in Indian Public Finance. M. Govinda Rao, Oxford University Press. © Oxford University Press 2022.
DOI: 10.1093/oso/9780192849601.003.0001

be settled. The consensus on what should be the role of the government to improve the welfare of the citizens has continued to elude. Nevertheless, governments exist, and they have to be financed.

The role of the government determines the functions undertaken by it. The provision of various services and the methods of financing them have varied consequences on the macroeconomy such as employment, incomes, and prices and microeconomic variables like relative prices impacting on the allocation of resources. The simple fact is that the markets cannot provide collective goods and services required by the people. In the absence of these basic 'public goods', markets cannot function. Such collective goods are 'non-rival' in consumption and non-excludable. As no person can be excluded from their benefits, this encourages the people to 'free-ride'. Since people will not reveal preferences for such goods, markets will not provide them. The provision of these goods requires collective action. In small groups, it may be possible to provide such collective goods through voluntary action by identifying the beneficiaries and making them pay for such goods and services. However, in large communities, voluntary action fails, and organized collective action is needed to determine the quantum of such goods to be provided and coerce people to pay for the provision of such goods through taxes.

The basic public goods which the markets cannot provide include protection of life and property of the people, formulation of rules for markets to function and enforce regulation to ensure fair competition and enforce contracts without which there will not be any incentive to save, invest, and grow. In developing societies, the governments have to address the issue of missing markets and correct imperfections to ensure that the markets function to ensure fair competition. It has to intervene to deal with the problems arising from information asymmetry and enable people to take informed decisions. It may have to intervene when the social benefits in the provision of a good or a service are much larger than the private benefits to ensure that the service in question is not underprovided. Most importantly, the governments have a major role in ensuring the socially desired state of distribution as the markets fail to redistribute incomes and wealth. It is also important to note that the method and quality of interventions by the government itself has implications for market incentives and distortions and, therefore, careful calibration of interventions is needed.

The economic role of the State has undergone tremendous change worldwide. The focus of the government in the 19th century was largely limited to the provision of public goods like defence and internal security and the required level of infrastructure required to expand their power of influence. In the 20th century, public perception of economic role of the State started changing. The democratic governments had to widen the economic role of the State to include socio-economic and redistributive agenda under pressure from the citizens. The Great Depression and the influence of Keynesian economics legitimized the expansion of the governments and the activist State in economic policy interventions became a fashion in the 1950s when many developing countries like India emerging from centuries of colonial rule wanted to improve the living conditions of its people. However, the increased public spending had to be financed by higher taxation or borrowing, which raised questions on their economic consequences. With public choice theorists raising concerns about the larger State impinging on the freedom of private enterprise, questions have been raised about the opportunity cost of State intervention in general and public spending in particular. Raising additional resources through taxation have become more and more difficult due to what Tanzi (2001) calls 'termites of the State' placing severe constraints on increasing the tax-GDP ratios. The termites emerge from the tax abuse through wilful avoidance and evasion of the tax facilitated by technological advances through digital and e-commerce companies, swift financial transactions escaping the scrutiny of the regulators, and emergence of multiple low-tax jurisdictions and tax havens.

This book is an attempt to analyse public finance policy in India in terms of its history and macroeconomic and microeconomic impacts. Unfortunately, there is no comprehensive book analysing the public finance policies in Indian context, and most of the analysis on some specific aspects of public finance have to be drawn from the Economic Surveys published by the Ministry of Finance presented along with annual budgets or some academic articles on specific aspects of public finance (Rao, 2018) or in the edited works on various aspects of public finance. This book is an attempt to fill this gap through a unified treatment of the issues relating to public spending, its financing through taxes and borrowing and its consequences. Given the largeness of the country and demarcation of the fiscal domains between the Union and the States, the issues of sharing of resources, overlapping fiscal domains, and other intergovernmental relationships also become a part of the study of Indian public finance. The book also deals with the impact of the most devastating pandemic of the century, government's response to the crisis and the implications for the medium term.

1.2. Some Reflections on Indian Public Finance: Important Messages

The important messages in the book are: (i) It is important to analyse State intervention through the prism of opportunity cost without ideological predilections; (ii) the State needs to intervene when the markets fail and areas of market failure in developing country like India with a large proportion of young population, and with features like missing markets and asymmetric information may be wider; (iii) more interventions do not necessarily entail increased public spending. Public expenditure is required only when the market failure requires public provision of services, redistribution, or for macro-stabilization. In other words, the nature of State intervention will depend upon the nature of market failure. (iv) The State interventions are beneficial to the population if it is complimentary to and improves the functioning of the markets. The objective of the intervention should not be to compete with or to replace the markets or to constrain the market development. (v) Considering the demographic profile of India, the State has a very important role in human development, which is critical from the viewpoint of enhancing productivity and improving income distribution; (vi) technological changes have substantially changed the areas of market failure and the ways in which the government needs to intervene. This calls for a periodic review of the role of the governments. Most activities which were once advocated for government provision for reasons of natural monopolies no longer require public provision as technology has made it possible to have decentralized provision as is seen in the case of telecom, electricity distribution, and even running of railways. Technological changes have narrowed the scope of public provision, expanded the scope of co-provision with the private sector (through public–private partnerships), and regulation requiring different capacity in terms of knowledge and skills by governments. (vii) Provision of public services does not require the government to produce the inputs needed. It can buy such inputs from the market and provide the intended service. (viii) The focus of the government in providing public services should be on achieving the outcomes rather than purchasing inputs. This implies that productivity is as important (if not more) as the volume of public spending. (ix) High mobility of capital and capital embodied in labour and increased international competition to attract them have dented the ability of the tax system to bring about significant reduction in inequality. The implicit incentive to evade taxes when the marginal tax rates are high has led to levying the taxes at reduced marginal tax rates. Thus, over the years, the focus of tax policy has shifted more to minimizing administrative, compliance, and distortion costs and the burden of ensuring equity or reducing inequality has substantially shifted to the public spending side of the budgets. This implies that the focus on the direction of benefits and productivity in public spending are extremely important to ensure equity. (x) The electoral politics tends to reduce the time horizon in policymaking. The focus on the short-term political gains results in inherent instability in calibrating fiscal policy and often the burden of financing expanding expenditure requirements is pushed to the unenfranchised next generation through borrowing. Therefore, it is important to ensure stability and sustainability in public finance which not only requires understanding of the impact of borrowing by the government on the cost of borrowing of the rest of the economy but also to ensure that the social productivity in public spending is at least as high as the rest of the economy. (xi) It is important to take into account both direct and indirect effect of financing public expenditures from borrowed funds. Borrowing by the government by resorting to financial repression can result in serious disincentives and distortions and can create hurdles in regulating the financial sector (Acharya, 2020). (xii) As against market failure requiring government intervention, it is important to create systems and institutions to safeguard against the government failure. These are only some of the messages that emerge from the analysis of various aspects of public finance.

The size and pattern of public expenditures and the sources and methods of financing them impact on the lives of people and businesses in a variety of ways. The spending has to be financed by either taxes or charging fees and selling assets or by borrowing and each of these methods has different economic consequences. Right from the cradle to the grave, governments, through their programmes of spending and financing them, impact on people's lives. By drawing resources from the people to finance the public goods and services, they impact on their disposable incomes, savings and investment, and overall level of economic activity, income, and employment. We want the governments to protect our lives, ensure property rights, enforce contracts to create enabling conditions for the markets to function, ensure adequate provision of services with significant externalities, undertake measures to contain negative externalities, redistribute incomes to lift the people from the morass of poverty and regulate the markets to make them act fairly. At the same time, we need the governments that promote businesses and not replace them. It is the businesses that generate economic activity and productively employ the workforce. Thus, the subject of public finance has both macro level and micro level implications, and it is necessary to understand its various aspects to calibrate economic policies.

Despite its importance, the study of public finance has not received the attention it deserves in India. Much of the discussions on the various aspects of public finance are based on impressions and opinions and not on analytical reasoning. In fact, there is considerable noise and 'festivity' around the presentation of the budget by the Union government and opinions are expressed on the appropriateness of taxes and adequacy of spending on various sectors even as we know that almost 70 per cent of the public expenditures is incurred at the State level. Similarly, most observations on tax policy are simply 'opinions' and not based on received theories or best practice approaches. Often, a claim is made that indirect taxes are distortionary because they distort the choice between taxed and untaxed goods and services. But income taxes too distort the choices between income and leisure. There are arguments that corporate incomes must be taxed at high rates for equity reason. However, as capital is internationally mobile, in open economies, high taxes may cause the flight of capital resulting in loss of employment as it might drive the corporations out of the country. In such a case, the tax on capital may actually turn out to be a tax on labour (Harberger, 1962). Despite a lot of focus on reducing inequalities of income and wealth through taxation, the impact of tax policies in reducing inequalities has been found to be negligible. Reducing inequality is important and focus on human development through universal education, health coverage, and skill development can be better instruments to reduce inequality and poverty. In India, the focus of public finance has often been the Central government's fiscal operations ignoring the fact that India is a Union of States, and their respective roles are specified in the Constitution and the States are significant players raising about 38 per cent of revenues and implementing 58 per cent of total expenditures.

There are very few comprehensive analytical studies on various aspects of public finance in India. This book is an attempt to present an overview of Indian public finance and analyse some of its specific aspects. Hopefully, the book will kindle greater interest among the students and scholars to explore the subject in greater depth and bring out fresh insights into this much neglected branch of Indian Economics and help the policymakers in undertaking reasoned and considered policy decisions.

1.3. Market Failure and Government Intervention

The analysis of public finance begins with the role of the State versus the markets. A competitive market is supposed to ensure Pareto efficient allocation of resources in the sense that no one can be made better off without someone else being made worse off. However, there can be several instances of the failure of the markets to bring about efficient allocation of resources and in such cases, Government intervention becomes necessary. Of course, not all market failures are addressed by spending and raising resources. It is important to first understand the nature of the market failure and then design and implement the right type of intervention needed. Even in providing such goods and services, it is not necessary that Governments should produce them. If private sector can provide such services more efficiently, the targeted people can be given cash vouchers to choose their purchase from alternative providers.[1]

[1] Kingdom and Panagariya argue for giving cash vouchers to the parents of the school-going children so that they can educate their child in better private schools rather than sending them to poorly run government schools. Similar arguments for giving cash vouchers for the poor

It is also well known that markets fail to bring about socially desired distribution of incomes and governments will have to undertake redistribution. Market failures arising from asymmetric information, missing markets, and uneven distribution of market power resulting in predatory competition will have to be addressed through setting rules and regulations and implementing them. Therefore, governments will have to assess the type of market failure, nature of intervention required to address the failure, and create enough capacity to implement the interventions. There are also other types of State interventions such as of ensuring access to information and regulating the functioning of the market to ensure fair competition and these do not necessarily entail the budgetary operations.

Thus, the subject of public finance deals with the processes and effects of raising revenues and incurring expenditures by the government for providing the services not provided by the market.[2] Provision of public services is called for when the markets fail to provide them or when the markets do not provide them in required quantity. The interventions to prevent predatory competition or to promote efficient competition or those intended to overcome asymmetric information in the market require regulation. The intervention can take the form of public provision, subsidization or tax concessions, or regulation. It is also important to realize that public provision does not mean public production. The government can procure the goods and services from the market and provide them or provide vouchers to the targeted people to purchase such goods and services from the market.

In this book, an attempt is made to provide an overview based on the studies done on various aspects of public finance in India. The attempt is to undertake a positive analysis of government finance in raising revenues and spending. Until 1991, India pursued the public sector

can be made for availing healthcare or even rations in the public distribution system. See Geeta Gandhi Kingdom and Arvind Panagariya (2020), 'Heart of the Problem: NEP 2020 charts new road map, but fails to make public schoolteachers accountable'. https://timesofindia.indiatimes.com/blogs/toi-edit-page/heart-of-the-problem-nep-2020-charts-new-road-map-but-fails-to-make-public-schoolteachers-accountable/.

[2] This is also called fiscal policy. 'Fiscal' is a Latin word meaning treasury and the policies which are calibrated through the operation of treasury is called fiscal policy.

dominated, heavy industry based, import substituting planned development strategy. However, since then, the role has been evolving though the vestiges of the past strategy continue to understand the level and patterns of public spending and its implications. It is important to trace these developments to analyse the role of public spending have evolved over the years to accommodate the requirements of the private businesses to promote stable, sustainable, and inclusive development of the country. It is hoped that the study will be useful to the students in their pursuit at understanding the issues of allocation of resources between the government and the private sector. Hopefully, the scholars will find it a useful starting point for further in-depth pursuits into research in various aspects of public finance. Similarly, it is hoped that the policymakers will find the analysis useful in designing and implementing various instruments of public finance.

In any case, the role of the government is determined through the political process and the role of the analyst is to bring out the consequences of these actions. The conclusions on the feasibility or successes and failures will have to be drawn on the basis of opportunity costs and counterfactuals. The areas of market failure are large in a developing country like India and, therefore, the government will have an important role in providing public and merit goods as well as in undertaking redistribution. It is important to find solutions to government failure as well and it is in this regard, public finance specialists will have to subject government finances to detailed scrutiny.

Once the contours of public finance are defined by the role of the government, the issue of raising resources becomes important. Public goods are 'non-rival' in consumption and 'non-excludable' and the difficulty in revealing preferences for them makes the determination of market price impossible. These characteristics also lead to 'free-riding'. Ensuring optimal provision of these goods is possible only when the people are forced to make compulsory payments. However, in a perfectly competitive economy, levying taxes would result in distortions. Therefore, the design and implementation issues in tax policy should aim at raising revenues by minimizing distortions. The question is, what are the essential characteristics of a good tax policy and how has India fared in designing and implementing such a policy?

1.4. Plan of the Book

The book begins with a discussion on the role of the State and its implications for public finance. The need for the government is to intervene when the markets fail. This includes provision of collective goods which the markets fail to provide, redistribute incomes which the markets do not undertake, and regulate the markets to ensure a fair conduct. The nature of market failure determines the nature of intervention by the State and choice of the intervention is critical in determining its effectiveness. It is in the provision of public services in which the markets fail, the instruments of public finance namely, public spending and the methods of financing are deployed.

In Indian context, historically, public spending policy has evolved in the backdrop of planned development strategy. On the expenditure side, in India, the planned development strategy required expanded role of the government. The important issue to be analysed is whether the level and composition of public spending is in line with the objective of maximizing welfare of the people by accelerating development. At the same time, the positive analysis of public expenditures should analyse the influence of special interest groups in determining the size and composition of expenditures. Public expenditures get impacted by 'political budget cycles'. There are conflicting factors at work—the expenditures that bring in short-term political gains versus those that impact on long-term development.

Ensuring macroeconomic stabilization is an important function of the government. The focus on macroeconomic management received focus after Lord Keynes showed that full employment is not a given when there are downward inflexibilities in interest rates and wage rates. It brought out the role of the government in maintaining the level of economic activity to fully employ the resources in the economy and to even out cyclical fluctuations. However, this also provided the scope for massive expansion of budgets financed through deficits resulting in the building up of indebtedness. The Keynesian argument was extended to claim that internal public debt did not entail any burden on the future generation as it was only the transfer of income from taxpayers to bond holders until James Buchanan in his seminal book *Public Principles of Public Debt* showed that there is an opportunity cost of borrowed funds and when these funds are not used to generate the return from efficient alternative use, it entails a burden on the future generation. Therefore, there is no difference between private or public debt or internal or external debt. The issue of debt sustainability and stability has become important as financing expenditures by borrowing often leads to crowding out private investment by drafting in overwhelming proportion of available savings for public spending and accumulation of debt pre-empted large portions of revenues for interest payments. Furthermore, unless the borrowed funds are used for generating income yielding assets intergenerational equity concerns arise. This has underlined the need for creating systems and institutions of checks and balances in terms of setting fiscal rules and monitoring to ensure that the governments do not borrow to unsustainable levels.

How should public services be delivered in large and heterogeneous countries with diverse preferences? Providing public services to cater to diverse preferences takes us into the realm of fiscal federalism. The first-generation theories elaborated on the welfare gains from fiscal decentralization and the second-generation theories argued for decentralization from the point of view of accountability. The implementable rules of fiscal decentralization deal with the issue of assignment of tax powers and expenditure functions, mechanism to deal with overlapping assignments. Although the 'Wicksellian' principle requires matching revenue–expenditure decisions at the margin, assignment according to comparative advantage necessarily results in the mismatch between revenue powers and expenditure functions and therefore, intergovernmental transfers become unavoidable. Thus, while the general purpose transfers are needed to 'enable' the states to provide comparable levels of public services assigned to them at comparable tax rates, the rationale for specific purpose transfers is to 'ensure' a normatively given minimum standard in respect of specified services that are considered meritorious or those having high degree of externalities. It is important to analyse the system of assignments, mechanisms to deal with overlapping assignments, promoting cooperation and regulate competition among the states and the design and implementation issues pertaining to intergovernmental transfers.

The book is planned to present the story of public finance in a sequential manner. The second chapter makes a more detailed exposition of the role of the state vis-à-vis the market. This helps us to define the contours of government intervention and its implementation through budgetary actions. It will also help in putting the debates on the normative and positive aspects of public finance in perspective. This is followed by the analysis of public expenditure trends and their allocative and technical efficiency aspects in Chapter 3. With the children in the age group of 0–14 constituting 35.4 per cent of the population, it is important to focus expenditures on items that would empower this group to reap the gains from demographic dividend. Failure to do so could result in demographic disaster instead of dividends. The detailed analysis of tax design and reform is discussed in Chapter 4. The chapter brings out the theoretical underpinnings of optimal taxation, and keeping the best practise approach in the background, reviews the trends in tax policy and reforms. The cross-country empirical analysis shows that the tax-GDP ratio in India is low by international standards and the reasons for this are analysed and reform issues brought out. The recent reform of the implementation of Goods and Services Tax (GST) is discussed in Chapter 5. The reform is characterized as the reform of the century and will lead to a 'good and simple tax' but is still evolving and requires further reforms until the revenue and efficiency gains from the reform are achieved. This is followed by the analysis of deficits and debt at Union and State levels and the role of rule-based fiscal policy is discussed in Chapter 6. Besides analysing intergenerational equity aspects, the chapter attempts to demonstrate the problems of credibility of budget numbers and bring out the legal and institutional mechanisms needed to enforce the rule-based fiscal policy. The analysis of Indian fiscal federalism is discussed in Chapter 7. This is followed by the chapter on intergovernmental transfers in India in Chapter 8. The last chapter is on Indian Public Finance in Pandemic times. It brings out the fiscal constraints and challenges faced by India during the unprecedented crisis caused by the Coronavirus pandemic.

2

The Contours of the State

Public Finance and Public Choice

The purpose of government is to enable the people of a nation to live in safety and happiness. Government exists for the interests of the governed, not for the governors.

—Thomas Jefferson

2.1. Why Do We Need Governments?

Almost three centuries ago, David Hume stated that the institution of government is one of the finest and most subtle inventions possible in the world to pursue common interests of individuals living in a community. The most important common interest relates to the provision of goods and services which are marked by jointness in supply and commonly required by everyone in the group. These are indivisible and no one can be excluded from their benefits and, therefore, they have to be provided through a collective action by the beneficiary groups. Resolution of these externalities is necessary to ensure optimal provision of such goods and services and improve the welfare of the community.

Thus, the critical element for collective action in the provision of public goods is externalities. Coase (1960) in his celebrated article argued that in a small community, once the property rights are clearly defined, the externalities can be resolved through bargains between the parties through voluntary action. In small communities, collective goods with limited benefit span can be provided through voluntary action. Ostrom (1985) and others have emphasized the importance of community organizations in successfully managing common property resources. However,

Studies in Indian Public Finance. M. Govinda Rao, Oxford University Press. © Oxford University Press 2022.
DOI: 10.1093/oso/9780192849601.003.0002

bargaining and coordination to resolve spillovers between different agents involve coordination and transaction costs and is subject to asymmetric information regarding costs and benefits of externality. As Olson (1965: 2) states that, unless the number of individuals in a group is small, or unless there is coercion to make individuals act in their common interest, '*rational, self-interested individuals will not act to achieve their common group interests*' (italics in the original). Thus, in large communities with diverse preferences resolving externalities through voluntary action is simply not feasible due to high organization and transaction costs and lack of enforcement mechanisms.[1] It becomes necessary for the governments to intervene and provide them. Thus, the governments must intervene when the markets fail to deliver some goods due to their benefit span (externality) and indivisible nature. Voluntary action fails when large groups are involved. Such 'public goods', by their very technical nature, are non-rival in consumption and non-excludable. The non-excludability makes revelation of preferences impossible and gives rise to 'free-riding' behaviour requiring the people to make compulsory payments (taxes) to finance them. In doing so, the government makes people to part with their entitlements for private goods.

Thus, public finance comes into play to provide public goods and finance them by collecting taxes. These goods are characterized by jointness in supply (non-rival) and infeasibility of exclusion (non-excludability). Because of this, people do not reveal their preferences for the good and voluntary action in their provision could lead to 'free-riding'. Ensuring safety and security and enforcing property rights is the classic case of public goods provision.

Mancur Olson's story of a Chinese warlord provides an interesting argument for the basic public good provision (Olson, 1993). In the early 20th century, a considerable part of China was infested with roving bandits and such a regime could not support economic growth due to lack of incentive to accumulate and uncertainty regarding life and property left no incentive for saving and investment by the people. However, Feng

[1] The small communities can be organized into collective action for provision of public goods with limited benefit span. Religious communities organize themselves for collective action for a common form of worship (Churches, temples, or mosques). A group of like-minded individuals can organize themselves into providing 'club goods'. However, collective action for providing public goods with large benefit span has to come from the state. See Olson (1965: 98).

Yu-hsiang, an enterprising warlord with exceptional bravery, defeated the much feared bandit, White Wulf, and assured to provide safety and security to the people in his jurisdiction in return for paying a share of their incomes. Thus, the first blessing of the invisible hand came into operation and this made a transition from roving banditry to stationary banditry or dictatorship replacing anarchy. The change resulted in providing the basic public good, namely, protection of life and property of the people. This created incentive for saving and investment which is a precondition for economic growth. However, the nature and quality of growth were determined by the dictator and, therefore, was not 'encompassing'. The objective function of the stationary bandit was to maximize his gain and he had no incentive in ensuring 'encompassing' development and he will not care for redistribution. Therefore, Olson concludes that only under participatory democracy encompassing growth is possible. The important point is that we need a government to provide basic public good, namely, ensuring safety and protecting their property rights. However, in a democratic society, for 'encompassing' growth, the State will have to be much more than providing merely basic public goods. It will have to undertake redistribution, ensure a stable macroeconomy, provide physical and social infrastructure needed to generate the externalities, and deal with asymmetric information.

2.2. Public Finance and Public Choice: Contrasting Views on the State

The mainstream normative public finance literature sees the government as a benevolent entity and a social guardian actively intervening to increase people's welfare. They are required to ensure the societies' desired supply of goods and services with externalities, provide those goods and services which are considered 'meritorious', redistribute incomes, ensure fair competition in the markets, create markets when they do not exist, and intervene to prevent problems arising from information asymmetry. In contrast, the Public Choice proponents do not consider governments as maximizing the welfare of the people. When the agents of the government, be it bureaucrats or politicians, maximize their own welfare, society's welfare is not maximized. Besides, they constrain the freedom of people. They are necessary in clear cases of market failures like the provision of basic collective (public) goods and redistribution. Brennan and Buchanan (1980) consider that as the governments have the monopoly power to tax, the agents of the government could expand the government to make them leviathans. Both bureaucrats and politicians may use the monopoly power to tax by the government to expand their sphere of influence to maximize their own power, income, and wealth rather than enhancing public interest.[2]

The ideas about the role of the State in the economy have been changing over the years. Adam Smith, in his *Wealth of Nations* in 1776, confined the role to the core functions of defence, protection to life and property, administration, justice, and large public works. However, over the next hundred years, there was a steady increase in State activity which led to Adolf Wagner to formulate the law of increasing state activity in 1896. According to Wagner, as democratic and progressive nations industrialize, the share of the public sector in the national economy increases faster than increase in incomes. The rising public spending is due to (i) increased social activities of the state, (ii) higher administrative and protective actions, and (iii) increase in welfare functions. Peacock and Wiseman (1961) after a detailed analysis of public expenditures in the United Kingdom during 1891–1955 formulated the 'displacement effect' hypothesis to explain step-like increases in public expenditure-GNP shares during wars and depressions. As ideas about 'tolerable burden of taxation' is always lower than those on the 'desirable level of public expenditure', many desired expenditures during normal times are held in check. However, during social upheavals like wars and depressions, ideas about tolerable burden of taxation go up to finance these contingencies and once they are over, many of the public spending programmes which were thought to be desirable but could not be implemented earlier become feasible and get executed to result in step-like movement in public expenditure-GNP ratio.

Despite steady increase on public spending over the years, much of the mainstream literature advocated limited State activity until 1926, when

[2] There was a fascinating discussion on the contrasting visions on public choice and public finance in a week-long symposium in the University of Munich in 1998 between James Buchanan who considers that an expanded government can become a leviathan and Richard Musgrave who thinks that governments do have a larger role in improving the welfare of the people by providing 'merit goods'. See Buchannan and Musgrave (1999).

Lord Keynes, in a book titled *End of Laissez Faire*, advocated expanded role of the State. The New Deal programme taken up by President Roosevelt to resurrect the economy ravaged by the Great Depression became a model, and the intellectual underpinning for that was provided by Keynes's (1936) *General Theory of Employment, Interest, and Money* which advocated an active fiscal role for the government to ensure full employment when the wages and interest rates show downward stickiness and prevent self-correcting equilibrium in labour and financial markets. The smoothening of cyclical fluctuations in economic activity and maintaining full employment require increased public spending. The 'functional finance' role advocated by Keynes created an era of activist governments. The newly independent countries, eager to accelerate development, followed the State-dominated planned development strategy.

In contrast to this, Hayek (1944) took the view that the expanded role of the State is a road to autarchy. Economic planning results in individuals losing freedom to determine their economic future. As bureaucrats and politicians taking decisions and exercise economic choices on their work, nature of economic activity, consumption, and investment, individuals are merely seen as tools of the State. The loss of economic freedom that came with planning can result in the loss of political freedom leading inevitably to the 'road to serfdom'. Thus, views on the desirable role of the State have oscillated between viewing it as a benevolent social guardian requiring an expanded turf to a malevolent institution in which the agents of the government maximize their own welfare rather than that of the people. For the latter, the State is necessary but should have a minimalist agenda. In some ways, the two views represent the normative and positive aspects of State activity.

2.3. Types of Market Failure and Government Intervention

While the role of the State continues to be a controversial area, there is full agreement on the need for the State to intervene to provide the public goods which can be called the core functions. These include protection of life, defence and internal security needed to protect the life and property of the people, ensuring property rights and enforcement of contracts. Thus, there is not much controversy about the need for government intervention in activities such as defence, internal security, judiciary, infrastructure, and science and technology. Even in the provision of these services, there is consensus that the State should not be engaged in the production of all the inputs required for the provision. It could purchase them from the market and provide them as required.

In addition to the core functions, the State has a role in ensuring a fair competition in the market and protection of people from flagrant abuse of market power. Promotion of market competition, promoting transparency, generation and dissemination of information to reduce the scope for information asymmetry, creation of markets where they do not exist are some of the other areas where the State has an important role. However, in these too, the nature of government intervention is ensuring effective regulation rather than getting into production–distribution processes.

The traditional argument attributed an important role for the State in getting into production–distribution activities in the case of natural monopolies. It was felt that lumpy investment required in the case of some industries with declining marginal cost over large volume of output gives it a monopoly status. Electricity, telecoms, railways, and airlines are some of the examples. However, the developments in technology have made it possible for the private sector to provide most of these services in a competitive environment. States' role in these cases is to ensure fair competition, and this could be done through regulation rather than getting directly involved in the production or distribution.

Another case of market failure is in incomplete markets. In developing countries, most of the markets are missing or incomplete. Often farmers have very little option than to sell their produce to the middlemen because rural markets are not connected, the middlemen form cartels and often they are forced to sell their commodities to the money lender or middlemen, or they do not wait until the produce gets a better price because they have to repay the loan contracted by the moneylender/middleman at usurious terms. Incomplete markets can also cause extreme volatility in prices which need to be stabilized. Similarly, credit and insurance market in rural areas are non-existent and if they do exist are usurious. Thus, intervention in cases of incomplete markets such as support price programmes, stabilizing farm prices, accessibility of loans at reasonable rate of interest to farmers, and loans to finance education is required.

There is a set of goods which do not strictly fall into the category of pure public goods, but the society desires that these should be provided by the government. Analytically, the choice between pure public and private goods is made by aggregating individual choices or 'social welfare function' in the Samuelson' model or though the voting mechanism as in Musgrave's (1959) construct. However, the 'merit goods' are not pure public goods; they can be provided in the market. Since they are meritorious to people's lives, it is the duty of the State to provide the desired minimum standards of these goods and services to every individual. Market failure is because individuals are unable to exercise their choice rationally in respect of these goods either because their benefits are not immediately known (education and healthcare) or these goods generate externalities resulting in social benefits (costs) exceeding (reducing) private benefits (costs) or this is the best way to achieve redistribution. However, according to public choice theorists, 'The state does not exist as an organic entity independent of the individuals in the polity. The state does not act as such, and it cannot seek its own ends or objectives' (Brennan and Buchanan, 1985: 22).

Another important area where State action is desired on the grounds of market failure is redistribution. Markets do not correct inequalities in the distribution of incomes and wealth and government intervention is necessary to bring about a socially desired state of distribution outcomes. Musgrave's formulation of the budget assumes existence of a 'desired' or 'proper' state of distribution and works on separate tax-transfer mechanism for achieving it (Musgrave, 1959). There are, however, difficulties in determining the proper state and this has to be done through a political process as the market process fails. In a democratic polity, the presumption is in favour of 'equality' but that itself can be subject to different interpretations such as equality in economic welfare or equality of opportunities. There are difficulties in making interpersonal comparisons of welfare as well.

Budgetary policy is not the only way in which distributional changes can be made. There are instruments such as the minimum wage legislation, price fixation and controls, subsidization policy, and tariff policy.

However, tax-transfer policy is considered superior as it involves minimum interference in resource allocation, unless non-neutrality itself is the objective. Thus, achieving the desired state of distribution through a progressively designed tax system with minimum adverse incentives on work, saving and investment and making direct cash transfers to the identified poor are superior to controls on prices and output and subsidizing certain commodities and services.

While the instances of market failure pointed out above require State intervention, it is important to choose the type of intervention required to deal with the market failure. Provision of public goods, merit goods, and redistribution require budgetary policies whereas issues of ensuring competition in the market, environmental protection, and information asymmetry will require effective regulation. Again, experiences have shown that the interventions should not be to replace the markets but to strengthen them to ensure fair competition. There is also an agreement on the fact that the State should not be engaged in the production of goods and services. It could purchase the required inputs for the provision of public services from the market. Credible and timely rewards and penalties do not exist in the government and in this environment, the States; involvement in the market activities would be inefficient.

2.4. Indian Development Strategy and Role of the State

Economic role of the State in independent India was circumscribed by the planned development strategy. This entailed public sector dominated, heavy industry based, import substituting industrialization, and public finance instruments were assigned a central role in this strategy. The specific objectives of fiscal policy were to raise the level of saving, particularly public saving to finance increasing levels of investments required to accelerate growth of the economy, to influence the magnitude and direction of economic activity as determined in the plans and to bring about reduction in inequalities in income and wealth.

However, questions have been raised on the effectiveness of fiscal policy in achieving the intended tasks.[3] Although there was a significant expansion of the public sector, it failed to generate the level of public savings and the resources required for investments. A considerable proportion of public sector spending had to be financed from borrowing, often from the Reserve Bank of India, and that led to large deficits and debt besides other adverse economic consequences including inflation. The emphasis on import substitution meant that production and perpetuation of inefficient production systems with low quality, high priced, non-standardized products to the consumers. Public spending failed to create physical and social infrastructure required to propel private investments to accelerate growth and reduce poverty to the desired extent. The large draft on household savings increased the cost of making investments for the private sector and automatic monetization of deficits put pressure on prices. The problem of poverty continued to persist as public finance policies did not provide competitive levels of infrastructure necessary to raise the level of economic activity required to generate productive employment and did not empower the workforce with the required human capital through education, skill development, and healthcare. The strategy was unviable and when the balance of payment situation reduced the drop in foreign exchange reserves to meet just three weeks' imports, requiring the government to physically lift gold reserves to secure forcing exchange, the market-based reforms became imperative and the State had to open up the activities for the markets to function.

Although the reforms professed to create primacy of the markets in resource allocation, the vestiges of the planned economy have continued. Most prices are still determined according to government fiat rather than through the market mechanism. The financial repression arising from the primacy of the governments in borrowing has continued. Public sector continues to occupy a predominant role in several sectors including finance. Attempts to privatize many unprofitable and non-strategic sectors have met with only limited success. The best government has been able to do is to disinvest some shares in profit-making companies

[3] For a detailed evaluation of the fiscal policy in planned development strategy, see Bagchi and Nayak (1994).

while continuing to retain the majority share and management control. Although the present Prime Minister unequivocally stated when he assumed office in 2014 that the government's business is not to be in business, there has been very little headway in disentangling. In short, there is much that needs to be done to review the role of the State to make it a catalyst in development and a promoter of efficient markets.

2.5. Concluding Remarks

The controversy over the role of the State versus Market continues to rage. Those who view the State as a social guardian or a benevolent entity maximizing the welfare of the people would like to justify the expanded role, while those who would like to contain the State to its minimalist role see it as constraining individual freedom and an instrument of political and bureaucratic capture. In some ways, this is a controversy over the normative and positive roles of the State.

The State is required to intervene when the markets fail to ensure efficient allocation of resources. The area of market failure is much more in a developing country than in mature market economies. Besides public goods and redistribution, the State also must step in when the markets are missing or incomplete. The State must intervene when there is information asymmetry. It has to also ensure efficient competition in the markets exist. Technological developments have made it possible for the State to recede in favour of the markets in the case of natural monopolies. However, technological developments have also necessitated State interventions in some cases to ensure information dissemination.

The nature of State intervention required depends on the nature of market failure. In cases of providing public goods, merit goods, and redistribution, public finance policies become relevant. In cases where intervention is called for it may be a combination of providing the public service or tax–subsidy policy when social benefits or costs exceed private benefits or costs, and enforcement of regulation. Ensuring efficient competition in the market requires regulation and not tax-expenditure programme. Even when the intervention takes the character of public spending for providing public or merit goods, it is important for the State to avoid producing the goods required for the provision. It is more efficient to procure them from the market. In undertaking redistribution, it is more efficient to have cash transfer to targeted groups rather than subsidizing certain items consumed by the poor in the interest of neutrality.

The real role of the State in any country is determined by the history. After observing the experience of the Soviet Union in leap frogging growth after the second World War, the activist role of the State in development policy among the developing countries was a fashion in the 1950s. While countries like Korea changed the course and moved from market displacing role of the government to market enforcing role to achieve fast development, India continued with dirigiste until 1991 when it became clear that resource allocation according to centralized planning is neither desirable nor feasible. However, despite market-based reforms undertaken since 1991, the vestiges of the planned development strategy have continued with dominant public sector activity and pervasiveness of price and output controls. Despite knowing the pitfalls of continuing with the dominant public sector, it has been difficult for the government to vacate activities which can legitimately be carried out by the markets mainly due to the influence of special interest groups. Thus, we have continued business presence of the government in the airlines, hotels and restaurants, telephones, textiles, drugs and pharmaceuticals, and even a travel agency generating losses year after year requiring infusion of funds from taxpayers' money.

3

Public Expenditures in India

Trends and Issues

'Economy does not lie in sparing money, but spending it wisely'
—Thomas Henry Huxley

3.1. Introduction

The volume and composition of public expenditures is determined by the role of the government in the provision of public goods, merit goods, engagement in macroeconomic management and redistribution. There are services which cannot be priced and some others for which the price charged is less than the average cost. The government must spend money in providing these services and as these cannot be priced, they have to be financed by levying taxes on people or borrowing from the market which will have to be serviced and repaid by the future taxpayers. In addition to providing these services, the government must undertake redistribution and it should have an administrative machinery for provision of services and undertaking regulation and supervision of markets.

The basic precondition required for the businesses to function is the protection of life and property and enforcement of contracts. Creating congenial business environment also requires creation of a governance system to formulate and implement rules and regulations for the working of the markets and a legal system and judiciary to formulate laws and enforce them. Thus, the first focus of the governments should be to incur expenditures to evolve an efficient system of governance comprising of responsive administration, effective force to ensure safety and security (defence and internal security), judicial mechanism to enforce property

Studies in Indian Public Finance. M. Govinda Rao, Oxford University Press. © Oxford University Press 2022.
DOI: 10.1093/oso/9780192849601.003.0003

rights and contracts swiftly. In addition, in a democratic polity, the government is required to undertake functions as required by the electorate and these require public spending.

In Indian context, in the initial years after independence, public expenditure policy had to be dovetailed to the planned development strategy. Almost two centuries (from 1757 to 1947) of colonial rule[1] were marked by prolonged stagnation as the policies were designed entirely to serve the interest of the colonial power. To resurrect the impoverished economy in independent India, the government required rapid development. Low standard of living, large mass of the poor, absence of a vibrant private sector, poor state of infrastructure, low levels of saving and investment, and pessimism on the capacity to export—all these factors warranted the adoption of planned development strategy. The government chose to adopt public sector dominated, heavy industry based, import substituting industrialization strategy to accelerate economic growth. Fiscal policy was required to play an important role in raising the level of saving and investment, redistribute incomes to reduce inequalities in income and wealth, and channelize the direction of economic activities as determined by plan priorities.[2] In a situation where public sector was required to play a dominant role, public expenditure was a key instrument to raise the level of capital formation and redistribute incomes besides providing the basic public goods. The government had to incur significant volumes of public investment in social and physical infrastructure to create generalized externalities and as the level of taxes was low, a considerable volume of investment had to be financed from borrowing not only from the market but also from the Reserve Bank of India.[3] Dissenting voices on this strategy were few and the mainstream opinion favoured this.[4] Despite making considerable progress over the last 70 years, the infrastructure deficit continues to be huge, and the volume of

[1] East India Company set its foot in India in 1612 and went on expanding its sphere of influence until 1757 when the Company rule of the country began.

[2] For a detailed discussion on the role of fiscal policy in the planning process in India, see Bagchi and Nayak (1994).

[3] Automatic monetization of the deficit by borrowing from the RBI was the accepted practice until 1997 when an agreement was signed between the Governor of the RBI and the Union Finance Secretary.

[4] B. R. Shenoy in his comments on the Second Five-Year-Plan document circulated to the group of 20 economists had warned about the dangerous macroeconomic consequences of having large plans without resources. See https://indiapolicy.org/debate/Notes/shenoy.PDF.

public investment required to build the competitive levels of physical infrastructure and social services is large.

According to the Economic Survey 2018–2019, India, with a relatively young population, promises significant demographic dividend with the proportion of working age group of population (20–59 years) peaking at 59 per cent in 2041. According to the 2011 Census, India's population in the age group of 0–14 years constitutes over 35 per cent of total population. Unless significant efforts are made in human development through investments in education and healthcare, the potential demographic dividend might turn out to be a demographic disaster. Similarly, the creation of efficient levels of physical infrastructure such as power, connectivity and transport and communication networks, irrigation, and urban infrastructure are essential for the industry to compete internationally. While a part of this can be attempted through public–private partnerships, the government has to make substantial direct spending in cases where such partnerships are infeasible.

The transformation of public outlay into outcome in terms of services is tenuous and often public spending itself is interpreted as a measure of public service delivery. Public spending only results in the purchasing of the inputs by the government, and these will have to be converted into outputs which eventually determine the outcomes. The transition from inputs to outputs depends on the productivity in transforming inputs into outputs. Productivity is determined by 'allocative efficiency' and 'technical efficiency'. Prioritizing the allocation decisions between different public goods and services as desired by the people determines allocative efficiency. Technical efficiency is achieved when different inputs (labour and other inputs) are used in optimal combinations and appropriate technology is used for delivering services.

Even when public expenditures are incurred efficiently, it may not result in the desired level of outcomes. This is because, efficiency in spending may create efficient level of outputs, not outcomes. Efficiency in outcomes is determined by a number of exogenous factors in addition to efficient outputs. For example, outcomes in education in terms of learnings are determined by a number of factors in addition to inputs like opening of new schools and spending on teachers or outputs like enrolment ratio. Improvement in health indicators like longevity of life, child, and maternal mortality rates depends not merely on efficiency in public expenditures but on many other factors. While it may not be possible for the governments to control the exogenous factors determining the outcomes in the short term, the best they can do is to ensure output efficiency and put in place the policies changing the structure of incentives and accountability towards outcome targets. Not surprisingly, many exercises evaluating public expenditure programmes emphasize transforming expenditures to outputs rather than outcomes. Sometimes, even this becomes difficult due to lack of information and the evaluations stop at measuring the input purchases. In the case of education, for example, often, achievements are shown in terms of the number of schools created and teachers appointed. Similarly, in the case of health spending, number of hospital beds created and appointment of health workers are taken as proxies for health service delivery.

3.2. Public Expenditure Trends in India

A notable feature of trends in public expenditure presented in Table 3.1 is its stability over the last three decades since 1991. The public expenditure-GDP ratio was 26.6 per cent in 1990–1991, marginally declined to 25.6 per cent in 2000–2001. Following the stimulus given during the global financial crisis in 2008–2009, the expenditure increased to 28.3 per cent in 2009–2010, but with the withdrawal of the stimulus, it declined to 26.4 per cent in the next year. It continued to fluctuate around 26 per cent until 2014–2015. However, the expenditure increased to 27.5 per cent in 2015–2016 and further to 29.3 per cent in 2016–2017 and in 2018–2019, it marginally declined to 28.3 per cent. In fact, even during the pre-reform period, particularly since the mid-1990s, the public expenditure-GDP ratio hovered around 25–26 per cent.

The trend in public expenditure brings out five important features. First, contrary to Wagner's law which states that public expenditure-GDP ratio increases with increases in per capita incomes, the ratio has remained broadly at the same level even as per capita income has increased from Rs. 27,449 in 1990–1991 (at 2011 prices) to Rs. 105,687 in 2018–2019. Despite the increase in per capita income levels, public expenditure-GDP ratios have continued to hover around 26–28 per cent. Second, the fluctuations in public expenditures do not seem to have a clear relationship with change in the parties in power. This is perhaps because

Table 3.1 Public Expenditure Trend in India: Aggregate and States' Share.

	1990–1991	2000–2001	2009–2010	2010–2011	2011–2012	2012–2013	2013–2014	2014–2015	2015–2016	2016–2017	2017–2018
Per cent of total expenditure (Centre and States) to GDP											
General services	12.13	13.81	13.84	12.87	12.91	12.41	12.79	12.79	13.85	13.76	13.51
Social services of which	5.28	5.24	6.39	6.36	6.43	6.61	6.34	5.80	5.49	6.31	6.41
Education	3.19	3.12	3.35	3.42	3.64	3.22	3.25	2.93	2.99	3.02	3.10
Healthcare	1.24	1.25	1.37	1.31	1.35	1.21	1.27	1.21	1.29	1.50	1.52
Economic services	7.34	5.61	7.45	6.51	6.05	5.69	6.99	7.58	8.95	8.23	7.94
Total expenditure	26.63	25.57	28.27	26.39	26.54	26.64	26.29	25.61	27.47	29.33	28.44
Per cent of state government expenditure to GDP											
General services	4.51	5.94	5.62	5.32	5.56	5.20	5.50	5.43	6.23	6.64	6.66
Social services of which	4.42	4.30	4.87	4.83	4.98	5.27	5.01	5.17	4.80	5.54	5.59
Education	2.68	2.61	2.48	2.55	2.59	2.49	2.57	2.62	2.68	2.86	2.82
Healthcare	0.99	1.09	1.00	0.93	0.93	0.94	0.95	1.11	1.16	1.33	1.33
Economic services	4.02	3.44	3.93	3.47	3.60	3.80	3.87	4.46	5.57	6.11	5.54
Total expenditure	12.95	13.67	14.42	13.63	14.13	14.27	14.38	15.07	16.59	18.29	17.79
Share of the States in total expenditure											
General services	37.14	42.99	40.59	41.32	43.04	41.89	43.02	42.50	44.95	48.28	49.31
Social services of which	83.78	82.07	76.25	75.99	77.45	79.68	78.99	89.16	87.43	87.71	87.16
Education	83.97	83.58	74.02	74.51	71.33	77.49	79.11	89.47	89.73	94.89	91.03
Healthcare	79.75	87.26	73.05	70.83	69.19	78.29	74.84	91.75	90.34	88.13	86.98
Economic services	54.84	61.29	52.71	53.33	59.48	66.78	55.44	58.89	62.27	74.27	69.75
Total expenditure	48.64	53.47	50.99	51.63	53.24	53.57	54.71	58.86	60.40	62.35	62.56

ideological leanings of political parties on issues relating to aggregate public spending do not seem to be very different. Besides, difficulties in raising additional resources and concerns about higher borrowings seem to have constrained the governments to limit their aggregate spending pattern. Third, over the years, the current expenditure comprising of consumption and transfers component of public expenditures has shown a steady increase while investment component of public expenditures has declined. Fourth, while the children in the age group of 0–14 constitute over 35 per cent of population, investment in human capital continues to be low. Finally, there is no evidence of differences in public expenditure pattern associated with electoral cycles. The exception to this, however, was in 2009–2010 when the ratio increased to 28.3 per cent following the farm loan waiver, increased coverage of National Rural Employment Guarantee from 200 districts to all the districts and implementation of pay commission's recommendations following the announcement in the 2008–2009 budget, which was the election year. Of course, this is only an anecdotal evidence and more rigorous work on this is needed to reach firm conclusions.

The expenditure composition in terms of functional categories too has remained broadly the same since 2000–2001. The spending on social services constitutes about a fifth of total expenditures and this has remained broadly at the same level throughout the 28-year period since 1990–1991. In contrast, there have been some variations in the share of general services as well as economic services. The increase in the share of general services in certain years was by reducing the share of economic services. In most of the years, general services accounted for 48–50 per cent of total expenditures and, in these years, the share of economic services varied around 27–28 per cent. However, in years when the share of general services increased to 54 per cent as in 2000–2001 and after 2015–2016, the share of economic services declined to about 21–22 per cent and much of this was the compression in capital expenditures. The Constitution assigns predominant responsibility for providing social services—particularly education and healthcare to the States and yet, expenditure on social services has been just about 20–25 per cent of the total throughout the period and as a ratio of GDP, has been around 5–6 per cent. As was pointed out in the previous chapter, children in the age group requiring significant investments in education and healthcare constitute over 35 per cent of the population, but expenditure relative to GDP on education constitutes a measly 2.8 per cent and on healthcare 1.3 per cent of GDP. According to United Nation's Human Development Report, 2013, even in the least developed countries, public health expenditure was 1.7 per cent of GDP in 2010. The expert norms for public spending on education and healthcare as a ratio of GDP are stated to be 6 per cent and 3 per cent, respectively.[5] Considering the low level of GDP, the per capita expenditure on health and education is extremely low and this explains the government's failure to provide adequate health and education infrastructure. Per capita expenditures on education and public health are abysmal particularly in low income States like Bihar and Uttar Pradesh where the proportions of children in the 0–14 age group are the highest.

Interestingly, the share of the States in defraying public expenditures is much higher than that of the Centre (Table 3.1). As a ratio of GDP, the share of States has shown a steady increase from 13 per cent in 1990–1991 to almost 18 per cent in 2017–2018. In terms of total expenditures, the increase in the share of States' expenditure in the total is just a little less than 50 per cent in 1990–1991 to about two-thirds of the total expenditures in 2017–2018. Interestingly, the States' share in total expenditures was broadly stable from 1990–1991 to 2010–2011 at about one-half, but thereafter, it increased sharply to 62.7 per cent in 2017–2018. A predominant part of the increase in the proportion of State expenditures was on economic services. The share of the States' spending on economic services increased from 55 per cent in 1990–1991 to 59 per cent in 2010–2011, but thereafter accelerated sharply to constitute almost 70 per cent in 2017–2018. Thus, overwhelming proportions of spending on both social and economic services are incurred at State levels. Ironically, while the presentation of Union budget receives enormous attention by the media and public, the States' budgets receive very little attention.

As mentioned above, States account for 87 per cent of spending on social services and their share of spending on education and healthcare is close to 90 per cent. Of course, this includes the spending on various

[5] The requirement to spend 6 per cent of GDP was first made by the Education Commission chaired by D. S. Kothari in 1966 (India, 1966) and was reiterated by the Saikia Committee (India, 1997) and Tapas Majumdar Committee (India, 1999). Similarly, the Planning Commission appointed High-Level Expert Group on Universalizing Healthcare chaired by Dr. Srinath Reddy recommended that public expenditure should be increased from 1.2 per cent of GDP in 2012–2013 to 2.5 per cent at the end of the 12th Five-Year-Plan and to 3 per cent by 2022 (India, 2012).

Central Sector and Centrally Sponsored Schemes (CSS). There are 13 Central Sector Schemes, and these are entirely funded by the Union government. The CSS are the shared-cost programmes between the Union and States initiated by the Union government. There are 28 CSS, of which six are classified as 'core of the core' with full funding by the Union government, 20 'core' schemes with the funding ratio of 60:40 between Union and States in the case of general category States and 90:10 in the case of Northeastern and Himalayan States and 2 'optional' schemes with the funding ratio of 50:50. Thus, these schemes are predominantly funded by the Central government but implemented by the States.

Both Reserve Bank of India and the Government of India classify spending on social and economic services as development expenditures and on administrative services as non-development. This is a little curious for, the spending on administrative services is for the provision of basic public good like ensuring safety and security of life and property, enforcement of property rights and contracts and creation of administrative machinery for the regulation and supervision of markets without which development is not possible. In fact, as was pointed out in Olson's story, ensuring security of life and property rights is basic incentives needed for accumulation and growth and yet these are christened as 'non-development' expenditures. Generally, it is assumed that the expenditures incurred on general administration and protection of property and enforcement of contracts are 'non-developmental', which is debatable, until clear norms are established on what is the ideal level of expenditures on these services. At the same time, all expenditures on social and economic services are considered 'developmental' which include large amount of spending on subsidies which change relative prices and create unintended resource distortions. It is important to be careful in drawing conclusions on the 'development' or 'productive' nature of expenditures. Interestingly, the IMF denotes capital or investment expenditures as developmental expenditures.

The composition of expenditures shows that spending on basic 'public goods' namely, ensuring safety and security, protection of property rights, and enforcement of contracts (defence, administrative services, and pension payments) has been broadly stable (Table 3.2). It was 5.9 per cent of GDP in 1990–1991, increased to 6.3 per cent in 2000–2001, and was 6.1 per cent in 2017–2018. Within this category, the expenditure on defence has shown a steady decline from 2.6 per cent in 1990–1991 to 1.6 per cent

Table 3.2 Development/Non-Development Expenditure Trend in India—Functional Categories (Per Cent of GDP).

	1990–1991	2000–2001	2009–2010	2010–2011	2011–2012	2012–2013	2013–2014	2014–2015	2015–2016	2016–2017	2017–2018
Non-development expenditures											
Interest payments	4.26	5.64	4.90	4.51	4.67	4.60	4.78	4.70	4.73	4.71	4.73
Defence services	2.63	2.28	2.19	1.98	1.96	1.83	1.81	1.75	1.64	1.61	1.53
Administrative services	2.37	2.21	2.16	2.02	2.12	1.96	1.91	1.94	2.28	2.06	2.03
Pension	0.88	1.78	2.15	2.13	2.04	2.16	2.12	2.19	2.19	2.39	2.42
Food subsidy	0.42	0.58	0.96	0.87	0.88	0.91	0.89	1.01	1.04	0.91	0.87
Other non-dev expenditure	1.56	1.32	1.48	1.36	1.24	0.93	1.24	1.18	1.94	2.04	1.90
Loans and advances	0.34	0.08	0.01	0.01	0.02	0.02	0.02	0.02	0.03	0.02	0.02
Total non-dev expenditure	12.13	13.81	13.84	12.87	12.91	12.41	12.79	12.79	13.85	13.76	13.51
Development expenditure											
Social and community services											
(i) Education, scientific research	3.19	3.12	3.35	3.42	3.64	3.22	3.25	2.93	2.99	3.02	3.10
(ii) Medical and public health	1.24	1.25	1.37	1.31	1.35	1.21	1.06	0.96	1.05	1.23	1.21
(iii) Social security and welfare	0.24	0.30	0.68	0.74	0.89	1.05	0.84	0.77	0.27	0.32	0.37
(iv) Urban development	0.13	0.18	0.50	0.38	0.49	0.42	0.30	0.29	0.33	0.49	0.50
(v) Other social services	0.47	0.38	0.49	0.50	0.50	0.82	0.35	0.25	0.26	0.47	0.39
Total: Social and community services	5.28	5.24	6.39	6.36	6.87	6.72	5.80	5.21	4.90	5.53	5.57

Continued

Table 3.2 *Continued*

	1990–1991	2000–2001	2009–2010	2010–2011	2011–2012	2012–2013	2013–2014	2014–2015	2015–2016	2016–2017	2017–2018
Economic services											
(i) Agriculture and allied services	2.00	1.42	1.96	1.86	1.88	1.75	1.61	1.76	1.94	2.62	2.75
(ii) Industry and minerals	0.66	0.31	0.57	0.85	1.14	1.25	1.02	0.74	0.53	0.54	0.44
(iii) Power, irrigation, flood control	1.72	1.55	1.57	1.36	1.51	1.50	1.40	1.53	1.94	2.05	2.00
(iv) Transport and communications	1.12	1.31	1.78	1.74	1.65	1.28	1.37	1.36	1.50	1.50	1.53
(v) Other economic services	1.08	0.38	0.48	0.71	0.89	1.19	0.55	0.43	0.68	0.82	0.78
Total: Economic services	7.34	5.61	7.45	6.51	6.05	5.69	6.99	7.58	8.95	8.23	7.94
Loans and advances	1.70	0.70	0.47	0.50	0.57	0.40	0.33	0.39	0.75	0.89	0.32
Total: developmental expenditure	14.31	11.55	14.31	13.38	13.49	13.83	10.52	9.68	9.56	10.96	10.86
Transfer of funds	0.18	0.21	0.12	0.14	0.15	0.40	0.33	0.39	0.75	0.89	0.32
Total expenditure	26.63	25.57	28.27	26.39	26.54	26.64	26.29	25.61	27.47	29.33	28.44

Source: Indian Public Finance Statistics, Ministry of Finance, Government of India.

in 2017–2018. Spending on administrative services as a ratio of GDP has shown a marginal decline from 2.4 per cent in 1990–1991 to 2.2 per cent in 2000–2001, but thereafter it has been fluctuating at a little over 2 per cent. The decline in defence and administrative expenditures was offset by sharp increases in expenditures on pensions from 0.9 per cent in 1990–1991 to 1.8 per cent in 2000–2001 and to 2.4 per cent in 2017–2018. Even in general services, the States' share in expenditures has increased from 39 per cent in 1990–1991 to 41 per cent in 2010–2011 and further to 49 per cent in 2017–2018. Thus, about a half of administrative expenditures is incurred at the State level.

Interest payment is the consequence of accumulation of debt from past borrowings. When revenues are stagnant, increase in interest payments crowd out expenditure on other items as they take the first charge on revenues. In Indian context, interest payments constituted 16.6 per cent of total expenditure in 1990–1991, increased to 23 per cent in 2000–2001 and thereafter gradually declined to 22 per cent by 2017–2018 largely due to the calibration of rule-based fiscal policy. As a ratio of total expenditures, interest payments constituted 22 per cent in 2000–2001 and declined to 18 per cent by 2017–2018. In terms of claiming resources, interest payments constituted 28 per cent of the aggregate tax revenue and 23 per cent of total revenues in 1990–1991. It increased to 40 per cent of tax revenue and 35 per cent of total revenue in 2000–2001. However, it declined gradually to constitute 27 per cent of tax revenue and 22 per cent of total revenue by 2017–2018. In other words, more than a quarter of tax revenues have to be spent on simply servicing the debt.

An important feature of trends in public spending over the years is a notable increase in subsidies and transfers. At the Central level alone, subsides as a ratio of GDP more than doubled from 1.2 per cent in 2000–2001 to 2.5 per cent in 2012–2013. The largest component of subsidy is on food followed by fertilizer and petroleum products. Food subsidy arises from difference in the cost of supplying foodgrains to the fair price shops which includes the cost of procurement, storage and transportation, and the realizations of revenues from the sale through the public distribution system at the rationed price. Similarly, fertilizer subsidy arises when the government subsidises the fertilizer companies to provide urea at the administered price. The costs of production in naphtha-based fertilizer companies and in those which were set up before 1992 are much higher than the new and gas-based companies and, therefore, to supply fertilizers at the price determined by the government for farmers, such old and inefficient companies are given the subsidy. Oil subsidy is given when the government is unable to increase the price of distillates in keeping with the costs. This happens when the international price of crude oil increases and the government is unable to increase the price of distillates for political reasons. In addition, there have been significant increases in transfers for employment guarantee, nutritional scheme, and assistance for construction of houses (*Indira Awas Yojana*), cash transfers to farmers (PM-Kisan), and so on, over the years.

Redistribution to low-income groups or certain groups of disadvantaged sections through direct cash transfers is preferable to providing relief through subsidizing commodities and services. This is because subsidy entails changes in relative prices and results in unintended resource allocation consequences. Subsidy on power results in changes in cropping decisions and unregulated exploitation of underground water with serious ecological consequences. Subsidizing fertilizers can result in its excessive use damaging the soil health and even underground water quality.

At the State level too, there have been a proliferation of various subsidies and transfers which, besides nutritional schemes and food subsidy, include giving away of television sets, laptops, and even food processors and grinders in some states. The focus of poverty alleviation strategy seems to be the short-run appeasement of the poor by giving them consumption entitlements for immediate electoral gains rather than long-term policy of ensuring employability and productivity growth in them. Perhaps, it is time to eliminate all the subsidies and, instead, the governments should think in terms of rolling out basic minimum income by excluding those families who pay income tax and Goods and Services Tax (GST), employees in the formal sector, and those owning cars and two wheelers.

In addition to the explicit subsidies, there are implicit subsidies from under-pricing of the goods and services delivered by the government. The most important implicit subsidy by the States is by not charging for the electricity used in irrigation pumps by farmers. Most of the States, with some notable exceptions like Gujarat and West Bengal, have rolled out free power to the farmers. In some states, the supply of power to farmers is done through separate feeders and in most states it is not metered. This can lead to misclassification of the theft of power as agricultural consumption. There have been several attempts at reform and the latest is called the Ujwal Discom Assurance Yojana (UDAY) initiated in 2015 asking the States to take over 75 per cent of the outstanding loans of their power distribution companies and initiating a time-bound action plan to reduce aggregate technical and commercial losses (AT&C), but this has not helped to reform the system. The latest attempt is to make power reform as a condition for availing additional borrowing space in the context of the financial distress faced by the States due to the economic collapse following the lockdown declared in response to the spread of the coronavirus pandemic.

Competitiveness of domestic producers depends on the availability and quality of physical infrastructure, but the trend in public spending on this is not very different. Capital expenditure by the Central government as a ratio of GDP has, in fact, declined from about 4 per cent in 2003–2004 to 1.8 per cent in 2011–2012 and much of the increase in capital expenditure seen is actually at the state level. The aggregate capital expenditure of the state governments increased during the period from a little over 0.5 per cent to about 2.2 per cent during the same period. Indeed, a considerable part of the Central government's capital expenditures on sectors such as coal, oil, and power now are being incurred by Central government enterprises and in sectors such as roads, public–private partnership is resorted to. The sharp decline in the revenues at both Central and State levels following the lockdown declared in response to the coronavirus pandemic is likely to compress capital expenditures further. A conservative estimate of the loss of tax and non-tax revenue at Central and State levels due to adverse economic impact of the pandemic is estimated at about 6 per cent of GDP and the additional borrowing panned by the Centre and provision made for the States will cover just about 4 per cent of GDP. As the easiest item to cut by the governments is capital expenditures, there will be substantial reduction in aggregate budgeted capital expenditures of about 4 per cent of GDP in 2020–2021.

The most notable shortcoming in the public expenditure trend is the low allocations made for both education and healthcare. With children in the age group 0–14 constituting 35.3 per cent of the population, the future of India depends on the government ensuring their development in terms of nutrition, healthcare, and education. The country cannot think of reaping the demographic dividend unless this generation is healthy and made productive through skill development and education. Unfortunately, this is the group not franchised and they do not seem to matter for governments. Healthcare is a State subject in Indian Constitution, but there has been a historical neglect of the sector. The experts have stated that the government expenditure for healthcare should be 3 per cent of GDP, but the actual expenditure is just 1.2 per cent. Estimating expenditures to conform to the norms of healthcare services set by the Ministry of health and family welfare in terms of the number of sub-centres and health centres and the personnel to be required according to population in different States, the government expenditure should be about 2.5 per cent as has been estimated by the High Level Committee on Universal Health Coverage appointed by the Planning Commission (India, 2011). Out-of-pocket expenditure is four times the government expenditure and this is one of the prime reasons for people falling under poverty. Healthcare is major sector with market failure due to very high asymmetric information and, therefore, requires substantial allocation and effective regulation of the market. Instead of building the health infrastructure and training healthcare workers, the government has taken the easy option of providing insurance through Ayushman Bharat, a centrally sponsored scheme. Unless basic health infrastructure is developed, the tertiary care expenditure on health cannot be controlled. The absurdity of neglecting the primary healthcare has become glaringly evident with the spread of coronavirus, and the governments had to run for cover as the pandemic spread fast. They had to spruce up the infrastructure by creating beds even in railway compartments.

The situation is not very different in the case of education. Although education is in the concurrent list, overwhelming proportion of spending is done at the State level. The total expenditure on education is estimated at 3.1 per cent of GDP as against the norm of 6 per cent stated by the Education Commission. Despite some of the Union Finance Commissions recommending grants for education to improve allocation to the sector and even after the government of India started the Sarva Shiksha Abhiyan, an elementary education financing programme financed by the cess collected from central taxes, the allocation has remained low at about 3 per cent of GDP. There are many ills affecting the sector, particularly in terms of poor learning outcomes as brought out from the Pratham reports every year, but not much progress has been seen. The problems afflicting the sectors needs a separate detailed analysis which is beyond the scope of this book. Suffice it to state here that in an economy which has a predominant young population, it is a short-sighted policy not to ensure adequate allocation for human development to secure their future.

Again, with per capita expenditure on both education and healthcare in different States closely related to their per capita GSDP, in States where the proportion of children to total population is higher, the per capita expenditures are substantially lower. For example, per capita expenditures on healthcare in 2016–2017 varied from Rs. 671 in Bihar to Rs. 2164 in Telangana and Rs. 2084 in Haryana. Similarly, per capita education expenditure varied from Rs. 1726 in Bihar to Rs. 4967 in Kerala. Thus, not only that the expenditures on education and healthcare are low but also they tend to increase inequalities in education and healthcare. This does not bode well for the future of this country.

Improvement in human development is an important mechanism to reduce inequalities in the country. Inequalities in the distribution of assets is the main reason for inequalities in income levels and living standards and one important mechanism through which the inequalities can be reduced is to endow those with low asset ownership with human capital. The analysis shows that the level of public spending on education and healthcare in States with higher concentration of poverty is lower. These are also the States with larger proportions of children in the age group of 0–14 which implies that the high inequalities will continue to persist. Furthermore, much of the expenditures incurred in public schools are for payment of salaries of teachers which hardly transforms into educational learning. Even when expenditures on education are incurred, they do not result in learning. The ASER report brought out by Pratham for 2018–2019 shows that as many as 53.2 per cent of Standard 1 children in government schools cannot read letters and 45.6 per cent cannot recognize the numbers from 1 to 9, and the corresponding number in private schools is 23 per cent and 17.3 per cent, respectively.

From the viewpoint of regional equity, the distribution of state-level expenditures is extremely important. The analysis shows that inter-state differences in per capita spending on social and economic services are high and are increasing over the years. Although since 2003–2004 the growth of expenditures in low per capita income states have been higher than those in advanced states, the per capita expenditure on these services continues to diverge. In 2011–2012, for example, per capita development expenditure in Bihar, the lowest per capita income state at Rs. 4900, was only 66 per cent of the average of per capita expenditures on these services in general category States. In fact, per capita developmental expenditures in Haryana, the State with the highest per capita income, was 2.4 times that of Bihar. This means that if the unit cost of providing these services is the same, developmental services for citizens in Haryana would be 2.4 times those of Bihar. Similar differences are seen in the case of education, healthcare, and economic services (Panagariya et al., 2014). The reason for this has to be found in the sharp interstate differences in the capacity to raise revenues and the inability of the transfer system to offset revenue disabilities.

3.3. Productivity in Public Expenditures

The transformation of public expenditures into outputs and outcomes depends on the productivity of public expenditures. As mentioned earlier, productivity in public spending to ensure efficient transformation of expenditures into outcomes depends on allocative and technical efficiency, targeting expenditures to intended groups, choice of appropriate technology to deliver public services, and assigning the task of delivery to appropriate levels of governments based on the principle of comparative advantage. One of the biggest challenges in ensuring efficiency in public spending is to create effective system of incentives and accountability. The composition of public expenditures in terms of economic and functional categories determines allocative and technical efficiency. While higher capital expenditures help in capital formation and creation of generalized externalities, higher wages, salaries, and pensions increase the unit cost of public service delivery. Subsidies tend to distort relative prices and should be employed to achieve a particular objective only when other less distorting options are not available. For redistribution, direct cash transfers to the targeted groups are less distorting than subsidizing the commodities and services consumed by the lower income groups.

The changes in the composition of public expenditure in India show that over the years, the composition of spending seems to have reduced the long-term productivity. The capital expenditures which formed almost

20 per cent of total expenditures in 1990–1991 have steadily declined to 14.3 per cent in 2017–2018 before marginally increasing to 16 per cent in 2018–2019. As a ratio of GDP, capital expenditures declined from 5.1 per cent in 1990–1991 to 3.9 per cent in 2018–2019. Similarly, the share of development expenditures (expenditures on social and economic services) in the total has shown a steady decline from 14.1 per cent in 1990–1991 to 10.9 per cent in 2017–2018. The three important items of non-development expenditure increase are (i) interest payments which as a ratio of GDP increased from 4.3 per cent to 4.8 per cent; (ii) pensions which increased from 0.9 per cent of GDP to 2.4 per cent; and (iii) food subsidy which increased from 0.4 per cent of GDP to 0.9 per cent.

Almost 60 per cent of the capital expenditures is incurred at the State level. By and large, until 2020–2021, the States, in the aggregate, were able to avoid having revenue deficits and the entire borrowing was used for incurring capital expenditures. Nevertheless, with steadily increasing committed expenditures in the revenue account, capital expenditures is seen as the residual since 2019–2020. Similarly, often, hard budget constraint at the State level displaces the much needed expenditures on the maintenance of assets adversely impacting the productivity.

The constraints on revenue limitations placed on borrowing combined with eagerness to please many constituencies result in taking up too many capital projects in the budgets by both Union and State governments year after year. This results in underfunding of the projects causing enormous cost overruns and delays in the completion of projects. Concerned with the trend, the government has entrusted the Ministry of Statistics and Programme Implementation to monitor the implementation of all projects. The report on project implementation delays brought out by the Ministry for 2020 shows that there were 1687 infrastructure projects each with a capital cost of more than Rs. 150 crore and their original cost was Rs. 21.45 trillion. Of these, 450 have been hit by cost overruns estimated at Rs. 4.28 trillion which was higher than the original cost by 20 per cent.[6] The problem is not confined to Central-level infrastructure projects

[6] See https://www.business-standard.com/article/economy-policy/450-infrastructure-projects-show-cost-overruns-of-rs-4-28-trillion-report-121012700043_1.html#:~:text=450%20infrastructure%20projects%20show%20cost,Business%20Standard%20News.

alone. At the State level too, the reports of the C&AG provide details of the cost and time overruns in the respective State reports.

Adverse impact on the productivity of public expenditure arises also from appeasing various constituencies for electoral gains. With the shortening time horizons and focus on electoral gains, political parties make promises of implementing plans to woo sections of electorate and implement these promises once they win the elections and come to power. Such electoral budget cycles are not uncommon even in developed countries. In the Union budget of 2008–2009, farm loan waiver was an important announcement, and its cost was estimated at Rs. 0.6 trillion. Subsequently, farm loan waiver has been announced in State elections in many States and in 2019–2020, the State budgets made a provision of Rs. 0.4 trillion for this purpose (RBI, 2020). Similarly, the announcement of one rank one pension in 2018 is estimated to cost Rs. 80 billion every year. With large corporates failing to repay the loans from the commercial banks, the government had to spend large amounts to recapitalize them. During the last 3 years, the government has spent Rs. 2.5 trillion for recapitalizing the public sector banks.

This brings us to the issue of financing to keep the public sector enterprises running. As discussed in Chapter 2, there is no rationale for the government to intervene in production–distribution activities when the private sector can perform. If there are market imperfections in these activities, the role of the government is to regulate. However, historically, the government has been running a number of enterprises from the planning era. Once started as a public enterprise, there will be resistance to privatize it. Not surprisingly, the government has been spending huge amount of money in providing funds to enterprises like Air India, BSNL, MTNL, Scooters India, and many others in non-strategic areas. At last, privatization of Air India is a relief to Indian taxpayers.

3.4. Concluding Remarks

Often, questions have been raised on the adequacy of public expenditures in India. The country suffers from huge infrastructure deficit. These generate generalized externalities. Of course, much more expenditures are needed to improve physical and social infrastructure in the country.

However, the question as to whether higher allocations to these services should be done by increasing the overall size of the expenditures or through reallocations from other less productive areas still remains.

Ironically, public expenditure allocation to various sectors in a democratic polity is determined considerably by pressure group politics rather than considerations of social productivity. Every interest group wants more to be spent on it by the government but not prepared to pay higher taxes. Whenever higher expenditure has to be incurred, the government has to finance it by borrowing which is tantamount to pushing the burden of financing the expenditure to the future generation. With outstanding debt of the government already high, pre-empting household savings for funding public spending can financially crowd out private investments and higher borrowings can only add to concerns about debt sustainability. While there is considerable need for higher volume of spending on both physical infrastructure and human development, inability to raise the tax-GDP ratio has been a major constraint.

Equally important issue with regard to public expenditures is its low productivity. It is possible to get better outcomes from the same level of spending reprioritizing the spending decisions, use of better technology, and ensuring greater accountability and incentives in the provision of services. The focus on reaping short-term electoral gains results in spreading expenditures thinly across a number of constituencies through subsidies and transfers rather than allocating expenditures in the long-term interest of augmenting the much-needed physical and social infrastructure.

It is possible to get better outcomes from the same level of expenditures on physical and social infrastructure by improving the productivity in spending. In other words, increasing outlays on infrastructure and social services does not necessarily promise proportionate improvement in service delivery. Ensuring better accountability and incentives can improve service delivery in labour-intensive services like education and healthcare. Using better technology too can be an important factor in improving productivity. Therefore, focus on merely expenditure levels may be misplaced.

4
Tax Policy and Reforms in India

We contend that for a nation to try to tax itself into prosperity is like a man standing in a bucket and trying to lift himself up by the handle.

—Winston Churchill

4.1. Introduction

This chapter attempts to review tax policy and reforms in India. Like other developing countries, India faces a major challenge of raising resources to meet public expenditure requirements while minimizing distortions. Taxes matter because they affect the citizens and businesses. Taxes change the way economic agents behave in a variety of ways. They reduce purchasing power of the people and impact on aggregate demand. They alter relative prices and allocation of resources. They determine the incentives to work, save, and invest. No one likes paying taxes. Some use ingenious ways to avoid them, some others unhesitatingly evade them, and most pay them grudgingly. Only a few consider it their legitimate duty to pay them.

Writing on economic policy, Keynes (1936: 570) stated, 'The ideas of economists and political philosophers, both when they are right and when they are wrong are more powerful than is commonly understood. Indeed, the world is ruled by little else. Practical men who believe themselves to be exempt from intellectual influences are usually the slaves of some defunct economist. Madmen in authority, who hear voices in the air, are distilling their frenzy from some academic scribbler of a few years back . . . . Soon or late, it is ideas, not vested interests, which are dangerous for good or evil'. However, the experiences

Studies in Indian Public Finance. M. Govinda Rao, Oxford University Press. © Oxford University Press 2022.
DOI: 10.1093/oso/9780192849601.003.0004

everywhere have shown that the impact of vested interests on tax policies is significant. Johnson and Myles (2011: 323) while summarizing the James Mirrless' review of the British Tax System state, 'In the real world, proposals for tax reform are constrained by politics. Those who loose from tax reforms tend to be vengeful while those who gain from them tend to be ungrateful. This can lead to tax policy, perhaps, more than any other policy, to a "tyranny of status quo"'. This chapter attempts to understand the challenges of overcoming this tyranny.

There are important reasons for reviewing Indian tax policy. First, despite several reform attempts in India, the ratio of tax to GDP has remained stagnant and in more recent years has even shown a decline even before the COVID-19 pandemic. The need for higher allocation to overcome the infrastructure deficit warrants identifying the reform areas in the tax system to increase revenue productivity. It is also important to contain fiscal deficits to conform to the FRBM targets on deficits and debt. Second, the need for reforming the tax system has arisen also from the desire to impart greater competitiveness to the economy. Third, the federal nature of the country has posed constraints in calibrating tax policies in a coordinated manner to evolve broad-based direct and indirect tax systems. The fragmented assignment of income tax with the Centre allowed to levy the tax on only the non-agricultural incomes has posed challenges to the compliance problem. The lack of coordination in calibrating the reform of indirect taxes levied by the Centre and state governments until the Goods and Services Tax (GST) reform was introduced in July 2017 has posed difficulties in evolving a harmonized consumption tax system in the country. Fourth, recent years have seen widespread frustration among the tax collectors about the ingenious ways of digital companies, e-commerce giants, and other multinational companies indulging in wilful avoidance of the taxes. Equally important are the complaints of businesses of the tax administration making unreasonable tax demands and indulging in what is often stated as 'tax terrorism'. Finally, the levy of GST by both Union and State governments and its management through the GST Council—an institutional mechanism invented for the purpose, is an exercise in coordinated calibration of consumption tax reform. Of course, the issues relating to the structure, operation, and institutional details of GST require a detailed review which is carried out in the next chapter.

On the issue of reforms, it is important to distinguish between minor changes in the tax system undertaken on an annual basis and the reform that is undertaken to change the nature of the tax system (Auerbach, 2008). Given the significant impact of taxes on economic activity, it is desirable to have a tax system that is simple, stable, and predictable. This requires that the changes in the tax system should not be disruptive. However, minor changes to take account of the conditions and conveniences of tax authorities and taxpayers may be necessary, but that cannot be called reform. The reform involves a shift in the direction of policy. In this chapter, the attempt is to analyse the major shifts in tax policy. At the same time, it must be noted that a reform is not an event; it is an ongoing process, particularly in a democratic polity, but there should be clarity in the direction of reform.

The present chapter analyses the trends and issues in tax policy and reform. The chapter draws from the earlier studies on the tax system undertaken by the author from time to time starting 20 years ago (Rao, 2000; Rao and Rao, 2005, 2010; Rao, 2015–2016; Rao and Kumar, 2018). Periodic analysis of the Indian tax system is necessary to take into account the changes in the economy including the development strategy, political landscape, changes in the structure of taxes, and application of technology to tax administration. There have also been considerable public discussions on the issue of reforming both direct and indirect taxes during the last few years. Besides the discussions on the replacement of multiple commodity taxes with a destination-based value-added tax (VAT) on goods and services, there were two discussion papers on the Direct Taxes Code and this indicates the urgency of reforms in both direct and indirect taxes. Therefore, a detailed review of the tax system in India is timely.

The principal objective of tax policy in a developing market economy is to raise revenue in an equitable manner and with minimum distortions. The tax system needs to be reformed to increase revenue productivity (in terms of the tax-GDP ratio) and to remove significant distortions arising from the pursuit of multiple objectives. Keeping in view the principles of an efficient tax system based on advances in the theory of tax reform and the best practice approaches, the tax system needs to be reformed to make it revenue productive, transparent, predictable, and to minimize distortions.

4.2. What Makes a Sound Tax System?

Tax policies stand on the tripod of three equally important and interdependent legs—the architecture, engineering, and management (Bird and Zolt, 2005). 'Architecture' provides the design of tax policy conforming to the objectives. The 'engineering' aspect relates to the mechanics of applying the design, which are influenced by the nature and quality of the systems and institutions involved in tax collection. The 'management' aspect of tax policy determines the implementation strategy and action taken, which depend on the political support, competence of the administration, application of technology in administration and the information system. A tax policy is only as good as it can be effectively administered. In the real world, tax policy is affected by a host of factors, including, *inter alia*, the role of the State, level of development, administrative capacity, efficiency in spending, and interest group politics. As economic, administrative, and political conditions vary across countries, and the responses of relevant economic agents to tax changes are non-uniform, each country has to choose a tax system that fits in with its specific conditions. However, the general principles are helpful to design and reform tax policies.

The thinking on tax policy and reforms has undergone significant changes over the years. The traditional view was that income tax was a major instrument to reduce inequalities in incomes and, therefore, it should be a preferred instrument for raising resources. It was employed to serve as an instrument to reduce inequalities by applying extortionary rates. Therefore, income tax was preferred over indirect taxes and inequality was sought to be reduced by taxing not only the incomes but also the accumulated wealth. Often the wealth taxation took the form of taxing it at the time of the death of the individual as inheritance is considered as an unearned income and taxing it did not affect the incentives.

The optimal tax theory, however, brought out the adverse incentives from levying the tax at high rates. The theory posits that the optimal tax rate schedule depends on the distribution of abilities. In the absence of lump sum taxes, the search for the second-best solution shows that marginal tax rates increasing with income to tax the people having high abilities and that could result in disincentives in their effort to earn more income. As shown by Mirrlees (1971), high marginal tax rates lead to large economic distortions relative to the revenue raised. Further research has shown that the distortions can be significant when the labour supply is relatively inelastic, which implies that the distortions from high marginal tax rates can affect wage rates, thereby defeating the very purpose of reducing inequality (Feldstein, 1995). Given the difficulties in getting the information on abilities and efforts, it is suggested that a flat tax may be close to being optimal.

In the case of commodity taxes, Ramsey (1927), in an early contribution, showed that distortions can be minimized by levying higher tax rates on commodities with low compensated price elasticity of demand. However, the difficulty in collecting information for designing such a tax system was simply unsurmountable and administering such a tax with several rates was well beyond the capacity of tax administrations. Rate differentiation can also provide scope for lobbying by special interest groups. In addition, such a tax system was politically infeasible because of its regressive nature.

While there is a large body of research on optimal tax theory, the practical application of them for designing the tax system has not been commensurate. Indeed, the perfect and costless information assumed in those models does not simply exist. The models do not consider the administrative and compliance costs. They focus on determining the tax bases and rates and fail to take account of the issues of enforcement capacity. Furthermore, they analyse behavioural responses in consumption and production decisions and not the responses in terms of avoidance and evasion of taxes. There is also an implicit assumption that people understand and rationally react to the tax system and, therefore, governments have no reason to manipulate the perceptions of the people (Slemrod and Gillitzer, 2014).

It must, however, be admitted that the results of optimal theories of direct and commodity taxes provide useful guidance in calibrating the real-world tax systems. As stated by Hahn (1973: 106), 'optimum formulas are either guides to action or nothing at all'. Despite this pessimism, it is obvious that the theoretical advances have helped to understand what constitutes a desirable tax system and to develop the best practice approaches to calibrating tax policies.[1] One of the most important lessons from

[1] The most recent attempt to distil balanced and well-grounded tax reform proposals in the United Kingdom of Great Britain and Northern Ireland was the Mirrlees Review. See Johnson and Myles (2011) and Gordon (2011).

optimal tax theory is that distortion from a tax is an exponential function of the tax rate. This has led to recommending uniformity and simplicity in designing and reforming taxes. While traditionally, the Haig–Simons income tax was considered the bedrock of the tax system, there is much less consensus on that today in view of the undesirable economic effects of capital taxation. In fact, there has been a movement towards 'dual' income taxation with capital income taxed at lower and less progressive rates (Auerbach, 2008). Notably, in many countries, the pendulum has swung in favour of indirect taxation in favour of a broad-based VAT on GST. Even as income taxes continue, the steep progressivity of over 90 per cent marginal rate that existed in most countries including the United States and the United Kingdom in the 1950s and 1960s, is no longer fashionable.

The most important objective of tax policy is to raise revenue by minimizing the three costs associated with taxation, the cost of collection, the compliance cost, and the distortion costs, as people change their behaviour in response to tax policy. To minimize administrative and compliance costs, the tax system must be simple, predictable, and transparent and the tax policy must not be loaded with multiple objectives but, instead, designed mainly to raise revenue. To raise the same amount of revenue with lower tax rates, tax bases must be broadened with minimum exemptions and preferences and an effective administration and intelligence system needs to be in place to ensure compliance. While raising revenue is important (taxes exist primarily to meet this objective), the focus of tax policy and reforms should be to enhance long-run revenue productivity and not to meet short-term exigencies through ad hoc changes in the bases and rates.

Thus, Bird and Zolt (2008) argue that the best practice approach to tax policy and reform requires that governments move towards a broad-base, low-rate approach, have a simple and transparent tax system, and avoid arbitrary tax differentiation across people and economic activities. The distortions increase exponentially with the tax rates. As a result, most countries desist from levying taxes at high rates. Thus, the preferred strategy for raising a given amount of revenue and putting in place a simple and transparent system is to broaden the base, reduce the rate, and minimize rate differences. In the same vein, an important piece of advice given to most developing countries is to levy a broad-based and simple GST at a single rate. The structure of the tax needs to be simple, and should be within the capacity of the tax administrations to administer and enforce.

In most developing countries, including India, tax policy is deployed to achieve many objectives, in addition to raising revenue in an equitable manner. In India, the tax system is complicated by providing exemptions and preferences for meeting a variety of objectives including incentivize savings in specified instruments and investment in particular sectors, achieving balanced regional development, augmenting infrastructure, enhancing exports, and encouraging the development of small and medium industries. Even when the assigned objectives are clear, such as promoting investment or exports, it is difficult to ascertain their effectiveness. Most often, they are redundant and ineffective and only contribute towards making the tax system more complicated. They create new avenues for avoidance and evasion of taxes. Often, they result in an uneven distribution of tax burden with domestic companies bearing a higher burden than foreign companies. Although experience suggests that sound macroeconomic factors, competitive infrastructure, effective governance, and stable and predictable policies are the most important determinants of investment, most countries continue to extend a variety of incentives to attract investment, which not only causes significant revenue losses from tax expenditure but also tends to distort resource allocation.

The major challenge is to design a tax system that incorporates fairness in its impact. The most important lesson from optimal taxation is that the distortions in the tax increase exponentially with tax rates and, therefore, even when the tax is seen to be progressive, the adverse effects on economic activity and employment may negate the progressivity. Furthermore, too much attention to the fairness of individual taxes is misplaced. When the tax system is designed to reduce distortions, it may contain some individual taxes that can be viewed as being regressive. What matters is the effect of the tax system as a whole and not the impact of individual taxes on the distribution of income (Bird and Zolt, 2005, 2008; Johnson and Myles, 2011).

The general presumption is that as indirect taxes are regressive, direct taxes should be designed to reduce inequalities. Accordingly, the traditional approach is to design highly progressive personal income tax and levy high rates on corporate income. This has, however, come into serious questioning. First, a progressive income tax structure with high marginal rates in an open economy can have an unintended effect of migration of capital and the tax on capital might turn out to be a tax on labour. Furthermore, high marginal tax rates can have serious disincentives and in an open economy to work, save, and invest. Second, it is possible to design non-regressive consumption taxes by exempting essential unprocessed food items. Third, the effectiveness of personal income tax in reducing inequality itself is doubtful. This is because only a small proportion of the population pays income tax in developing countries. In most of those countries, income tax is neither comprehensive nor progressive and much of the revenue comes from withholding taxes, with very little of it emanating from self-employed businesses, which can be attributed to a poor information system and the existence of a large unorganized sector. Furthermore, progressive tax systems are not costless. They increase administrative, compliance, and even more economic efficiency costs, and when the distortions are considered, the adverse impact on economic activity on the income of the poor may outweigh the gains from progressivity.

Empirical studies in developed and developing countries have shown that the tax system has not been effective in redistributing incomes. The study by Pechman (1985) using alternative assumptions about the distribution of burden of individual taxes for the period 1966–1985 shows that the tax system of the United States is not significantly progressive. Similarly, a careful study of the tax system of Chile by Engel et al. (1999) indicates that the tax system is moderately regressive with the Gini coefficient higher at 0.4881 when the incidence of tax is taken into account as compared to 0.4861 without the tax. In India, there are no comprehensive studies taking into account the distribution of tax burden to all taxes. There were studies on the incidence of indirect taxes (Chelliah and Lal, 1978) which assumed full shifting of the tax burden on the consumers and concludes that the tax burden was mildly progressive. On income taxes, with the number of taxpayers constituting only 3 per cent of the population, any attempt to alter the distribution is not likely to make changes in disposable incomes across a large stretch of the Lorenz curve. Furthermore, concerns about distorting incentives to work, save, and invest at higher marginal rates have forced many countries including India to levy the tax at moderate marginal rates. On corporate income tax, there is also the need to keep the tax system competitive to avoid the flight of capital. Therefore, the focus of redistribution in fiscal policy needs to shift from reducing the income of the rich to increasing the income of the poor and that has to be accomplished through spending in human development and direct anti-poverty interventions which have to be carried out in the expenditure side of the budget.[2]

In recent discourse on tax systems, discussion, on the issue of an appropriate tax base-income versus consumption has resurfaced. Most versions of consumption tax avoid taxing normal returns on savings or capital or both. Of course, applying an expenditure tax may not be an option; also, it is not possible to impose a zero effective tax rate on the returns to capital. Nevertheless, a consensus among tax theorists is that labour and capital income should be taxed differently because of the different effects they have on taxation. In fact, Auerbach et al. (2010) recommend the replacement of the present system of corporation tax with a destination-based VAT on goods and services with labour costs deductible in addition to the input costs.

While doing away with the idea that corporation tax would be politically unacceptable in all countries, the discussion brings out that a comprehensive VAT on goods and services is an important instrument in any modern tax system. The tax has been found to be particularly important to overcome a decline in revenue when developing countries try to rationalize import duties. This is demonstrated in the study by Keen and Lingthart (2002), which shows that a revenue-neutral tariff reduction accompanied by a price-neutral GST enhances revenue and efficiency. An increase in revenue arises from the self-enforcing nature of the tax. An increase in efficiency arises, as it avoids distorting the input prices and to that extent, reduces production inefficiency (Keen, 2007). Emran and Stiglitz (2005), however, contend that GST on recorded transactions, when combined with weak administrations in developing countries, can work as a tax on the formal sector. In contrast, Keen (2007) considers GST as one of the least costly ways of taxing the informal sector because

[2] As Harberger (2003: 13) argues, 'Society is not going to bring about major changes in the income distribution by operating either on the tax side or on the expenditure side of the budget of the public sector . . . it is more realistic to think of the struggle against poverty to be a major goal'. He recommends that that should be done by helping the poor to meet their basic needs and providing opportunities for advancement by ensuring access to education and health care to those who cannot afford it. For similar arguments, see also Bird and Zolt (2008).

of its self-enforcing nature. In effect, so long as the gains from participating in the formal market are greater than the tax loss, the taxpayer prefers to stay in the formal market. The basic Harberger reform package for developing countries that are price takers in the international market includes, among other things, a uniform tariff and a broad-based VAT (Harberger, 1990). As Bird and Gendron (2007) argue: 'On the whole, while further theoretical and particularly empirical research on the effects of VAT in developing and transitional countries is needed, the case for a VAT in such countries remains solid'.

Accordingly, a good tax system is the one that minimizes administrative, compliance, and distortion costs to the economy. It should have broad base, low marginal rates, and less differentiated rates with a simple structure. Fairness in tax policy should be judged in its totality and not individual taxes. Furthermore, the focus of fiscal policy should shift from reducing inequality to alleviating poverty, which is more effectively done through the expenditure side of the budget. An important component of a good tax system is a comprehensive GST. It is not enough to focus on the design of the tax structure; building capacity and orientation in tax administration is equally important. A good tax system is supported by a good information system not only to enforce the tax but also to calibrate changes with full information. A hallmark of good tax administration is the taxpayer service, which not only builds confidence among the taxpayers but also improves compliance. Use of information technology promotes transparency and provides information for the enforcement of taxes.

4.3. Tax Revenue Trends in India

The tax-GDP ratio in India increased from less than 10 per cent in the 1970s to 14 per cent in the 1990s and 16.5 per cent after 2008–2009. As shown in Table 4.1, the highest ratio was 17.5 per cent, achieved in 2007–2008. Due to the reduction in the consumption tax rates in the wake of global financial crisis, the ratio declined to 15.5 per cent in 2009–2010 and thereafter gradually recovered to 16.5 per cent in subsequent years. The important point is that the tax-GDP ratio has been stubbornly stagnant since 2008–2009. The decline in the ratio after 2008–2009 by two percentage points was mainly due to lower central tax collections, partly

Table 4.1 Trends in Tax-GDP Ratios at Union and State Levels (Per Cent).

Year	Centre			States			Total		
	Direct	Indirect	Total	Direct	Indirect	Total	Direct	Indirect	Total
1950–1960	1.57	2.77	4.33	0.65	1.69	2.34	2.22	4.46	6.68
1961–1970	1.93	4.49	6.42	0.44	2.48	2.92	2.37	6.97	9.34
1971–1980	2.21	6.21	8.42	0.26	3.71	3.97	2.47	9.91	12.39
1981–1990	1.96	7.77	9.74	0.20	4.79	4.99	2.17	12.56	14.73
1991–2000	2.64	6.21	8.85	0.16	4.97	5.13	2.80	11.18	13.98
2007–2008	6.26	5.63	11.89	0.13	5.43	5.56	6.39	11.06	17.45
2010–2011	5.63	4.55	10.19	0.16	5.99	6.15	5.79	10.55	16.34
2016–2017	5.54	5.65	11.19	5.23	0.68	5.91	10.78	6.32	17.10
2017–2018	5.85	5.35	11.19	4.35	1.06	5.41	10.19	6.41	16.60
2018–2019 (RE)	6.31	5.38	11.70	4.57	1.43	6.00	10.88	6.82	17.70
2019–2020 (BE)	6.34	5.34	11.68	4.45	1.67	6.12	10.78	7.02	17.80

Note: The data for 2014–2015 refer to a revised estimate for the government and budget estimate for the states.

Source: India, Ministry of Finance. Public finance statistics (various years, for 2013–2014 and 2014–2015; budget documents of the government and Reserve Bank of India (2016).

due to lowering of the rates of excise duties as a part of the stimulus given during the global financial crisis. Although in subsequent years, the ratio recovered to some extent, it never reached the 2007–2008 level.

The aggregate tax-GDP ratio follows broadly the trend in Central tax ratio. The highest tax-GDP ratio was reached in 2007–2008 (11.9 per cent). Following the lowering of the union excise duty rates as a stimulus in response to the global financial crisis, the ratio declined to 9.9 per cent in 2011–2012. In subsequent years, there was a marginal increase to reach 11 per cent in 2018–2019. However, slowdown in the economy and poor implementation of GST led to a sharp decline in the ratio to 9.8 per cent in 2019–2020. As the GDP contracted by 7.3 per cent in 2020–2021 due to the pandemic, the tax revenue declined to at 9.8 per cent.

The composition of Central tax revenues shows two distinct trends. First the share of direct taxes has shown a steady increase over the years. In 1991–1992, the revenue from direct taxes constituted just about 23 per cent of total gross tax revenue of the Centre and this has steadily increased to about 55 per cent in 2018–2019 (Table 4.2). Thus, the share of indirect taxes has shown a steady decline during the last three decades. Second, within indirect taxes, the share of international trade taxes has shown a sharp decline. In 1991–1992, revenue from customs duties constituted almost a third of total tax revenue of the Centre, but in 2018–2019, its share was just 5.7 per cent.

Revenue from state taxes as a ratio of GDP has steadily increased, albeit at a slow rate, from 5.5 per cent in 2008–2009 to the highest level of 6.6 per cent in 2014–2015, but thereafter declined to 5.4 per cent in 2017–2018. An important reason for the steady increase in the tax-GDP ratio at the State level is the high price of oil distillates and as the sales taxes on these are ad valorem, the revenue yield was high until 2015 when the oil prices declined sharply.

The composition of State taxes shows a steady decline in the share of direct taxes mainly due to declining revenues from land revenue and agricultural income tax (Table 4.3). The revenue from tax on agricultural land and incomes as a ratio of total state tax revenues declined from 5.7 per cent in 1991–1992 to 2.4 per cent in 2018–2019 and total revenue from direct taxes which includes revenue from the taxes on transfer of property (stamps and registration) declined from 14 per cent in 1991–1992 to 11.5 per cent ion 2018–2019. It is also seen that revenue from sales

Table 4.2 Trends in Tax-GDP Ratios: Union Government (Per Cent).

Year	Corporation tax	Personal income tax	Total direct taxes	Customs duty	Excise duty	Service tax/ GST	Total indirect taxes	Total tax-centre
1991–1992	1.17	1.00	2.26	3.30	4.17	0.00	7.55	9.81
1995–1996	1.34	1.27	2.74	2.91	3.28	0.07	6.31	9.07
2001–2002	1.55	1.36	2.94	1.71	3.08	0.14	4.98	7.94
2005–2006	2.74	1.55	4.30	1.76	3.01	0.62	5.62	9.95
2006–2007	3.36	1.97	5.34	2.01	2.74	0.88	5.88	11.03
2007–2008	3.87	2.17	6.05	2.09	2.48	1.03	5.93	11.89
2008–2009	3.79	1.88	5.68	1.77	1.93	0.55	4.51	10.75
2009–2010	3.78	1.89	5.68	1.29	1.59	0.90	3.94	9.64
2010–2011	3.84	1.79	5.63	1.74	1.77	0.91	4.53	10.19
2011–2012	3.58	1.83	5.42	1.66	1.61	1.09	4.43	9.87
2012–2013	3.52	1.94	5.48	1.63	1.74	1.31	4.74	10.25
2013–2014	3.45	2.08	5.54	1.51	1.48	1.35	4.39	9.96
2014–2015	3.37	2.15	5.53	1.49	1.46	1.33	4.33	9.89
2015–2016	3.34	2.27	5.61	1.48	1.62	1.49	4.64	10.27
2016–2017	3.15	2.37	5.52	1.46	2.48	1.65	6.17	11.69
2017–2018	3.34	2.51	5.85	0.75	1.52	2.70	5.01	10.86
2018–2019	3.50	2.49	6.00	0.52	1.21	2.60	4.95	10.95
2019–2020	2.74	2.36	5.10	0.54	1.18	2.50	4.31	9.41

Note: 1. Total direct taxes include revenue from other minor taxes such as estate duty and wealth tax.

2. Total taxes include Union Territory taxes also.

Source: Budget Documents, Ministry of Finance, Government of India.

Table 4.3 Trends in Tax-GDP Ratios in States (Per Cent).

Year	Tax on land and agri. incomes	Stamps and registration	State excise duties	Sales tax/VAT	Taxes on transport	Other taxes	Total States' own tax
I. Non-special category states							
1991–1992	0.13	0.48	0.96	3.72	0.53	0.34	6.31
2001–2002	0.09	0.57	0.84	3.80	0.57	0.18	6.31
2005–2006	0.09	0.84	0.83	4.26	0.61	0.19	7.04
2010–2011	0.13	0.83	0.91	4.26	0.54	0.19	7.07
2011–2012	0.12	0.89	0.97	4.60	0.54	0.16	7.47
2012–2013	0.12	0.92	0.98	4.76	0.58	0.19	7.75
II. Special category states							
1991–1992	0.47	0.09	0.59	1.49	0.24	0.12	3.47
1995–1996	0.18	0.09	0.63	1.49	0.28	0.13	3.10
2001–2002	0.13	0.18	0.76	2.23	0.46	0.24	4.12
2005–2006	0.06	0.32	0.65	3.28	0.47	0.18	5.13
2006–2007	0.06	0.40	0.64	3.42	0.45	0.14	5.31
2007–2008	0.06	0.31	0.64	3.49	0.40	0.18	5.29
2008–2009	0.09	0.24	0.61	3.37	0.47	0.19	5.16
2009–2010	0.08	0.23	0.64	3.29	0.52	0.14	5.06
2010–2011	0.10	0.22	0.63	3.49	0.48	0.15	5.21
2011–2012	0.07	0.25	0.68	3.93	0.52	0.24	5.90
2012–2013	0.09	0.28	0.73	4.01	0.47	0.23	5.99

III. All states							
1991–1992	0.33	0.46	0.94	3.60	0.52	0.15	6.15
1995–1996	0.50	0.53	0.75	3.10	0.47	0.14	5.66
2001–2002	0.18	0.55	0.83	3.70	0.56	0.09	6.18
2005–2006	0.19	0.81	0.82	4.20	0.60	0.09	6.93
2006–2007	0.18	0.91	0.82	4.28	0.56	0.10	7.05
2007–2008	0.16	0.89	0.82	4.16	0.52	0.10	6.88
2008–2009	0.15	0.75	0.85	4.12	0.52	0.11	6.69
2009–2010	0.16	0.72	0.88	3.99	0.52	0.10	6.57
2010–2011	0.19	0.80	0.89	4.22	0.54	0.13	6.96
2011–2012	0.17	0.85	0.95	4.56	0.54	0.12	7.38
2012–2013	0.19	0.88	0.97	4.71	0.58	0.12	7.65

Source: Annual Articles on Finances of State Governments, Reserve Bank of India, and Finance Accounts of Different States.

taxes constitutes almost two-thirds of the States' own tax revenue and within sales taxes, the share of petroleum taxes was significant. In 2018–2019, sales taxes on petroleum products accounted for 23.8 per cent of the States' own tax revenue. As mentioned earlier, petroleum product taxes are not included in the GST and are not subject to input tax relief. The cascading caused by these taxes is significant. The revenue from alcohol taxes was 12.7 per cent of the States' own tax revenue in 2018–2019, which is a little lower than in 1991–1992 (15.3 per cent).

How does India's tax-GDP ratio compare with other countries with a similar level of development in mobilizing revenue? A number of studies have estimated the tax potential using cross-country regressions.[3] These studies estimate the tax potential by running a regression with tax-GDP ratios as the dependent variable and a vector of taxable capacity variables as independent variables. The predicted tax-GDP ratio obtained by substituting the actual values of the determinants in the estimated equation is taken as the tax potential and the ratio of actual tax-GDP ratio to the predicted value is taken as tax effort. The predicted value represents the potential tax-GDP ratio according to the average relationship between tax collection and its determinants across countries.

More recent advances in estimating tax potential extend beyond the simple regression approach mentioned above. Estimates can be made of the tax potential not on the basis of average behavioural relationships but also by using the stochastic frontier analysis (Cyan, Martinez-Vazquez and Vulovic, 2013; Langford and Oldenburg, 2016). Under this approach, the envelope for the tax-GDP ratio is estimated by employing tax frontier determinants representing taxable capacity and effort. The relevant frontier for the country represents the highest tax ratio that would result for a given set of determinants.

The empirical studies, by and large, show that the actual tax-GDP ratio in India is much lower than its potential. Bird and Zolt (2005) show that in 2000, the average tax ratio for the middle-income countries (per capita income ranging from US$1000 to $17000) was 22 per cent. A more recent study, conducted by the International Monetary Fund (IMF), covering 174 countries, shows that the average tax ratio for lower middle-income countries (per capita gross national product (GNP) ranging from $995 to

[3] For a more recent study, see Le et al. (2012).

$3945) for the period 1980–2009 was about 18 per cent (IMF, 2011). In comparison, the ratio in India was much lower. After reaching 17.5 per cent in 2007–2008, the ratio declined to 15.5 per cent in 2009–2010 and has been hovering between 16.2 and 16.5 per cent over the past years.

To empirically estimate the extent of under-taxation in India, Rao and Kumar (2018) estimated the potential tax-GDP ratio for India based on the cross-country relationship between tax ratio and per capita income in a regression model. The details of the econometric analysis relating tax-GDP ratio to per capita income, urbanization, revenue from natural resources, and consumer price index shows that, India should have raised about 19–20 per cent of GDP. The details of the econometric exercise are presented in Appendix 4.A1.

This estimate, as mentioned above, is based on the observed average cross-country relationship between the tax-GDP ratio and its determinants. In contrast, Langford and Oldenburg (2016), based on the stochastic frontier analysis, estimate the potential at 28.4 per cent. While this is the highest that can be raised, from the policy perspective, the government should at least try to enhance the tax ratio to the average level of 19.3 per cent. Surely, a country that aspires to accelerate its development has to substantially augment its public spending on physical infrastructure and human development. As mentioned in the previous chapter, with about 35 per cent of its 1.3 billion people in the age group of 0–14 years, the expenditure on education and healthcare relative to GDP must be much higher than 3 per cent and 1.2 per cent, respectively. The country has to increase significantly money spent on physical infrastructure and a large proportion of it must come from the budget. It is estimated that for financing the Sustainable Development Goals set for 2030 to achieve sustainable development goals, the tax-GDP ratio should be increased to about 20 per cent of GDP, which is close to the estimate of the tax potential in this paper. It is, therefore, important that efforts are made to increase the fiscal space by increasing the tax-GDP ratio at least to the average levels.

4.4. What Ails the Indian Tax System?

The low revenue productivity of the Indian tax system has been a matter of concern and despite several rounds of reforms the tax-GDP ratio has remained stubbornly static. The highest tax-GDP ratio at 17.5 per cent was reached in 2007–2008 and it declined to 15.5 per cent following the reduction in the consumption taxes due to global financial crisis. Although it recovered to 16.5 per cent subsequently, it has remained stagnant.

The low and stagnant tax-GDP ratio in India is mainly due to the failure to address the reasons for narrow tax bases. The important reasons keeping the tax bases narrow are (a) the fragmented Constitutional assignment between the Union and States, (b) wide-ranging tax preferences, (c) multiplicity of objectives incorporated into tax policy, resulting in complications in the tax laws, wide avenues for evasion and avoidance, and large and increasing amounts held in disputes, (d) tax abuse by multinational companies, resulting in base erosion and profit shifting, and (e) poor capacity of the tax administration, including the information system, to effectively administer and enforce the taxes.

(a) Constitutional Assignment and Narrow Base

The low revenue productivity of the Indian tax system is mainly attributable to the narrow tax bases. There are a variety of reasons rendering the tax bases narrow and these include the fragmented Constitutional assignment, wide-ranging exemptions, concessions and deductions, complications and ambiguities in the tax laws due to multiplicity of objectives assigned to tax policy resulting in large and increasing amounts held in disputes, mechanisms of the multinational resulting in base erosion and profit shifting, organizational shortcomings, and the poor capacity of tax administration including the information system to effectively administer and enforce the taxes.

Inability to levy a comprehensive income tax in India lies mainly in the Constitutional assignment. The assignment of the tax on incomes from agriculture to the States has resulted in the Union government levying tax only on non-agricultural incomes. The States do not levy the agricultural income tax except incomes from plantation crops. Even the corporates making investments in agricultural sector do not have to pay the tax. There have been a number of studies estimating the potential from taxing agriculture and the study by Rao and Sengupta (2012) for 2008–2009 estimates the potential at 0.6 per cent of GDP. The exemption to the agricultural sector prevents the levy of comprehensive income taxation and provides easy avenue for the evasion and avoidance of the tax.

(b) Tax Exemptions and Preferences

The second important reason for the narrow base of taxes is a plethora of exemptions, concessions, and deductions given in direct and indirect taxes. As mentioned earlier, Indian tax system has been loaded with several objectives. A close look at the number of objectives pursued by the tax system is enough to understand the complications and its ineffectiveness in achieving any. The tax system besides raising revenues is required to fulfil a number of objectives such as incentivizing savings, promoting exports, achieving balanced regional development, promoting investments in infrastructure, expanding employment, promoting scientific research and development, and encouraging cooperatives and charitable activities. Similarly, the excise duty is supposed to provide preferential treatment to activities like promotion of small-scale industries by keeping the threshold high, promoting backward area development and units in special economic zones. Incorporation of all these objectives in tax laws creates enormous avenues for evasion and avoidance, and no one can be sure how much of these objectives are achieved if at all. Having given all these concessions, when the companies take advantage of them and reduce their tax liability, the government comes up with a minimum alternative tax.

Since 2006, Government of India has been publishing estimates of revenue foregone from various tax concessions in the budget. For 2014–2015, the budget estimates the revenue foregone at a staggering Rs. 5.89 trillion. Of this, Rs. 3.01 trillion is on account of customs and Rs. 1.85 trillion is on account of excise duties. These are at best indicative and there are shortcomings in the methodology employed. The difference between the rates specified in the tariff schedule and the actual rate applied on the value of imports is taken as the revenue forgone in the case of customs duty. Indeed, when an essential commodity is imported due to domestic shortage, the government applies lower rates in public interest. There is question of the right level of customs duty itself because that is simply the protection given to the producers. In a sense, all import duties are equivalent to taxing people to subsidize to domestic producers. Similarly, the exemptions given to imports used in the processing for re-exports should not be included in the revenue forgone for all exports should go without any domestic taxes to ensure competitiveness to producers. Similarly, exemptions are given to a large number of goods and services in GST not only because they are consumed predominantly by lower income groups but also for administrative and a variety of other reasons.

Nevertheless, the revenue foregone estimates bring out glaring impact of various incentives on revenue productivity. The revenue lost on account of concessions in corporate income tax in 2018–2019 was estimated at Rs. 1.04 trillion. Of this, the concessions on export profits for units located in special economic zones was Rs. 228.9 billion and Rs. 182 billion was foregone on account of concessions given to companies in the power and infrastructure sectors and another Rs. 48 billion for companies located in Northeastern and Himalayan States. In the case of personal income tax, total revenue forgone on account of tax concessions was Rs. 951 billion of which concession to savings schemes was Rs. 670 billion and Rs. 46.3 billion was accounted for health insurance schemes. Interestingly, the incentive given to savings in specified instruments may not add much to additional savings as, once the required amount is saved for 5 years, that may simply be reinvested.

(c) Revenue Concentration from Petroleum Products

An important development of the tax system over the years is the heavy reliance on collecting excise tax revenue from petroleum products. In 2018–2019, revenue from petroleum tax by the Central government constituted 11.1 per cent of its gross tax revenue and 28.2 per cent of the revenue from domestic consumption taxes. The government has found it easier to levy the tax as the demand for petroleum products is price inelastic and the resistance to the tax is much less. At the State level, the sales taxes on petroleum products in 2018–2019 constituted 23.8 per cent of States' own revenue. In fact, both Centre and State governments resorted to imposing additional taxes on petroleum products after the coronavirus pandemic struck to make up for the revenue losses due to the lockdown.

Petroleum products constitute a major input for transportation and higher taxes on these items increase transportation cost of producers and consumers alike. As these products are not included in the GST, there is no input tax relief to the producers impacting on their competitiveness adversely. Interestingly, when the international price of crude oil declines, the Governments find it attractive to increase domestic taxes to garner more revenue and the consumers do not get any benefit from the lower international price. It is necessary to reduce the rates of these taxes and also include these items in the GST to reduce the burden on the consumers.

(d) Low Productivity of Property Tax

One of the major shortcomings of the Indian tax system is the low revenue productivity from property taxes. In most multilevel fiscal systems, property tax plays an important role in financing local services. It is also a preferred means of financing local services because and is relatively immobile and therefore less distorting, visible, simple, and easy to administer at the local level. This is an important instrument to link revenue–expenditure decisions at the local level because it is largely a benefit tax and for that reason, it is supposed to evoke greater degree of compliance. It is also argued that fiscal differentials at local levels get capitalized into property values and a part of the gain can be harnessed in terms of the property tax (Oates, 1969).

Despite visibility, localized nature, and stronger linkage of the tax with beneficiaries of services, the tax on immovable properties has not been successful in India. In contrast to OECD countries which, on average, raise about 2 per cent of GDP from property taxes and developing and transitional countries where the average is about 0.6 to 0.7 per cent, the amount of tax raised through property taxes in India is negligible. The available estimate based on the sample surveys of municipalities for the Thirteenth Finance Commission for 2006–2007 showed that revenue collections from the tax ranged from 0.16 per cent to 0.24 per cent of GDP. The revenues have not only been low but also stagnant over the years.

There are a number of reasons for the low revenue collections from property tax and its slow growth. The most important reason is the poor coverage of the tax and its low collection efficiency. Poor coverage is due to (i) wide-ranging exemptions; (ii) poor information system and lack of up-to-date registry of land and properties by municipal bodies; (iii) existence of vacant properties.

Exemptions vary from State to State and from one municipal body to another, but there are some common alities. Article 285 of the Constitution provides exemption to all properties belonging to the Union government. The big metropolitan cities also have large unauthorized buildings and properties not included in the municipal register which, while availing the municipal services, do not pay the tax. Other important exemptions include places of religious worship, educational institutions, charitable institutions, ancient and historical monuments, burial and cremation grounds, government land and buildings set apart for free recreational purposes, offices of trade union associations, buildings and lands of urban development authority constituted under the respective state government acts, institutions providing free medical relief and education, and certain types of vacant lands and buildings. In addition, there may be exemptions and concessions for the properties owned by ex-servicemen and their families.

Poor information system on properties is another important reason for the low revenue productivity. Lack of clarity on property ownership or tenancy rights and a cadastre that uniquely identifies properties and their owners is a major constraint. In addition, ambiguity in ownership and tenancy rights and inability to adopt market-based valuation place constraints in increasing the revenue productivity of the tax. Most municipal bodies have not made attempts to update the registers relating to property ownership and tenancies nor do they coordinate with the registration department for getting information on the properties transferred and their values.

Many municipalities have simply not updated their property tax registers and many properties are simply not included in the tax base. The Administrative Reforms Commission has noted that only about 60–70 per cent of the properties in urban areas are actually assessed (India, 2015 b). The Commission recommended the matching of the properties paying the tax with those in the Geographical Information System (GIS) to identify those properties not paying the tax.

The problem of low coverage of properties is compounded by poor collection efficiency. This arises from the actual values of properties assessed are significantly lower than the market values and increases in the value of properties on account of both improvements to existing properties and increase in prices are not adequately captured in the tax base. Often assessed values are as low as 8–10 per cent of the market values and on an average about 30 per cent of the market values in 36 largest municipal corporations. Any attempt to increase the value from such a low base to resemble market values will meet with severe opposition (Rao and Rao, 2008).

(e) Tax Abuse by Multinational Corporates

The fifth important factor eroding the base is the way in which multinationals operate in the country. 'Base erosion and profit shifting' by multinational companies is a worldwide phenomenon. Multinational companies indulge in a variety of ways to avoid taxes. Creating a web of complex subsidiaries and shifting the profits to subsidiaries in low-tax jurisdictions and taking advantage of tax treaties is a common method employed. Manipulating prices in related party transactions, or what is usually referred to as transfer pricing to reduce the tax liability is another method used. Although there are 'arm's length pricing rules' to deal with the transfer pricing issue, it is difficult to apply them in practice when intangible assets, such as trade names, goodwill, brand recognition, or intellectual property, such as patents, copyrights, brands and trademarks, and business methodologies, are involved. Multinational companies also act as intermediaries in product sales and distribution, make loans and interest payments, and charge fees to one another for activities, such as management services, treasury services, and investment services, to reduce the tax liability.

Tax avoidance by multinational companies is a global phenomenon. There is overwhelming evidence of this tax abuse even in developed countries, such as the United Kingdom, the United States, and member States of the European Union (EU). This prompted the Group of 20 (G-20) countries to request the Organisation for Economic Co-operation and Development (OECD) to develop a base erosion and profit shifting system action plans in September 2013. OECD has come up with 15 action plans for countries to follow in its various reports. However, those proposals do not go far enough. In fact, there is considerable unease among the developing countries about the OECD proposals because of the discussion on this in OECD is dominated by developed countries and the representatives of multinational enterprises and the interests of developed and developing counties do not always converge.

The Independent Commission for the Reform of International Corporate Taxation (ICRICT), a group of leaders from government, academia, and civil society created to promote reforms, in its review of the action plans states that they are a patchwork of existing approaches. Multinational enterprises are essentially unified firms organized to maximize profits across jurisdictions and treat them as independent entities, making the application of the arm's length principle for transfer pricing meaningless. Large multinational enterprises are oligopolies; there are no comparable local firms that can serve as benchmarks. In addition, the OECD action plans fail to deal with the problem of shifting profits through the exploitation of intangible assets mentioned above. The ICRICT (2018) declaration calls for a paradigm shift. In the declaration, it is stated that to seriously attempt to stop base erosion and profit shifting, there must be a change in the mindset that a multinational enterprise is comprised of separate independent entities. The ICRICT has recommended that a multinational enterprise and its subsidiaries be considered as a single firm and that its worldwide profits to individual countries should be allocated according to an agreed formula that includes such factors as employment, sales and resources used, and fixed costs. Almost all multinational enterprises are listed on the stock market and would not understate their worldwide profits. It should, however, be noted that formulary allocation can result in tax competition by individual countries to attract investment in their jurisdictions. To avoid such a race to the bottom, a consensus on a minimum tax rate be reached.

However, the challenges of arriving at a consensus formula at the international level are formidable, as the interest of countries is not single peaked. When there are differences, multinational enterprises tend to play one country against another. Accordingly, even though taking the unitary approach and applying a formulary apportionment remains the goal, the Commission recommends interim approaches with a single entity as the centrepiece of reform. The important point is that forcing the multinational enterprises to pay legitimate taxes, particularly to developing countries, is a formidable task. While this is work in progress, the way forward is not to treat the affiliates of multinational enterprises as different entities but to consolidate their profits and allocate them based on a formula. This also requires a change in the global system of tax governance to ensure universal membership and an open and democratic structure. There is a strong basis behind bringing international taxation matters under the United Nations aegis, as this institution alone can provide the sanctity for rules based on the principle of sovereignty of all countries. The recent G-20 agreement to levy 15 per cent on the profits of the multinationals makes some progress in dealing with the issue.

In Indian context, there is considerable evidence to show that multinational companies have been indulging in abusive tax practices. Patnaik and Shah (2011) show that the effective corporation tax rate on multinational companies is significantly lower than domestic companies. Rao and Sengupta (2014), in their more detailed study, indicate that during the period 2006–2011, the effective interest rate paid by multinational companies was higher than the market rate and the amount of tax paid per unit of borrowing was lower. A more recent study, conducted by Petr and Prats (2013), is based on sample data of multinationals in India. It shows that those entities report 1.5 per cent less profits, pay 17.4 per cent less in taxes per unit of asset, pay 30.3 per cent less taxes per unit of profit, and have 11.4 per cent higher debt ratios than companies with no connection to tax havens. The Government of India has passed the General Anti-Avoidance Rule and has been applying it. Nevertheless, building administrative capacity to enforce tax payments by the multinational enterprises remains a major challenge.

(f) Low Capacity of Tax Administration

Tax administration is a critical element in the tripod of tax systems, namely architecture, engineering, and management. In fact, Milka Casanegra

(1990: 179) states that in developing countries Tax administration is tax policy'. According to Richard Bird (2004), 'The best tax policy is worth little if it cannot be implemented effectively'. However, the issue of tax administration is not just about its effective implementation. It has to do with ability to enforce the tax on complex dealings of taxpayers, particularly the multinational companies, the attitude of the tax administration towards taxpayers, the taxpayers' confidence and trust with the tax administration, and clarity in laws to avoid discretion to tax administrators.

By all accounts, Indian tax administration does not evoke much confidence and trust that a modern tax administration requires. There have been a number of reports on the reform of the tax administration beginning with Report of the Tax Reforms Commission (1991). The careful studies by Das-Gupta and Mukherjee (1998), Bagchi et al. (1995), and more recently The Reports of the Tax Administration Reforms Commission (India, 2014, 2015) have dealt with various aspects of the reform of tax administration in detail. The issue is one of implementation of reforms which requires political will rather than identification of reforms areas.

The important problems of tax administration in India have to deal with (i) lack of autonomy; (ii) morale of tax administrators arising from organization structure of administration, the prospects of progression in the careers of administrators, their subjugation to general administrators; (iii) organizational problems of separation of direct and indirect tax administration into Central Board of Direct Taxes (CBDT) and Central Board of Excise and Customs renamed as Central Board of Indirect Taxes and Customs (CBIC), their independent functioning and lack of coordination between the two; (iv) area-wise rather than functional divisions and lack of functional specialization including developing intelligence system; (v) lack of information system and use of technology for tax administration; (vi) perverse incentive from setting targets to tax administrators and judging their performances based on the fulfilment of the targets; (vii) poor capacity to forecast revenues and its adverse impact on expenditure management at both Union and State levels; (viii) lack of clarity in tax laws and wide discretion to tax officials and build-up of huge amount of revenues; (ix) adversarial attitude of the tax administration towards taxpayers essentially as tax evaders rather than agents who collect the tax from the people on behalf of the tax departments.

While the problems with both the organizational set up and the functioning of the tax administration are well known, there have been some attempts to address them. After the introduction of GST, the taxpayer number for GST was linked to permanent account number of Income tax and it is hoped that in the future, there will be better coordination of the two departments to undertake scrutiny of both income tax and GST. Another important reform has been the requirement for electronic filing of the returns and payment of refunds directly to the accounts of the taxpayers. The government has also given instructions to the CBDT that they should not appeal to the income tax appellate tribunal if the disputed amount is less than Rs. 50 lakhs to avoid piling of cases in the tribunal and adding to tax arrears. The recent rescinding of retrospective tax amendment on capital gains taxation on transactions in other countries is an important decision which is likely to infuse greater confidence in the stability of the tax system, These are only small initiatives, and by and large, the tax administration does not invoke much confidence among the taxpayers to improve the voluntary tax compliance.

4.5. Recent Reforms and the Way Forward

Direct and indirect taxes must be reformed at the national level and the state level in India to boost the revenue productivity of the tax system to raise the tax ratio required for development. Some of those reforms can be implemented immediately, whereas others can be carried out only in the medium and long term. Some of the reforms can be set easily, while for others, the challenges associated with carrying them out are formidable.

As emphasized by Johnson and Myles (2011: 323):

> In the real world, proposals for tax reform are constrained by politics; those that lose from tax reforms tend to be vengeful while those who gain from them tend to be ungrateful. This can lead in tax policy, perhaps more than in any other areas of public policy, to a 'tyranny of the status quo'. There is always a tension between what is economically desirable and what is politically practical.

The most formidable task in developing a comprehensive income tax in India, as pointed out earlier, is the fractured assignment system. While it may not be easy to integrate income from agricultural and non-agricultural sectors, the practical solution may be to enter into an agreement with the states. Under such an agreement, tax would be levied according to applicable rates on the income declared as agricultural income after allowing deductions for crop insurance premiums while computing the agricultural income and distributing the proceeds to the states from which the income originates. This, however, is not going to be easy, as it would face a wild political storm. Nevertheless, this type of agreement should be in the reform agenda for the medium term. Ways and means must be found to tax the income from corporations involved in farm activities and a mechanism is needed to provide a check against mis-declaring non-farm income as agricultural income to evade the tax.

The first discussion paper on a direct taxes code was a well-thought-out document. Many of the suggestions contained in it, particularly those relating to grandfathering the tax exemptions and concessions merit consideration to broaden the base, increase revenue productivity, and reduce unintended distortions in resource allocation. It is also important to work on a time-bound plan to effectively apply the general anti-avoidance rules applied to multinational companies. To develop the capacity to administer it, a special unit may be created and a time-bound plan for building capacity should be followed. Indeed, there is need to overhaul the administrative framework to enable functional specialization and coordination among various tax departments, including sharing of information. However, the transition is not likely to be easy. In the short term, it would be advisable to create specialized agencies, such as the one for administering the general anti-avoidance rule and, effect proper administrative divisions into various functionally specialized groups from the prevailing region-based divisions. The reform process needs to be initiated with the intention to simplify and rationalize the tax system with a view to broaden the base, simplify the tax by weeding out various tax preferences, strengthen the information system and technology-assisted enforcement.

An important reform undertaken recently relates to the Corporation tax. The Finance Minister in his Budget Speech in 2014 had stated that the rate of company tax would be reduced to 25 per cent in phases to make it competitive. It was reduced to 25 per cent for companies with turnover up to Rs. 4 billion by 2018–2019. However, in the Budget presented in July 2019, the new Finance Minister brought it down to 22 per cent if tax concessions are not availed and the tax rate for new companies was reduced to 15 per cent and the rate of minimum alternative tax (MAT) was reduced from 18 per cent to 15 per cent. This is an important reform in the direction of broadening the base and reducing the rate, though reducing the MAT rate does not make much sense as the objective should be to make availing concessions less attractive. In the 2020–2021 budget, the option was given to avail concessions and pay higher rate of tax or not avail concessions but paying tax at lower rate in the case of personal income tax as well.

Regarding indirect taxes, following more than 14 years of discussion, the Government has implemented a major tax reform by consolidating a number of national and state indirect taxes to introduce GST at both the national and state levels. The reform was unveiled with much fanfare at midnight on 1 July 2017 and has been touted as and promised to be a 'good and simple tax' and the 'one nation, one market, one tax'. The tax is still evolving, but the experience so far has not justified that claim. The tax has three components, a general GST, a state GST, and an interstate GST. The tax is administered by a seamless input tax credit mechanism throughout the country with interstate transactions subject to the interstate GST and a clearing house mechanism ensuring that the tax accrues to the state of destination. A separate body, the GST Council, was constituted with representation of Central and State finance ministers and chaired by the national finance minister. It makes all decisions relating to the structure and operational decisions. Given the far-reaching consequences of this reform, the evolution and implementation of GST are discussed in a separate chapter.

The recent tendency to increase tariffs, however, is retrograde. After the experience of import substitution strategy by providing high protection through tariff and non-tariff barriers, it was dismantled since 1991 to make the Indian manufacturing more competitive. However, during the last 3 years, the protectionist trend has been pronounced in the name of 'boosting domestic production', 'incentivizing domestic value addition', and promoting 'make in India'. In the 2018–2019 budget, import tariffs were increased on 46 consumer goods to provide, 'adequate protection to the domestic industry'. The subsequent budgets in 2019 and 2020 have maintained the trend of increasing tariffs. This is clearly retrograde and will have adverse effects on productivity and competitiveness in the medium and long term. A major problem with the Indian tax system has been the lack of predictability in tax policy. The decision to amend the law to levy capital gains tax on offshore transactions retrospectively in 2012 after the government lost the Vodafone case in the Supreme Court has been criticized extensively. This was a major plank on which the present ruling party criticized the then government, but it took over 7 years for it to withdraw the amendment. The retrospective amendment has sent a wrong signal to foreign investors and its withdrawal signals an investor-friendly approach.

Appendix 4.A1. Estimation of Taxable Capacity in India

Rao and Kumar (2018) estimate India's taxable capacity in a cross-country econometric analysis. Based on the availability of continuous time series data for the variables employed, a panel of 115 countries for the years 2005 - 2015 was chosen. The variables used to determine taxable capacity in the equation are the ratio of urban population to total population, the consumer price index for inflation, per capita income in purchasing power parity (PPP) dollars, and the share of revenue from natural resources. These variables were collected from WDI (World Development Indicator) database of the World Bank. The log of the per capita income in the estimation is used.

Tax potential is analysed by estimating the equation of the form:

$$\left(\frac{T}{Y}\right)=c+\left(\frac{Rn}{R}\right)+Ln\left(\frac{Y}{P}\right)+U+Inf+\in$$

where *T/Y* denotes tax-GDP ratio, *Y/P* represents per capita GDP, *Rn/R* represents the share of revenue from natural resources in total revenues, U denotes the share of urban population to total population, and Inf denotes consumer price index inflation. Tax revenue data are the sum total of the tax revenue being generated at different levels of government(s) in a country. While *Y/P* represents the ability of the people to pay taxes, *Rn/R* takes into account the need to raise tax revenue is lower in countries that derive substantial revenue from natural resources.

The results of the estimated regressions are presented in Table 4.A1.1. The predicted value of tax-GDP ratio (year 2015) for India based on the above estimates using pooled data, fixed effect, and random effect model are 20.16, 19.27, and 19.008, respectively. The Hausman test suggests use of fixed effect model estimates according to which India should have generated a tax-GDP ratio of 19.27 per cent in 2015, as compared to its actual ratio of 16.5 per cent.

Table 4.A1.1 Estimated Tax-GDP Ratio Using Panel Data.

	Pooled estimate (robust SE)	**Fixed effect estimate**	**Random effect estimate**
Intercept	−29.876 (2.039)***	5.869 (3.015)**	−0.529 (2.831)
Share of revenue from natural resources in total revenue	−2.009 (0.174)***	−0.229 (0.111)**	−0.400 (0.108)***
Urbanization	0.047 (0.014)***	0.151 (0.041)***	0.141 (0.029)***
Log (per capita income in PPP $ terms)	5.564 (0.276)***	0.995 (0.411)***	1.73 (0.375)***
Inflation	0.036 (0.037)	−0.039 (0.012)***	−0.035 (0.012)***
Note: Hausman test indicates use of fixed effect model over the random effect model			
Number of observations	1178	1178	1178
Predicted value of Tax-GDP ratio for India (year 2015)	20.16 (0.30)	19.27 (0.92)	19.008 (0.90)

Note: Standard errors are in parenthesis. ***, ** denote 1 per cent and 5 per cent level of significance, respectively.

Source: Estimated by the author.

5

Goods and Services Tax in India

Progress, Performance, and Prospects

> To put the point in zoological terms, VAT is neither a gorilla nor a chimpanzee but rather a genus like 'primates'.
>
> —Bird and Gendron (2007: 10)

5.1. Introduction

The Goods and Services Tax (GST) in India has been variously described as 'one country-one tax', 'a game changer', and 'a reform of the century'. The implementation of a standard invoice-credit destination-based value-added tax (VAT) on goods and services in a large and diverse federal country at both national and subnational levels ruled by different political parties is a remarkable achievement. Almost all the countries that have implemented GST have taken considerable time to settle down, and even in Canada, the VAT on goods and services implemented at both federal and provincial levels almost 30 years ago is still evolving (Bird, 2012). The challenge of implementing such a reform at national and subnational levels in India involving the Union government, 28 States, and three Union Territories with legislatures with different ruling parties is formidable. The reform of this nature is a great experiment in cooperative federalism and required a States manlike stewardship.[1]

[1] In the Gulati Memorial lecture delivered in 2011, Rao (2011) had stated, 'reform of this nature involving both Centre and States is an experiment in cooperative federalism and requires stewardship by the Statesmen' (Rao, 2011).

Studies in Indian Public Finance. M. Govinda Rao, Oxford University Press. © Oxford University Press 2022.
DOI: 10.1093/oso/9780192849601.003.0005

As of 2018, of the 193 countries with UN Membership, 166 including all OECD Member countries except the United States of America had implemented the VAT on goods and services in one form or another. Most of the developing countries have replaced their cascading domestic trade taxes with VAT to reduce distortions or as a measure to recoup revenue loss arising from the reduction in tariffs on joining the WTO. The GST was expected to be a money machine and was found to be an appropriate instrument to offset revenue losses from reducing tariffs.[2] Once introduced, only five countries have repealed the VAT only to reintroduce it with improvements.[3] Not surprisingly, IMF has been a leading change agent (Bird and Gendron, 2007) of the reform and this has generally been an important reform component for the countries participating in the Fund programme (Keen, 2009).

In most of the countries, transition to the VAT/GST has been relatively smooth because the tax is essentially levied by the Central government. Even when federal countries like Australia or Germany levied the VAT, it was at the Central level. The only other examples of subnational foray into GST are Brazil, Canada, and the EU and even after years of experience in these countries, the reform is still a work in progress. In the case of Brazil, the tax is levied on the basis of origin principle in the case of interstate trade and there is no conceptual and administrative clarity in the federal and State versions of VAT. Besides the problems with cross-border trade and interstate tax exportation, it has significant compliance, administrative, and distortion costs (Bird and Gendron, 2007; Varsano, 2000). In the EU, all 27 member states levy the VAT because its adoption is a condition for the membership. It is a destination-based tax, but the issue of cross-border trade continues to be a subject of discussion (Cnossen, 2010; Keen, 2009). Furthermore, there is no uniformity in the structure of the tax among the member countries in terms of thresholds, exempted goods and services, and the structure of rates. In fact, the standard rate of VAT in EU varies from 15 per cent to 25 per cent with a mean of 19.4 per cent and except for Denmark, every other

[2] Keen and Lockwood (2010: 148) test in a cross-country analysis test whether the introduction of VAT in countries has led to increase in revenue conclude, 'The impression that emerges is that adoption has increased revenue and improved effectiveness in the large majority of countries that have implemented the VAT and would do so too for most of those have not'.

[3] Bird and Gendron (2007) cite the cases of Belize, Ghana, Grenada, Malta, and Vietnam which repealed the VAT after implementing it, but then reintroduced it in improved form.

European country has one or more rates in addition to the standard rate (Bird and Gendron, 2007). In Canada, Bird (2012) argues that the transition has not been easy and even after 28 years of experience, it is still a work in progress. By 2011, six out of 10 provinces accounting for 80 per cent of the population have imposed some form of VAT. The reduction in the federal VAT rate in 2008 from 7 per cent to 5 per cent and the provision to retain the rate setting by provinces helped to enable some of the provinces to join in the harmonization exercise. Nevertheless, there are four different systems in Canada with (i) four subnational units (Alberta, 3 northern territories and North-eastern Territories of Nunavut and Yukon) not having any sales tax; (ii) five subnational governments (New Brunswick, Nova Scotia, Newfoundland, Prince Edward Island and Ontario) joining the VAT regime with Harmonized Sales Taxes (HST), with rates varying from 8 per cent to 10 per cent. In 2013, the cumulative GST rate varied from 13 per cent in Ontario to 15 per cent in Nova Scotia; (iii) two provinces (Saskatchewan and Manitoba) continuing to levy separate GST on the tax base including the federal tax; and (iv) one province—Quebec, levying VAT at 9.975 per cent and administering the federal VAT along with the provincial VAT. In British Columbia, the agreement to join the harmonization exercise was controversial and, in a referendum held on April 2013, the State reverted to levying the earlier provincial sales tax.

After several years of deliberations, India implemented the GST from 1 July 2017 with the participation of both Centre and all the States. The tax on the supply of goods and services replaced a number of domestic trade taxes. It is designed as a destination-based tax. There is a Central GST (CGST), a State GST (SGST), and an interstate GST (IGST), with the revenue from the latter put in a separate account to allow adjustment for input tax credit and finally settled to the States on the basis of final consumption through a clearing house mechanism. Thus, the GST in India is designed to be a destination-based tax with seamless input tax credit mechanism. The decisions relating to the structure of the tax are taken by a separate institution created by amending the Constitution—the GST Council, registration, payment, and submission of returns are to be done through the IT-enabled GST Network (GSTN) minimizing the interface between the taxpayer and the collector.

The GST has been implemented with very high expectations of achieving a simpler, more transparent, revenue productive, and less distorting tax.

Even after three and a half years of implementation, the tax has been evolving as the GST Council makes frequent changes. Nevertheless, the time is opportune to take stock of the progress in implementing the tax, analyse its revenue implications and economic impact, and identify further challenges and reform areas to reach the goal of raising revenue productivity and minimizing the three associated costs to the economy, namely, administrative cost, compliance cost, and the distortion cost.

5.2. Implementation of GST in India: Salient Features

International experience with the implementation of GST shows that there is 'no one size fits all' or a unique GST. There are different models with varying structure and implementation systems in different countries depending on what is politically acceptable. However, the general principles recommended by most experts are to (i) aim for a comprehensive base with few exemptions, credits, rebates, or deductions; (ii) do not use the tax system to achieve too many social and economic goals; (iii) keep the threshold at a reasonably high level to focus the administration on the 'whales' rather than 'minnows'. This will serve the purpose of not only minimizing administrative cost but also serve the cause of equity (Keen and Mintz, 2004); (iv) the tax structure should be simple to minimize administrative, compliance, and distortion costs; (v) continuously monitor the tax system, focus on basic tasks such as tax deduction at source and an ID number system; (vi) do not collect more information than that can actually be processed; (vii) actively encourage good record-keeping and aim at long-term goal of self-assessment. However, even as conventional wisdom on GST has been proved right, it is not always possible to strictly adhere to them. In fact, as Bird and Gendron (2007: 4) state, 'Some "bad" features—such as too high or too low thresholds, overly extensive exemptions, or multiple rates—may be essential to successful adoption in the first place'. At the same time, they caution, 'Such features may prove to be extremely difficult to remove'.[4]

[4] Bird and Gendron (2007) refer to the recommendation of a committee in Sweden to switch over to one rate of tax (from two), which was not accepted.

The invoice-credit, destination-based GST system is one of the few examples of subnational VAT. The implementation was preceded by considerable deliberations and consensus was built over 17 years. The earliest recommendation for the adoption of GST came first from an Expert Group on Taxation of Services (India, 2001), chaired by Govinda Rao, which was recommended again by the Task Force on Indirect Taxes (Chairman: Vijay Kelkar; India, 2003). Subsequently, the States moved over to the VAT on goods in 2005 replacing their cascading, type sales taxes and the Union excise duties were converted into a form of VAT called the CENVAT levied on manufactured goods. A separate tax on services was levied, initially on three services,[5] but the coverage was later progressively expanded, and in 2012, all services with a small negative list were included in the base. There were considerable deliberations in the Empowered Committee of State Finance Ministers to rationalize domestic indirect trade taxes and it was announced in the Union Finance Minister's budget speech of 2006 that the GST would be implemented from 2010. However, consensus on the structure of the tax could not be reached, and, finally, the reform was implemented from 1 July 2017.

Unlike in most of the countries where VAT was adopted for enhancing revenue productivity as it was considered to be a 'money machine' (Keen and Lockwood, 2010), the reform in India was mainly motivated by the desire to unify multiple trade taxes, reduce distortions, and harmonize the indirect taxes between the Centre and States. The short-term focus was to have a structure which is revenue neutral though in the medium and long term, it was hoped that better compliance would ensure higher revenue productivity.

The GST combines a number of Central and State taxes listed in Table 5.1. In some ways, the reform is a unique experiment in both Central and State governments giving up their tax autonomy in favour of harmonization of the domestic consumption tax system. The GST comprises of a Central GST (CGST), State GST (SGST), and interstate GST (IGST). The tax is designed to be destination based and the revenue from inter-state transactions is put in the IGST account and eventually distributed according to destination through a clearing house mechanism. The

[5] The three services chosen for taxation in the first instance were non-life insurance, telecom, and stock brokerage services.

Table 5.1 Central and State Taxes Subsumed Under GST.

Central taxes	State taxes
(i) Central excise duty (except five petroleum and tobacco products)	(i) State value-added tax (VAT)/sales tax (except five petroleum products and alcoholic liquor for human consumption)
(ii) Additional excise duty	(ii) Entertainment tax (other than the tax levied by the local bodies)
(iii) Service tax	(iii) Central sales tax (levied by the Centre and collected by the States)
Countervailing customs duty	(iv) Octroi[a] and Entry tax
Special additional duty of customs	(v) Purchase tax
	(vi) Luxury tax
	Taxes on lottery, betting, and gambling

Source: India (2019).

[a] Octroi is a tax on the entry of goods into a local area for consumption, use, or sale.

Constitution was amended to create GST as a joint tax of the Centre and the States (Article 269 A), to be administered by a new Constitutional body—the GST Council chaired by the Union Finance Minister and with Finance Ministers or other ministers nominated by the Chief Ministers of the States and Union Territories with legislatures as Members. The Union Revenue Secretary is the Secretary of the Commission, and a separate Secretariat was set up to oversee the functioning of the Council. The decisions taken in the council should have at least two-thirds majority.

The GST Council is an important institutional innovation and an experiment in cooperative federalism. The States agreed to give up their tax autonomy in favour of tax harmonization, but were unwilling to cede it to the Centre, but agreed to have a new institution created in the Constitution with participation by the Centre and each of the States. The Centre has one-third of the voting rights and each of the States has equal rights in the remaining two-thirds. The decision taken in the Constitution is required to have two-third majority. The GST Network (GSTN), a non-profit company, was created to provide common and shared Information Technology (IT), infrastructure and services to the Central and State Governments, taxpayers, and other stakeholders with the non-government financial institutions owning 51 per cent equity and the Centre and States, the remaining 49 per cent. Although it was decided to make it a fully government-owned company in March 2018, action on that is yet to be taken.

The threshold for registration was kept at Rs. 2 million in non-special category States and Rs. 1 million in special category States.[6] Later, the threshold was raised to Rs. 4 million for goods in the non-special category states, but for services it has continued at Rs. 2 million. For special category States, the limit for goods was raised to Rs. 2 million. Businesses are required to register in each of the States where it has branches. Interstate self-supplies are taxable. Administration of the tax was divided between the Centre and respective States. All taxpayers below Rs. 15 million were to be administered by the concerned State where they are registered and the responsibility for administering those above the Rs. 15 million was divided between the Centre and the respective States equally based on random selection. The dealers with less than Rs. 15 million also have the choice of paying a simplified tax at a compounded rate of 6 per cent (3 per cent each to the Centre and to the concerned State) on the turnover without any provision for input tax credit (ITC).

The implementation of GST was preceded by considerable deliberations including those on the structure of rates. The committee appointed by the Ministry of Finance with the Chief Economic Adviser as the Chairman (India, 2015a), suggested that the revenue neutral rate would be in the range of 15–15.5 per cent (Centre and States combined). It recommended that although India should strive towards a single rate in the medium term in keeping with international practice and to facilitate administrative and compliance ease, in the immediate context it could have a three-rate structure (excluding zero), comprising of a lower rate of 12 per cent, a standard rate varying between 17 and 18 per cent and a very high rate of 40 per cent on 'demerit' goods.

In the GST that was finally adopted, goods and services are classified according to harmonized system of nomenclature (HSN) and the tax is levied at 0 per cent, 5 per cent, 12 per cent, 18 per cent, and 28 per cent. There is no standard rate, but most services are taxed at 18 per cent. A special rate of 0.25 per cent is applicable on precious and semi-precious stones and gold is taxed at 3 per cent. The job work done in diamond industry is to be taxed at 1.5 per cent.[7] The items

[6] Mountainous states with international borders having very low tax bases are declared as 'special category states' by the National Development Council.

[7] The rate was 5 per cent but was brought down to 1.5 per cent in the 37th meeting of the GST Council on 20 September 2019.

classified as 'demerit' and 'luxury' items of consumption such as aerated drinks, automobiles, air conditioners and washing machines, cement, paint, marble, accommodation in five-star hotels, and tobacco products are taxed at 28 per cent. In addition to the basic rate, most items under the last category are subject to the compensation cess, the proceeds of which are used to pay compensation to the States for any loss of revenue arising from the implementation of GST (discussed next). The GST Council also acceded to the request of Kerala State and allowed a levy of a separate cess on financing reconstruction of infrastructure damaged by the flood of 2018. For smaller suppliers having turnover up to Rs. 15 million, a simplified tax on their turnover at 6 per cent (3 per cent CGST and 3 per cent SGST) without the facility of ITC was levied. The facility of paying the composition tax was extended also to restaurants and affordable housing under construction at 1 per cent and other housing at 5 per cent without the benefit of ITC.[8] The collections from the IGST are supposed to be kept in a separate account and allocated between the Centre and the States after adjusting their respective ITCs. Zero rating of the exports is done by the exporters paying the tax first and claiming refunds. The revenue from the compensation cess is supposed to be put in the Public Account and used to compensate the States for any shortfall in the promised revenue collections.[9]

To get the States to agree, the Central government agreed to compensate any shortfall in their actual revenues from the potential revenues from the merged taxes. This is estimated by taking 2015–2016 revenues from the merged taxes certified by the C&AG increased by 14 per cent every year for a period of 5 years. As mentioned earlier, the compensation was to be financed by a separate cess on the demerit and luxury items over and above CGST and SGST levied at rates varying from 15 per cent to 96 per cent of the tax rate applicable. The analysis of the trends in the state tax merged in the GST shows that to secure the agreement with the States, the Central government settled for a generous scheme of taking 14 per cent growth on the 2015–2016 base year collections although the actual growth was much lower (Table 5.2).

[8] Affordable housing is defined as tenements having a carpet area less than 90 square metres in non-metropolitan towns and less than 60 square metres in Metropolitan cities and having a value of less than Rs. 4.5 million.

[9] The budget has consolidated fund, contingency fund, and public accounts. Public account includes only those items for which the Government merely acts as a banker/trustee for custody. These are not subject to vote in the Parliament.

Table 5.2 Average Growth Rate of State Taxes Subsumed in GST.

State	2014–2015 to 2016–2017	2012–2012 to 2016–2017
Andhra Pradesh	3.5	1.2
Bihar	13.0	22.6
Chhattisgarh	8.7	10.5
Goa	10.5	10.2
Gujarat	3.6	8.5
Haryana	11.7	11.8
Jharkhand	13.1	13.5
Karnataka	10.7	13.3
Kerala	10.4	12.1
Madhya Pradesh	11.0	12.5
Maharashtra	9.4	10.6
Odisha	6.7	9.4
Punjab	5.9	9.6
Rajasthan	11.6	13.3
Tamil Nadu	6.2	11.2
Telangana	24.8	0.0
Uttar Pradesh	9.4	9.4
West Bengal	7.7	13.8
Aggregate—Non-special Category States	8.9	11.7
Special category states		
Arunachal Pradesh	36.3	28.8
Assam	12.5	10.2
Himachal Pradesh	11.6	11.9
Jammu and Kashmir	9.7	12.0
Manipur	8.0	12.8
Meghalaya	8.9	12.9
Mizoram	20.0	17.6
Nagaland	16.8	12.3
Sikkim	8.7	27.0
Tripura	10.1	10.9
Uttarakhand	13.5	14.5
Special category States	12.3	12.4

Source: Estimated from the State Finances: A Study of Budgets (Various Issues), Reserve Bank of India.

Table 5.2 presents 5-year and 3-year growth rates of the revenue from taxes subsumed in GST in different States. It is seen that the average growth rate for non-special category States for 3 years was 8.9 per cent and for 5 years it was 11.7 per cent. Similarly, for special category States, it was 12.3 and 12.4 per cent. Furthermore, considering that the nominal growth of GDP has since declined, most states are unlikely to show 14 per cent growth and will have to be given compensation. As a result, the Cess to be charged to compensate the taxes had to be high. It is seen that the revenue from compensatory cess constituted almost 8.5 per cent of the GST revenues in 2017–2018 and 8.3 per cent in 2018–2019.

The exemptions and rate structure of GST were determined to (i) ensure that the new levy did not cause any significant increase in consumer prices; (ii) the incidence of GST on individual commodities remained broadly similar to the total incidence of the taxes subsumed in GST; (iii) the rate structure chosen did not result in the loss of revenues. The GST Council set up a 'Fitment Committee', by nominating the officials of the Tax Research Unit of the Central Board of Indirect Taxes and Customs (CBIC) and some senior officials of the Commercial Taxes Departments from selected States. The Committee estimated tax rates on different commodities and services by adding the rates from State VAT with excise duty (CENVAT) (adjusted by adding post-manufacturing margins) and included other taxes subsumed in the GST to arrive at the cumulative rate and fitted the commodities or services to the closest of the four rates chosen. In the process, the opportunity to think afresh in determining the rates to remove the anomalies was missed. However, after implementation, in response to the reactions by the businesses, changes were made in respect of a number of commodities by reducing the tax rate from 28 per cent to 18 per cent and in some cases from 18 per cent to 12 per cent. The facility of composition was extended also to restaurants at 5 per cent without ITC from 12 per cent with ITC. Similarly, the compounding facility was extended to housing under construction as well. Further, even as the tax rates were designed to be uniform across States, the GST Council allowed the State of Kerala to levy a special cess to finance mitigation of the damage caused by the unprecedented flood in 2018–2019.

The taxpayers are required to electronically file a single return for CGST, SGST, IGST, and GST Compensation Cess. Initially, a fully automated system with 100 per cent matching of invoices for ITC was envisaged with taxpayers required to submit three returns GSTR-1, GSTR-2, and GSTR-3 every month and a final annual return at the end of the year. GSTR-1 was required to furnish the details of outward supplies. This information along with the information from tax deducted at source on government transactions and e-commerce supplies are shared electronically with the registered recipients in Form GSTR-2A based on which GSTR-2 was to be filed containing information on inward supplies. GSTR-3 was auto-populated with information from the two forms. However, the system failed because the businesses as well as service providers were not ready and the system itself could not cope with the large number of taxpayers. After repeated postponement, a separate simplified self-assessed summary form GSTR-3B was to be filled as a temporary measure. In July 2018, the GST Council announced that by 1 January 2019, a simplified new return will be rolled out and this has been postponed repeatedly and now the scheduled date is fixed as 30 November. In the absence of a proper return with details of invoices, the self-declaration done in GSTR-3B has continued to the basis for determining the tax liability. From 1 April 2021, the GST Council has tried to simplify the compliance by requiring the businesses with less than Rs. 50 million to file quarterly returns although the tax has to be paid monthly. The technology platform seems to be settling down and the returns planned initially are gradually being reintroduced.

Other features of GST in India include the introduction of e-way bill and reverse-charge mechanism. With the abolition of checkposts across the country after the introduction of GST, a system of web-based e-way bill has been introduced to ensure better compliance of the tax. From 1 April 2019, carrying the e-way bill by the person in charge of the vehicle carrying goods is compulsory for all interstate supplies of value more than Rs. 50,000. All the States have also enacted laws to carry e-way bills even for intrastate supplies, but with varying limits.

The reverse charge is applied on the registered supplier purchasing the taxable supplies from an unregistered supplier. However, looking at the complexity, the proposal was sought to be restricted to all daily transactions above Rs. 5000. In the notification issued in October 2017, the tax payable by the registered person for the supplies of goods and services received from the unregistered suppliers was exempted till 31 March 2018 and in August 2018, the proposal to levy reverse charge was further postponed until 30 September 2019. In a notification in February 2019, it was stated that the Government will specify the class of the registered persons and the categories of goods or services to be subject to reverse charge. However, so far, the Government has not specified the class of registered persons or the categories of goods and services on which the provisions are applicable.

Section 171 of the CGST Act stipulates that the benefit of any lower rate or reduction of GST as compared to the pre-GST existing rate on any supply of goods or services should be passed on to the purchaser by way of lower prices. Failure to do so is considered 'profiteering'. The aggrieved person or organization can make complaints against profiteering with proper evidence. To adjudicate the matter, the Act provides for the setting up of National Anti-profiteering Authority, Directorate General of Anti-Profiteering, and State-level Screening Standing Committees.

5.3. Impact of GST: Cost Savings, Productivity Gains, and Impact on Revenue

(a) Cost Savings and Productivity Gains

The implementation of GST is a major reform and three and a half years is too short a term to assess its impact. Besides, it has been undergoing continuous changes both in the structure and in operational details and in that sense, it is an ongoing reform. Furthermore, given the diversity of Indian federal polity, and the number of States with varying economic characteristics, politically acceptable reform that is implemented is far from being perfect, and it is still evolving. However, given the fact that it has been accepted by the stakeholders, the reform is likely to sustain, though as Bird and Gendron (2007) state, making the required reforms will be challenging.

To analyse the impact of GST, Keen (2013) employs a concept of 'C-Efficiency' in which the share of GST revenue in GDP is decomposed into the standard tax rate, value of consumption (excluding GST), and an interactive term—'C-efficiency'.[10] The latter is the ratio of GST revenue to the

[10] $V/Y = \tau_s E^c (C/Y)$ where V denotes revenue from VAT, Y denotes GDP, τ_s denotes the standard rate of the VAT, and C denotes consumption (valued at VAT exclusive prices). 'C-Efficiency' is estimated as: $E^c = V/\tau_s C$.

product of standard rate and consumption. Using this approach, Acosta-Ormaechea and Morozumi (2019) evaluate the VAT in the EU to conclude that a rise in VAT accompanied by a fall in income taxes promotes growth only when the VAT is raised through 'C-efficiency', and for a given amount of VAT revenue, rise in 'C-efficiency' offset by a fall in standard rate also promotes growth. In Indian context, however, it is not possible to estimate 'C-efficiency' to evaluate the reform for (i) three and a half years is too short a period for undertaking such an empirical analysis and although month-wise collection figures are available, there is no corresponding consumption estimate; (ii) with multiplicity of GST rates in vogue, it is difficult even to identify the standard rate.[11] Therefore, evaluation of the impact of GST has to be based only on anecdotal evidences.

There are some important gains from the GST implementation which are easy to identify though their measurement at this stage is difficult. The first is the fact that it has successfully unified several consumption taxes to reduce both administration and compliance costs. Second, it has succeeded in harmonizing the domestic trade taxes levied vertically between the Centre and States and horizontally between different States. Although the Constitution separates the tax powers of the Centre and States by listing various taxes either in the Union or in the State list, in effect there was concurrency and overlap between the Union excise duties and States' sales taxes. The introduction of GST merged these bases and taxed them together based on the value added. Furthermore, it has eliminated the race to the bottom indulged in by the States to attract trade and investments into their jurisdictions. Similarly, the uniformity in the determination of bases and tax rates as well as laws and procedures along with the elimination of various tax incentives for investment has helped to reduce interstate tax competition[12] and achieve a measure of harmonization. Although interstate suppliers have to deal with the laws of different States, the laws and rules have been made substantially uniform to reduce the compliance burden.

The most important gain from the tax has been the elimination of checkposts to enable unhindered movement goods across the country. This has paved the way for a nationwide market for goods and services.

[11] Unfortunately, GST Council does not share any data required for serious analysis.
[12] Now the tax incentives have to be given as reimbursement of the taxes paid.

According to the Ministry of Road Transport, post-GST, the long-distance travel time for trucks has been reduced by 20 per cent.[13] Abolition of checkposts has not only helped to reduce transportation time but also rent-seeking at the checkposts, which was particularly rampant in States where Octroi and entry taxes were levied. Equally important is the cost savings on account of changes in supply chain management. Earlier, the large companies chose to create branch offices all over the country and send their supplies by way of consignment transfers to avoid the interstate sales tax. With the taxes charged on the supply of goods and services under GST, interstate transactions attract IGST with seamless ITC and, therefore, there are no gains to be had by having branch offices and by sending the commodities through consignment transfers.

A major objective of GST was to minimize cascading of the taxes by providing seamless input tax credit through the production–distribution chain throughout the country. The introduction of GST has considerably reduced it cascading by eliminating it on account of central sales tax by simultaneously taxing the supplies at central and state levels and by providing more systematic input tax credit on interstate sales. Of course, the comparison is with respect to the situation prevailing prior to GST implementation and full realization of this will happen only when the coverage under GST is made comprehensive. This has also helped the exporters to eliminate domestic indirect taxes on exports more comprehensively to impart greater competitiveness.

The electronic administration envisaged under the GST was to eliminate the interface between the taxpayer and tax collector. Right from registration, payment of the tax by availing ITC, filing of returns and assessment, the entire process was designed to be electronically managed without any personnel interface. This was also supposed to ensure faster refunds to the exporters. The mechanism was required also to ensure better compliance with the tax as well. A strong technology platform was critical also for ensuring seamless credit on cross-border supplies. However, glitches in the technology platform have constrained the full realization of these benefits as will be discussed in some detail later.

[13] See https://economictimes.indiatimes.com/news/economy/policy/post-gst-travel-time-of-trucks-has-reduced-by-a-fifth-government/articleshow/59831749.cms?from=mdr.

Another important feature in Indian GST is the creation of the GST Council. This is an important innovation in fiscal federalism where both the Union and State governments pass on their fiscal autonomy to levy important consumption taxes to a joint agency in the interest of tax harmonization (Reddy, 2018). Any change in the structure would require the decision by the Council. A major vacuum in Indian fiscal federalism is the absence of an institution for intergovernmental bargaining, fostering cooperation, regulating competition, and achieving conflict resolution (Rao, 2020) and GST Council provides a model for achieving this in the sphere of tax harmonization. This experiment can be useful to deal with tax harmonization but also can be a useful guide to resolve issues relating to intergovernmental cooperation and conflict resolution. However, it is important to raise a word of caution at this stage. In fact, the decisions taken in the Council have been unanimous and the practice is being persisted with. This has also meant that important decisions requiring substantial changes are hard to be passed, and the reforms will be marked by the tyranny of status quo. Besides, the consensus decisions are likely to be suboptimal (lowest common multiple).

(b) Impact on Revenues

In the short term, the GST was supposed to be revenue neutral; it was expected that over time, higher compliance from self-policing nature of the tax would result in significant revenue productivity. Although three and a half years is a short term to make judgements on revenue gains or losses, particularly as a number of changes in the rates of tax have been made during this period, it helps to identify the measures needed in the short and medium term to improve revenue productivity.

The analysis shows that after the implementation, there has been a deceleration in revenues. For 2017–2018, the C&AG estimates the growth of GST of the Central government (CGST + UTGST + Central part of IGST) by taking into account the revenue from the taxes subsumed in it in the previous years and finds that the revenue actually declined by 10 per cent (India, 2019: 29). This is in spite of excessive drawing of IGST on Centre's account by appropriating unallocated balance in the IGST account into the Central government's consolidated fund. In addition, there was a shortfall in the transfer of the compensation cess into Public Account which was retained by the Centre (India, 2019: 28–29). Estimated effective tax rate (revenue from GST subsumed taxes to private final consumption expenditure) shows a decline from 10.3 per cent in 2015–2016 to 9.8 per cent in 2018–2019. The monthly average revenues in 2018–2019 were higher by the average monthly collection in the 8 months of 2017–2018 (August to March) by just 6 per cent. In 2018–2019, the actual collection from the tax fell short of the budget estimates by a substantial amount. There are only 5 months until October 2020, when the gross collection figures of GST exceeded the one trillion rupees mark.

It is also clear that even from the Central government's own point of view, there has been a significant shortfall in revenue collections. The budget estimate for 2018–2019 for the Central government was Rs. 7.43 trillion and the actual collection according to Controller General of Accounts was Rs. 5.81 trillion which was lower by Rs. 1.62 trillion or by 22 per cent (Table 5.3). Even as compared to the revised estimate, the actual collection was lower by 10 per cent. Even if the lower collections were on account of reduction in the tax rates from 28 per cent to 18 per cent on a number of items in November 2018 is considered, the extent of shortfall is worrisome.

The coronavirus pandemic has brought the issue of poor revenue collections and the associated difficulties for the Union government in paying compensation for the loss of revenues to the States to the forefront. As mentioned earlier, the Union had agreed to compensate for the revenue shortfall from the revenues from the state taxes subsumed

Table 5.3 Revenue Trends in GST of Central Government in 2018–2019.

Tax	Budget estimate (Rs. Billion)	Revised estimate (Rs. Billion)	Actual (Rs. Billion)	Shortfall in actual from budget estimate	Shortfall in actual from revised estimate
CGST	6039	5039	4575.35	−24.24	−9.20
IGST	500	500	289.47	−42.11	−42.11
Comp. cess	900	900	950.81	5.65	5.65
Total	7439	6439	5815.63	−21.82	−9.68

Source: Report of the Comptroller and Auditor General (p. 26).

in GST enhanced at 14 per cent every year. The States had budgeted the GST revenue for 2020–2021 at Rs. 6.5 trillion. The Union government estimated the shortfall at Rs. 3 trillion and after adjusting for the revenue collections from the Cess (Rs. 650 billion) the compensation payable was estimated at Rs. 2.35 trillion. The Union government split this amount as attributable to the 'Act of God' at Rs. 1.68 trillion and presented two options to the States. The first was to allow them to borrow Rs. 970 billion, which was later revised to Rs. 1.1 trillion under the special window to be opened by the RBI and both interest payments and repayments will be met from the future collections of the cess. In the second option, the entire shortfall of Rs. 2.35 trillion could be borrowed from the market and the States were to bear the interest cost, but the repayment will be adjusted against future collections of the cess. This was vehemently opposed by the States. After prolonged discussions, the Union government finally agreed to borrow Rs. 1.1 trillion and pay compensation to the States. The entire episode brought out the fragility of the agreement and casting serious questions on the future of Union State relationships.

The C&AG has made a detailed compliance audit of the technology platform. It observes that complexity of returns and the technical glitches have resulted in the roll back of the originally envisaged full invoice matching system of verification for ITC, using GST returns (GSTRs-1, 2, and 3). The GSTR-3B return, which was introduced as a stopgap measure is a summary return which does not provide the invoice-wise details needed for verification. The absence of proper technology-based verification is prone to ITC frauds. This has also led to continuation of avoidable taxpayer–tax officer interface. The report concludes, 'On the whole, the envisaged GST tax compliance system is non-functional' (India, 2019: 22). Further, the settlement of IGST to the States also could not be done properly as the system failed to generate the required modules such as appeals and refunds from the returns.

The C&AG's audit report also found several other problems which included (i) duplicate records in settlement ledgers; (ii) incorrect settlement of IGST due to erroneous entries in settlement ledgers; (iii) erroneous claim of ITC by one taxpayer accounting for 79 per cent of total ITC claim by all taxpayers for a month exposing the vulnerability of fraudulent claims. The inability to settle the IGST balance after adjusting for cross utilization of input tax credit between SGST, CGST, and IGST led to arbitrary allocation of IGST proceeds to the States in 2017–2018, using the 14th Finance Commission's formula for tax devolution or the original ratio of protected revenues which was clearly arbitrary (Bhaskar, 2019). The failure to firm up the technology platform is also one of the reasons for delay in the settlement of refunds to exporters.

Inability to match invoices to validate input tax credit must be rectified without much loss of time to improve the compliance of the tax. The issue must be dealt with in two ways. First, as argued by Keen and Mintz (2004), threshold should be kept high enough to optimize the collection of tax revenue. This not only helps the tax administration to focus on the large taxpayers but also serves the cause of equity as most of the low-income earners buy their requirements from small traders. Bird and Gendron (2007) after reviewing the experiences of different countries suggest a thumb rule of having a threshold of USD 100,000 for developing countries, and Rao (2011), in a paper written before GST was introduced, had suggested the threshold at Rs. 5 million. The originally set threshold at Rs. 2 million was low and later, it was raised to Rs. 4 million for goods, but for services, the threshold has continued at Rs. 2 million. The GST Council should revisit the issue to have a proper threshold after analysing the turnover range-wise number of taxpayers, their turnovers, and tax paid in each range. It is possible to devise the policing system to minimize the misuse of the threshold by mining the data from the returns. Furthermore, in GST, it does not make sense to have separate thresholds for goods and services.

Unfortunately, GSTN does not put the information of turnover range wise number of taxpayers, their turnover, and tax paid by them and efforts to collect the information did not bear fruit. The analysis based on the information collected for an 'average' State, Karnataka, presented in Table 5.4 shows that over 92 per cent of the taxpayers are in the turnover range of below Rs. 5 million and they account for just about 12 per cent of the GST paid. Increasing the threshold to Rs. 5 million will help to reduce the burden on the technology platform and leaves much more time for the tax administration to focus on bigger taxpayers.

The second issue relates to the desirability of 100 per cent matching of invoices. The early experience of 100 per cent matching of invoices in

Table 5.4 Turnover Range-Wise Number of Taxpayers and Tax Paid in Karnataka 2018–2019.

Turnover range (Rs. Million)	Number of taxpayers	Taxable turnover (Rs. Million)	Tax paid (Rs. Million)	Per cent of taxpayers	Per cent of turnover	Per cent of tax paid	Per cent of tax paid to turnover
<2	490357	1345112	62816	85.42	3.56	7.05	4.67
2–5	41865	1093451	44234	7.29	2.90	4.96	4.05
5–10	18635	1021396	39201	3.25	2.71	4.40	3.84
10–100	20379	3954303	162736	3.55	10.48	18.25	4.12
100–500	2150	3122868	152295	0.37	8.27	17.08	4.88
500–5000	607	4844476	214176	0.11	12.83	24.03	4.42
5000–10000	23	736016	28285	0.00	1.95	3.17	3.84
>10000	18	21627367	187728	0.00	57.30	21.06	0.87
Total	574034	37744989	891471	100.00	100.00	100.00	2.36

Source: Office of the Commissioner of Commercial taxes, Government of Karnataka.

Korea was stated to be not worth the effort (Choi, 1990).[14] The Korean experience showed that the practice was neither efficient nor effective. Therefore, the system was modified in 1988 to require inputting of output invoices above a threshold (approximately £175) and when the discrepancies between input and output invoices or between invoices and VAT returns were higher (approximately £2875), the practice of e-invoicing was adopted. A detailed analysis of Krever (2014) shows that comprehensive invoice matching system imposes very high compliance costs on taxpayers who are least likely to evade VAT and diverts administrative resources from audit processes aimed at uncovering suppression of sales or claims to ITC related to outputs.

Considering the problems faced, it may be appropriate to review the strategy and require invoice matching for the suppliers with turnover of more than some threshold (say Rs. 10 million, and for invoices more than Rs. 5000). Detailed audit can be carried out in cases where there are discrepancies. This will relieve the pressure on the technology platform, reduce the burden on the tax administration, ease information requirements from the taxpayer, and reduce their compliance burden and cost. Even if the threshold is not increased, confining the invoice matching to taxpayers with turnover more than Rs. 10 million will limit the invoice matching requirements to just 8 per cent of the existing taxpayers (Table 5.4). The key is to enforce the tax effectively on the big suppliers and then to leverage the withholding of downstream GST through standard administrative procedures without worrying too much about small suppliers. Of course, this creates incentive to hide below the threshold. However, as the technology stabilizes, the coverage may be extended. It is also possible to intensify information-based policing based on the tax returns of bigger taxpayers.

At the State level, it is difficult to infer the extent of shortfall in revenue collections due to the difficulties in estimating the base year estimates (some taxes like octroi, entry tax, and purchase tax are collected at local levels). Furthermore, arbitrary allocation of IGST makes it difficult to ascertain the actual collections. Thus, from the information available in public domain, it is impossible to find out how many of the States have

[14] Richard Krever (2014) provides very useful insight in the Korean experience. See also Bird and Gendron (2007: 170–171).

actually received the compensation and how many were able to collect more than 14 per cent increase over the base year.[15] Even the budget documents do not show the compensation received under a common revenue head. While some of them put it under GST, some others put it as grant from the Centre and club it under other grants. The data collected from the budget documents from the State governments presented in Table 5.5 show that most of the States had to be paid compensation according to the agreed formula. The States are concerned about the matter as after June 2022, they will not receive any compensation unless, the matter is revisited by the GST Council to extend the period of compensation.

Adhia (2019), the former Secretary of GST Council, presents a picture which is not very different.[16] The revenue shortfall from GST as compared to what the States should have collected from subsumed taxes escalated at 14 per cent in 2017–2018 was 16 per cent and it declined to 12 per cent in 2018–2019. Substantially higher collections in 2018–2019 were seen in the north-eastern states with Mizoram getting the highest increase of 62 per cent followed by Arunachal Pradesh (59 per cent), Manipur (35 per cent), Nagaland (24 per cent), and Sikkim (12 per cent). Among the non-special category states, Andhra Pradesh and Telangana which had a marginal surplus of 4 per cent and 1 per cent, respectively. All other non-special category states had to be given compensation. The deficits were the highest in Punjab (37 per cent), Karnataka (20 per cent), Haryana (16 per cent), and Gujarat (1 per cent). Among the low-income states, there were large deficits as in Chhattisgarh (25 per cent), Odisha (20 per cent), Bihar (18 per cent), Jharkhand (14 per cent), and Madhya Pradesh (14 per cent). The losses were within single digits in Rajasthan (8 per cent), Tamil Nadu (5 per cent), and Maharashtra (4 per cent). In some ways, this was to be expected as the growth rate factored in for determining the compensation was far too optimistic, much higher than the actual growth of taxes subsumed in the GST, and there was little that could contribute to improved compliance. This was before the pandemic struck. In 2020–2021, every State has to face significant shortfalls and the controversy relating to compensation created much distrust between the Centre and States.

[15] Efforts to get this information from the GST Council did not bear fruit.

[16] See https://www.business-standard.com/article/opinion/how-the-states-are-doing-post-gst-119090501480_1.html.

Table 5.5 Compensation Payments to States (Rs. Million).

State	2017–2018	2018–2019 (RE)	2019–2020 (BE)
Andhra Pradesh	5002		
Assam	9027.10	10000.00	10000.00
Bihar	30410.00	0.00	35000.00
Chhattisgarh	14830.00	37003.60	45064.10
Goa	0.00	0.00	0.00
Gujarat	36870.00	0.00	0.00
Haryana	11990.00	28000.00	30000.00
Himachal Pradesh	5390.00	27020.00	29000.00
Jammu And Kashmir	11370.00	25915.30	29543.40
Jharkhand	3690.00	7000.00	2580.00
Karnataka	62460.00	108000.00	172490.00
Kerala	17720.00	21000.00	0.00
Madhya Pradesh	0	0	33000.00
Maharashtra	14880.00		
Manipur	240.00		
Meghalaya	1240.00		
Orissa	20190.00	40740.00	48670.40
Punjab	40370.00	93749.40	86190.30
Rajasthan	25980.00	28250.00	0.00
Tamil Nadu	6320.00	42380.00	55820.00
Uttar Pradesh	21240.00	0.00	0.00
Uttarakhand	12830.00	0.00	30172.50
West Bengal	16876.40	19900.00	20000.00
All States	368925.60	488958.30	627530.70

Source: Budget documents of State governments.

Another important issue relates to the mismatch between the revenue from compensation cess and the amount distributed to the states as compensation. According to the Act, the collections from the Cess are to be deposited in the non-lapsable compensation fund to be placed in the Public Accounts from which the payments should be made. However, in 2017–2018, of Rs. 626 billion collected from the cess, only Rs. 561 billion was transferred to the fund and the remaining amount was appropriated by the Central government in the Consolidated Fund. The revised estimate of 2018–2019 shows that of the Rs. 900 billion collection as compensation cess, the Central government proposes to retain Rs. 582.85 billion and pass on the remaining to the fund. This raises questions of propriety.

There are a variety of reasons for the low-revenue productivity of GST, the principal ones being glitches in the technology platform and secondly, the design of the structure of GST. The report of the C&AG makes a detailed analysis of the technical glitches adversely impacting on compliance (India, 2019). Inability of the technology platform to verify invoices for ITC has the potential to create false claims and refunds. Similarly, inability to validate the registrations has led to the creation of several shell companies (some of them within the group) to issue fake invoices which eventually disappear leading to evasion of the tax. The fact that annual return filing date is being repeatedly postponed due to technical glitches does not serve the objective of validating ITC. In the absence of a clear trail, the assessment will be based entirely on trust and this provides opportunity for the unscrupulous businessmen to evade the tax. In fact, the annual return filing for 2018–2019 was repeatedly postponed. Similarly, inability to validate and debar the ineligible taxpayers from availing composition levy has also led to misuse of the facility. The Minister of State for Finance in his reply to a question in Rajya Sabha stated that since GST was rolled out on 1 July 2017, 9385 cases of tax fraud involving an amount of Rs. 456.82 billion have been detected by tax authorities and the amount of fraud detected in 2018–2019 was Rs. 379.46 billion and in the first 3 months of 2019–2020, 1593 cases involving Rs. 65.2 billion has been detected.[17]

The basic problem arises from the inability to deal with large number of assesses and the ambitious plan of having 100 per cent matching of invoices to avail ITC and settle IGST. As of end March 2019, the number of registered dealers was 12 million and total number of returns filed numbered almost 16 million. Matching every invoice issued by a dealer to verify ITC requires a robust pretested technology platform which the GSTN has not been able to erect. However, even though revenue collections have not reached the optimistic expectations, the loss has not been so large as to get worried, and as the States are fully assured of the

[17] Quoted from the report in Indian Express on 30 August 2019. https://indianexpress.com/article/business/since-gst-rollout-in-july-2017-45682-83-crore-fraud-detected-5833003/

buoyancy, the tax has come to stay. Thus, there is no fear of going back and efforts will have to focus on improving the system.

(c) Structure of the Tax and Revenue Impact

Does the introduction of GST lead to informalization of the economy? Pigott and Whalley (2001) argue that in an economy with a large informal sector, VAT tends to increase the tax on the formal sector leading to worsening of the distortions to reduce welfare. In the same vein, Emran and Stiglitz (2005) argue that in developing countries, VAT acts as a tax on the formal sector and shifting from tariffs to VAT could result in reduced welfare from informalization of the economy as at least under the former, inputs get taxed. However, Emran and Stigitz, in their analysis, do not take the real-world VAT, which involves payment of taxes on inputs on all exempted goods and the actual VAT is no less effective in taxing informal sector imports (Keen, 2007, 2009). The important issue, however, is that in an economy with a large informal sector, there can be adverse impact on revenue if the entre chain of transactions is kept outside the formal sector. This may be particularly important if the list of exemptions is large and the difference in the rates of tax between formal and informal sectors is high.

The best practice approach is to keep the list of exemptions in GST small to have a more comprehensive trail of transactions. The rationale for exempting many items or levying low rates on items considered necessities is to ensure equity in the distribution of tax burden. However, while exemptions or low rates of tax on such items may confer larger proportional benefit to the low-income groups, it could result in larger absolute benefit to high-income groups. This is an inefficient way of achieving equity as the exempted items are consumed also by the rich and, therefore, the better way to achieve equity is through the expenditure side of the budget (Keen, 2013) by making cash transfers and spending on items like education and healthcare.[18] In India, as many as 148 commodities under four-digit HSN classification and having

[18] Sonia Munoz and Stanley Song-Wook Cho (2004) using micro data on Ethiopia conclude, 'Even very poor countries can sometimes deliver the goods more effectively than poorly targeted exemption'. Quoted in Bird and Gendron (2007: n 13, p. 77).

almost 50 per cent weight in the consumer price index have been kept in the exempted list. The ostensible reasons for this are administrative ease, equity, and minimize impact on prices. Apart from unprocessed agricultural goods, a number of items are exempted for social reasons. Most food items including the processed items are exempt so long as they are not packaged and branded. The glaring examples of exempted services are transportation of goods and people in road, railways (except travel in first or air-conditioned class) and inland waterways, and courier services. Large exemptions not only lead to narrowing of the tax base but also informalization of the economy. Large exemption list lowers the input tax credit and this reduces the incentive to register and pay the tax. Thus, while the flour is not taxed, toasted bread and rusk are taxed at 12 per cent, and malt, biscuits, cakes, and pastries are taxed at 18 per cent. Given that the technology involved in their supply is not sophisticated, the high rate of tax drives the entire process of production and sale outside the tax net. It is not surprising that organized manufacturers of biscuits have been complaining about the fall in sales. While items like coffee beans and fresh tea leaves are exempt, coffee and its substitutes, tea, and dry ginger are taxed at 12 per cent. Unbranded food items such as savouries are not taxed, whereas branded items are subject to 12 per cent tax. De-oiled cakes used as cattle feed are exempt but other uses are taxed at 5 per cent. In fact, much of food processing can be carried out using simple technologies and, therefore, can remain outside the formal sector to evade the tax. There are many such examples.

Rate differentiation done for reasons of equity simply based on the perceptions about the consumption pattern may not only result in lower tax collections but can also have a serious adverse impact on employment and incomes. Many items such as building materials including cement and its products, marbles and granites, veneer and plywood, paints and varnishes, tiles, sanitary ware, motor cars and parts, refrigerators, air conditioners, vacuum cleaners, and even chocolates and razor blades are taxed at 28 per cent on the perception that these are luxury items. In fact, in addition to the basic rates, compensation cess at varying rates is levied on some of these items over and above 28 per cent tax to earmark the revenue for paying compensation to the States for any loss of revenues. These rates vary widely creating enormous rate differences among the commodities and services subject to the 28 per cent category. As shown in Table 5.6,

Table 5.6 Tax Rates on Motor Cars.

Type of vehicles	GST rate (per cent)	Compensation cess (per cent)	Total tax rate (per cent)
Petrol/CNG/LPG car less than 1200cc/length less than 4 meters	28	1	29
Petrol/CNG/LPG car less than 1200cc/length more than 4 meters	28	15	43
Petrol/CNG/LPG car over 1200cc (irrespective of length)	28	22	50
Diesel car less than 1500cc and length less than 4 meters	28	3	31
Diesel car less than 1500cc and length more than 4 meters	28	20	48
Diesel car over 1500cc engine capacity, greater than 4 meters length and ground clearance of 170 mm or more	28	22	50
Electric cars (all sizes including 2 and 3 wheelers)	12	Nil	12
Vehicles fitted for use as an ambulance	28	Nil	28

Note: The rates are as decided by the 31st GST Council meeting held in December 2018.
Source: https://www.paisabazaar.com/tax/gst-on-cars/

on motor cars alone, the cess varies depending on the engine capacity, length, and fuel use of the vehicle. In some cases, the total incidence of the tax works out to 50 per cent. Automobile industry with its ancillaries and downstream repair and services has enormous employment implication. Furthermore, as both motor spirit and high-speed diesel are kept outside the GST net and excise duties on them are levied at very high rates without input tax relief, this makes the entire system of transportation of both goods and people non-competitive.

The problem is high tax rates incentivize evasion of the tax by creating a grey market for such goods. This is particularly true of building materials in which the rate of tax levied is 28 per cent, but final tax on affordable houses is 1 per cent and other houses, 5 per cent without ITC. Since there is no paper trail on the input providers for the builders of these properties, they can purchase their inputs from the grey market and merely pay the compounded tax or not pay the tax at all as there is no paper trail. This can result in a huge loss of revenue. In the case of motor cars, high taxes could lead to higher prices resulting in lower demand. The problem is reinforced by the fact that motor spirit and diesel are not included in the GST base and this increases the cost of transportation. The fall in demand results in the loss of employment not only due to layoffs by the vehicle industry but also by the ancillaries and servicing of motor vehicles. Thus, the tax that is intended to fall on the rich may hurt the poor more. It is, therefore, important to assess the general equilibrium effects tax rates and their changes while designing the tax structure.[19]

In traditional cascading-type sales taxes, commodities and services predominantly used as inputs are taxed at much lower rates than outputs to minimize the cascading effect. However, as full input tax credit is given under the VAT, such distinctions should not be made. Actually, large rate differences provide incentives to evade the tax. Implementation of GST was an important opportunity to think afresh and determine the tax rates based on the first principles. However, when the fitment committee simply added the rates of merged taxes in GST to calculate the total rate for various commodities and services and fitted the items closer to the predetermined rates, it carried over the shortcomings of the prevailing structures. The earlier VAT in States as well as the excise duty on manufactured products levied by the Centre had lower rates of taxes on items considered predominantly as inputs. In the GST, as ITC is given, it is not necessary to tax the inputs at lower rates. In fact, when there is a large difference in the rates between the items considered as inputs and outputs, there can be an incentive to purchase the inputs and pay the tax but suppress the output and evade the tax. Thus, most metallic ore is taxed at 5 per cent, and metallic bars, sheets, tubes, and other products are taxed at 18 per cent and utensils are taxed at 12 per cent; a foundry owner can buy the ores by paying 5 per cent tax, manufacture bars, sheets, and tubes and sell it in the market and suppress his output and sale. The difference in the rates is 13 percentage points and along with the additional value added in the process of manufacturing and sale, the incentive from suppressing his output and sale is considerable.

[19] The automobile industry has been claiming that there have been massive lay-offs on account of various factors including high rate of GST.

5.4. GST and Continuing Distortions

(a) Multiple Rates

The predominant objective of GST implementation is to minimize distortions associated with the prevailing domestic consumption taxes. In particular, the reform was designed to reduce welfare losses due to deadweight losses arising from the cascading elements in both Central and state consumption taxes. Cascading creates a wedge between consumer and producer prices more than the tax element, alters relative prices in unintended ways, promoted vertical integration in businesses, adds to opacity, and reduces the competitiveness in international trade due to difficulties in relieving the input taxes from exports in a comprehensive manner.[20]

The conventional wisdom arising from conceptual as well as the best practice approach to designing GST is to keep the list of exemptions small and levy the tax at a single rate. The attempt to keep an additional lower rate on items predominantly consumed by low-income groups is an inefficient way of targeting and, therefore, the expenditure side of the budget can achieve the objective better (Keen, 2013). Jenkins et al. (2006) recommend a higher threshold on the grounds that it increases progressivity of the tax without distorting relative prices. The practice, over the years, has been increasingly to ley the tax at a single rate (Table 5.7) and in fact, the 13th Finance Commission advocated such a 'flawless' GST.

Despite the overwhelming expert opinion on the desirability to levy the tax at a single rate, the tax has to be designed based on societal preferences and political acceptability. As Bird and Gendron (2007) argue, there is no one size fits all (NOFSA) principle in designing GST. Even in the European Union, except for Norway, all other countries have (mostly) two rates and the proposal to switch over to a single rate based on the recommendation of an expert committee was shot down politically (Bird and Gendron, 2007). At the same time, adopting excessive rate differentiation complicates the structure, increases administrative and compliance costs, and accentuates distortions by altering relative prices in unintended ways. In fact, considering the fact that the States had only two

[20] For a systematic analysis of welfare loss from cascading, see Keen (2013).

Table 5.7 VATs with a Single Rate at the Time of Introduction.

Years	Number of new VAT countries	Percentage with single rate
Before 1990	48	25
1990–1999	75	71
1999–2011	31	81

Source: Keen (2013).

VAT rates implementation of GST, with four rates (excluding zero and special rates on precious metals and stones) and cesses at varying rates is excessive and it is important to move over to two rates sooner than later.

(b) High Rates of Tax and Anomalies

Not only that there is excessive rate differentiation but levying taxes at 28 per cent on consumer durables (like air conditioners, refrigerators, and automobiles and parts) and construction materials not only provides a good incentive to evade the tax but also creates distortions. One of the reasons attributed to deceleration in economic growth in the last few quarters is from slowdown in private consumption and high GST rate on consumer durables does not help to reduce prices to increase demand for them. While with the available information it is not possible to state to what extent GST is the cause of slowdown in consumption expenditure growth, reducing it to a lower level of 18 per cent could certainly help in arresting the deceleration while improving the structure of the tax. For 'sin' and 'demerit' goods, it may be desirable to have a separate excise rather than complicate the GST structure with additional rates. In the medium term, it makes sense to merge even the 12 per cent and 18 per cent to 15–16 per cent so that the GST will have two main rates—5 per cent and 15/16 per cent.

The problem with wide-ranging rate differentiation within a commodity/service group enormously increases both administrative and even more importantly, compliance costs. Both the producer and the seller dealing with different types of cars have to keep detailed accounts of sales of different types of vehicles and the input purchases. Strangely, the tax department has been levying the tax at 28 per cent even on imported auto-components like floor mats and ashtrays even as the tax rate on these manufactured domestically is 18 per cent.

The structure of GST with four main rates makes it complicated. When the levy of cesses is also considered, it is difficult even to count the number of rates. In the case of motor vehicles, rate differentiation is done on the basis of engine capacity, length of cars, their fuel base, and use. Table 5.7 presents some undesirable examples of rate differentiation. There are instances where the rate differentiation is done for the same commodity or service group based on the values (footwear, apparel, quilts, hotel tariff) for equity reasons. Differentiation is also made based on the nature of the commodity as in the case of fibres used in textiles (natural or man-made), based on whether the commodity is in the nature of input or an output and use of the commodity (oil cakes used as cattle-feed and others). The problem with multiple rate structure is that it is easily prone to misclassification. For example, silk and cotton fibre are exempt, other natural fibres are taxed at 5 per cent, and man-made fibres are taxed at 18 per cent (see Table 5.8). The food served in restaurants in hotels having room tariff less than Rs. 1000 per night is exempt, and in other restaurants, it is taxed at 5 per cent without the provision of ITC, whereas restaurant services in hotels with over Rs. 7500 room tariff per night and those in clubs and guest houses are taxed at 18 per cent.[21] Similarly, catering services were taxed at 18 per cent earlier and this was brought down to 5 per cent without ITC in the 37th meeting of the Council. Surely, it is not very difficult for the restaurants to classify catering as sales from the restaurants, nor is it difficult for a professional caterer to open a small restaurant to misclassify the same.

An important consequence of multiplicity of rates is the possibility of input taxes claimed for credit exceeding the output taxes payable and this requires refunds to be made. Such inverted rate structure occurs in the cases where the input tax rates are higher than the rates on outputs and the value added by the output supplier is not high. Textiles and housing sector provide examples of inverted duty structure. In textiles, the synthetic fibre is taxed at 18 per cent, yarn at 12 per cent, and cloth at 5 per

[21] Brought down to 12 per cent in the 37th Council meeting on September 20.

cent. This results in large refunds and the inability to provide these has posed problems to the manufacturers.[22] Similarly, in housing, most inputs are taxed at 28 per cent and affordable and other houses are either subject to compounded levy of 1 per cent and 5 per cent or if they want to claim input tax credit, 5 per cent and 12 per cent, respectively. Given the inverted duty structure, delay in getting the refunds has severely constrained their working capital.

(c) Cascading Element

In India, even after attempts were made to relieve input tax element in the consumption tax system by converting the States' sales taxes into VAT on goods in 2005, and Centre's excise duty into CENVAT, significant cascading elements had continued to persist. The excise duty was essentially a manufacturing stage sales tax cascading into wholesale and retail stages. There was no input tax credit mechanism between excise duty and sales taxes or the VAT levied at the State level. Sales taxes were levied on the excise duty paid value. There were a number of other taxes like interstate sales tax, octroi, entry tax, and purchase tax where there was no provision for relieving input taxes at all. Therefore, GST was considered as the most appropriate solution to provide ITC in a more comprehensive and systematic manner.

While the reform has helped to substantially reduce the cascading element in taxes, it falls well short of the desired. This is not because of the non-inclusion of financial services or real estate which is a problem even in developed countries (Bird and Gendron, 2007), but due to the exclusion of motor spirt, high-speed diesel, real estate, potable alcohol, and electricity from the GST. High-speed diesel and motor spirit contribute over 35 per cent of the revenues of Centre and the States and the GST Council simply did not take any risk by extending the coverage to these items. For ensuring a more comprehensive VAT chain, it would have been desirable to levy the GST and impose a separate environment excise to protect revenue.

[22] The President of CII has complained that the delays in the refunds have severely hampered working capital liquidity. See, https://economictimes.indiatimes.com/industry/cons-products/garments-/-textiles/textiles-sector-rues-synthetics-inverted-duty-structure/articleshow/67877119.cms?from=mdr.

The revenue from both Central and State cascading taxes constitutes a substantial proportion of revenues collected from internal indirect taxes. At the Central level, the excise duty collected on petroleum products constituted 40.3 per cent of the total internal indirect taxes collected and the revenue from cascading indirect taxes at the State level was 43.4 per cent aggregated for all non-special categories taken together. Even if the data on Andhra Pradesh and Goa are ignored because the former is a newly formed State and the latter is a very small state, the revenue from consumption taxes excluded from GST base varies from 33.6 per cent in Maharashtra to 54.6 per cent in Tamil Nadu (Table 5.8). As the States levy their sales taxes on the union excise duty paid value, the cascading element is substantial. Thus, the cascading impact of not providing ITC to natural gas, petroleum products, and electricity is significant and varies among sectors depending upon their direct and indirect use as inputs. Some sectors with substantial exports also face significant cascading, and this adversely impacts on their competitiveness. The cascading element in taxes is tantamount to imposing penalty on exports and eliminating such penalties was an important motivation for adopting GST in Canada. Furthermore, providing ITC for fuel provides incentive for businesses to report their sales. In fact, because of keeping fuel outside the GST base, the entire transport sector except air travel and air-conditioned and first-class train travel is exempted which renders the tax base narrower and adds to cascading.

In addition to the exclusion of these consumption taxes from the GST, ITC is not available on items exempted from GST, the compounded tax on the dealers with less than Rs. 15 million turnover, and compounded tax on services in restaurants and housing. The tax on affordable housing is levied at a compounded rate of 1 per cent and other housing at 5 per cent with no input tax credit. Large-scale exemptions and extending the benefit of compounding to cases such as supplies in restaurants and housing also deny ITC and add to cascading. Since most housing materials are taxed at 28 per cent, the dealers put the pressure to restore the original rate of 8 per cent and 12 per cent on these categories with ITC. Given the high tax rate on inputs, inverted duty structure in this case is unavoidable. Equally important is the fact that revenue from compensatory cesses constitute about 8 per cent of the GST collected and these are not subject to ITC.

Table 5.8 Examples of Anomalies in Tax Rates.

Item	Rate of tax (per cent)
1. Different tax rates on same commodity group	
Footwear value up to Rs. 1000	5
Value above Rs. 1000	12
Fibre:	Nil
Silk and jute	5
Cotton and natural	18
Man-made	
Readymade apparel:	5
Value up to Rs. 1000	12
Value above Rs. 1000	
Cotton quilts/piece:	5
Value up to Rs. 1000	12
Above Rs. 1000	
Hotels and lodges:	Nil
Tariffs up to Rs. 1000	12
Tariffs from Rs. 1000–Rs. 2500	18
Tariff from Rs. 2500–Rs. 7500	28
Tariff above Rs. 7500	
Restaurants	5
Catering	18
2. Rate differentiation according to the use of the article:	
De-oiled cakes:	Nil
Used as cattle feed	5
Other uses	
3. Rate differentiation according to stage of production	
Metallic ores (iron, manganese, copper, nickel, cobalt,	5
aluminium, lead, zinc, tin, chromium, tungsten, uranium,	18
thorium, titanium, precious metals, and others (from	12
2601 to 2617)	
Pig iron, ferro alloys, iron and steel and alloys of steel,	
uranium and powder, semi-finished products of iron and	
steel etc.	
Utensils, household articles	
Aluminium utensils, table and kitchenware or household	12
articles	18
Aluminium alloys, ingots, billets, wires, bars, rods, plates,	28
sheets, tubes, and pipes.	
Aluminium foil, doors, windows and their frames, and	
sanitary ware	

Source: GST Council.

5.5. A Summary and a Starting Point

Implementation of GST is a far-reaching reform involving 28 States with wide variations in development, 3 Union Territories with legislatures, and the Centre. It is not surprising that some bad features in the structure and operational details of the reform had to be accepted to get agreement from all governments. However, undertaking reforms to get rid of the bad features is a challenge and requires concerted efforts to convince all the benefits of improvement. Since the roll-out of the reform on 1 July 2017, there have been 45 meetings of the GST Council until September 2021 to decide on the changes in the structure and operational details of the tax in response to the demands by the trade and industry. Thus, GST has been evolving in India and will have to face many challenges before settling down to a stable tax system.

The reform was unveiled with much fanfare on the midnight of 1 July 2017 and was billed as a game changer and reform of the century. It was supposed to be entirely IT based without any interface between taxpayers and officials and requiring 100 per cent invoice matching for providing ITC. Trade and industry too accepted the reform hoping to have a simpler and cleaner tax with minimum compliance cost. Of course, the reform of this magnitude was expected to have teething troubles. While the reform has taken firm roots, after more than 42 months, the experience has also led to the moderation in expectations. It is now clear that significant additional reforms are needed in the structure of the tax to realize the potential gains from the reform.

Subsuming of a number of Central and State taxes has simplified the tax system to a considerable extent though much more remains to be done on this front. The system of online payment of the tax and distancing the taxpayer from tax collector has minimized the scope for rent-seeking and reduced the compliance cost. Although the jury on the overall reduction in the compliance cost of the tax is still out as the complications and insistence on online payment have required the taxpayers to take the help of tax consultants, reduction in rent-seeking is certainly an important positive. Administrative cost too is likely to come down as the Centre and State governments reorganize their administrative systems in the medium term.

Table 5.9 Cascading Element in States' GST.

State	GST (Rs. million)	Cascading taxes (Rs. million)*	Total (Rs. million)	Share of cascading taxes in total (per cent)
Andhra Pradesh	103960	427854	531814	80.5
Bihar	170297	102000.3	272297.3	37.5
Chhattisgarh	121510	70796.3	192306	36.8
Goa	32030	11281.1	43311.1	26.0
Gujarat	433976	342869.3	776845.3	44.1
Haryana	237600	148449	386049	38.5
Jharkhand	106000	64260	170260	37.7
Karnataka	426397	227973	654370	34.8
Kerala	270000	246605	516605	47.7
Madhya Pradesh	216931	177973	394904	45.1
Maharashtra	1053029	535565	1588594	33.7
Odisha	129748	109109	238857	45.7
Punjab	217717	125137	342854	36.5
Rajasthan	221540	229520	451060	50.9
Tamil Nadu	432764	519558	952322	54.6
Telangana	280518	303310	583828	52.0
Uttar Pradesh	529803	314783	844586	37.3
West Bengal	230600	130602	361202	36.2
All States	5557746	4265512	9823258	43.4

Note: Cascading consumption taxes include sales taxes on petroleum products, motor vehicle tax, passengers and goods tax, electricity duty and entertainment tax, and other consumption taxes excluding State Excise Duty.

Source: State Finances: A Study of Budgets of 2017–2018 and 2018–2019. Reserve Bank of India.

It is important to underline the gains from the implementation of GST. The most important gain is from the abolition of interstate checkposts erected to enforce taxes on cross-border transactions and intrastate checkposts erected to collect octroi and entry tax by local bodies. This has substantially removed impediments to the movement of goods across the country and is an important step in creating a national common market. In addition, it has helped to reduce the cost and time required for transportation of goods. The merger of interstate sales tax has helped to make the tax destination based and reduced tax exportation from the more developed producing States to the consumers in less-developed States. Besides, the merger of central sales tax has put an end to the practice of interstate consignment transfers and abolition of branch offices in different States established to avid the tax. The GST unlike the sales tax which is levied on the sale of goods and services is a tax on the supply of goods and services, and since there are no differences in the tax rates between States, there are no tax gains to be had in creating branch offices and this has made the supply chain management more efficient.

Another important gain from the tax is the reduced cascading due to more comprehensive ITC mechanism. The improvement over the past comes from the fact that the excise duty levied by the Centre was levied at the manufacturing stage and it cascaded into the final value at the point of retail sale. Besides, there was no systematic ITC mechanism for excise duty and service taxes. In the earlier tax regime, States' VAT on goods was levied on the central excise duty and service tax paid values. The inclusion of taxes like central sales tax, octroi, purchase taxes, and luxury taxes on hotels in the GST has minimized cascading from these taxes as well.

One of the major problems in Indian fiscal federalism is the institutional vacuum to minimize transitional cost of intergovernmental bargaining and conflict resolution and the GST Council provides an interesting institutional innovation for such a task. This is a model which can be employed to foster much greater understanding between the Union and the states and among the States *inter se* on matters requiring collaboration for mutual gains and also to resolve various conflicts between them. However, it remains to be seen how the institution will eventually shape. More importantly, the emphasis on building consensus to making changes in the tax system has resulted in delays in decision-making and suboptimal decisions in the structure of the tax even as the States' revenue is protected until 2022–2023. Given that GST is still evolving, and a lot of distance is yet to be covered, the tyranny of status quo due to indecision could be counterproductive.

While these gains are real and, in the medium term, could lead to improvement in productivity, much more needs to be done to realize the full potential of reforms. Besides, there are areas of concern both in the structure of the tax and in operational details and it is important to rectify them to realize both efficiency and revenue gains. The GST in India is still evolving. The GST Council has a number of players and so far, the decisions taken have been consensus; for the same reason often, the decisions have been suboptimal. Given the diverse representation of State Finance Ministers belonging to different political parties in the Council, it will take longer time and much more effort to undertake further reforms to achieve the goal of a stable, efficient, and productive GST. At the same time, it is useful to take stock of the important shortcomings in the system and list out the nature and direction of reforms.

The most important concern now is the stagnant revenues, and unless immediate steps are taken to increase the revenue productivity, the euphoria about GST will wane and there could be questions about the wisdom of undertaking reform itself. There has been a sharp decline in the buoyancy of Centre's GST as well as States' GST. The States are concerned as they stare at significant revenue loss after the 5-year period of payment of recouping the loss of revenue is over. Even before the pandemic, during the 5 months of 2019–2020, while the compensation cess collections amounted to Rs. 410 billion, the compensation actually paid to the States was Rs. 650 billion.[23] Thus, monthly shortfall was approximately Rs. 50 billion. This has three implications. The situation became alarming when the pandemic struck as the revenues declined sharply due to the lockdown and the issue of compensation became contentious. There have been other consequences of low revenue growth. First, inability to meet the compensation obligations from the cess collections has forced continuation of the levy. Second, unless revenue productivity improves, there will be pressure by the states to extend the period of compensation and the Centre. Finally, considering the low buoyancy in revenues, there will be hesitancy on the part of the GST Council to undertake reforms in the structure of the tax for fear of losing more revenues. Thankfully, during the last few months, particularly after October 2020 when the technology platform has stabilized, the GST revenues have shown higher buoyancy and the time is opportune to think of reforms.

The first important issue that the GST Council and GSTN together should address is to firm up the technology platform. The C&AG in its

[23] A report in Business Standard on 16 September 2019 titled, 'Auto-sector's rate cut hopes fade as GST cess collection declines', https://www.business-standard.com/article/economy-policy/low-gst-cess-collection-dampens-auto-sector-s-hopes-for-rate-cut-119091500720_1.html.

IT audit of GST has pointed out a number of shortcomings in the present system and the GST Council should take steps to plug these loopholes. It may be desirable to give up the task of 100 per cent matching of invoices to create a functioning platform considering the large number of taxpayers and zillions of invoices. It may be desirable to decide on invoice matching of large taxpayers with turnovers above Rs. 10 million which would eliminate almost 95 per cent of the taxpayers from compulsory invoice matching. Even for these taxpayers, the invoices above a certain value (say Rs. 5000) may be matched and when the discrepancies are found, detailed audit can be undertaken. For the remaining, the Central Board of Indirect taxes and State commercial tax departments can work out a modality of choosing 10 per cent of the taxpayers based on rick perceptions to undertake detailed audits. It should be possible for the technology platform to deal with invoice matching for fewer taxpayers and invoices. Once the technology is stabilized, the GSTN can extend the coverage. Along with technology platform, it is also important to create a system of real-time reporting from the banks about the payment of the tax to match the invoices.

Firming up the technology platform for invoice matching and the real-time reporting system will substantially reduce the problem of evasion through the fake invoices route and improve the compliance of the tax by increasing the probability of detection. It will also help to discharge speedy refunds to exporters. Furthermore, it will accurately settle the IGST to States based on the destination. After more than three and a half years of rolling out the GST, the GST Council has finally mandated that e-invoicing system must be used by all those taxpayers with more than Rs. 5 billion turnovers from September 2020 and that seems to have evoked better compliance. Not surprisingly, the revenue collections have been more than Rs. 1 trillion since September. In April 2021, the monthly collection at Rs. 1.4 trillion was the highest since the tax was implemented. While a part of the increase is due to the recovery of businesses in the economy after the lockdown was progressively relaxed, it could also be due to tracking the input invoices through better technology. The tax administration has been able to detect several cases of fake invoicing. Now compulsory e-invoicing requirement has been extended to all taxpayers with more than Rs. 1 billion turnover from 1 January 2021 and the revenues are expected to increase due to better compliance.

The reform in the structure of the tax is equally important and this is easier to carry out when the revenues are buoyant. To begin with, it would be useful to keep the threshold at Rs. 5 million to avoid too many small taxpayers with little liability. This, as was pointed out, also serves the cause of equity. Another area requiring immediate intervention is to transfer consumer durables, cars, and building materials taxed at 28 per cent into the 18 per cent category. The idea is to move away from the 28 per cent category altogether so that there will be only three rates besides exemption. At present, the revenue from this category including the cess is reported to be 22 per cent of total revenue from GST. In fact, 12 per cent and 18 per cent together contribute almost two-thirds of revenue collections. Transferring items like construction materials and automobiles from 28 per cent category into 18 per cent could help to revive these sectors which have been severely impacted by the lockdown. In the final part of the reform, the 12 per cent and 18 per cent categories can also be merged to simplify the tax system to have two rate categories (besides exemption). These reforms can be calibrated over a period of 2–3 years.

There are some 'demerit goods' or sumptuary goods such as tobacco and its products in the 28 per cent category. The proper method to treat these goods is to levy the GST at the standard rate and have a separate sumptuary excise. Over time, it would be desirable to adopt such an approach. At present, the supply of tobacco products is taxed at 28 per cent, but there are very high rates of compensation cess varying with the nature of the product. In the case of cigarettes, the rate of cess varies depending on the length of cigarettes. Of course, it is important to have high tax rates on them to discourage their consumption. However, the sumptuary objective can be captured by a separate excise levied by the Central government over and above the GST levied at 18 per cent. Another sumptuary item which is outside the ambit GST is the alcohol for human consumption. This is because the Constitution places the tax on alcoholic consumption in the State List and the States may not be willing to cede their power to tax and include them in the base in GST. Besides, some States follow the policy of prohibition which does not permit the consumption of alcohol in these states.

Minimizing distortions from cascading requires including the supply of all the items in the tax base. Therefore, over time it is important to include petroleum products and electricity in the base of GST. The major reason for keeping petroleum products out of GST base is their overwhelming contribution—almost 35–40 per cent of the revenue from tax on domestic consumption at both Central and state levels. As mentioned, it would be desirable to levy the GST on these products at standard rates and levy a separate excise for environmental reasons (Ahmad and Stern, 2011). This will satisfy both revenue and environmental causes. As regards electricity is concerned, the Constitution places it in the State list and the States should be persuaded to agree to make the necessary amendment of the Constitution to enable the levy of GST.

The large list of exemptions has eroded the base of GST and it is important to revisit the list to broaden the base. The present approach has been to exempt most of the items that are perishables and those considered necessities not only for administrative and equity reasons but also to ensure that the implementation of GST does not result in inflation. The exempted supplies have a weight of almost 50 per cent in the consumer price index. Equity is better served by making cash transfer rather than having an expanded list of exemptions. Besides, the entire passenger and goods transportation excluding air travel and air-conditioned and first-class train travel is exempt from the tax. Once a systematic approach is taken to taxing petroleum products, it should be possible to include these in the tax base. While exempting the tax may not be the appropriate method to deal with questions of equity, it may not be easy to prune the list politically. Nevertheless, it is important to minimize the list of exempted items with the passage of time.

There are infirmities in the rate structure prevailing at present and these should be rectified for reasons of both revenue and efficiency. As mentioned earlier, the supply of the same group of commodities is taxed at different rates depending on the price or their use and nature of purchase (consumption or take home; restaurant or catering). There are also rate differences based on the stage of production. It is important to review the rates and correct them for reasons of efficiency and better compliance.

Levying GST at both national and subnational levels can raise a number of issues and the overlapping responsibilities between the Central and State tax administrations will have to be dealt with as and when it becomes contentious. Besides these are some problems with the administrative arrangements. Although the laws and rules governing the administration are identical across States, the requirement to register in every State adds to the compliance burden. This can easily be avoided. Furthermore, interstate self-supplies attract the tax. The zero-rating of exports is cumbersome as it first involves the exporter paying the tax and later taking refunds.

One of the important reforms that the GST Council should undertake is to have a proper technical and a research team to analyse and design the structure of GST including exemption, rates and revenue, and economic implications of changes in the rates, matters dealing with administration including registration, forms, filing of returns, payment of the tax, assessment, audit, and enforcement. Similarly, estimation of revenue implications from changes in the rates requires measurement of the effect of rate changes on the demand for the commodity or service. In fact, a strong research team is important to see the implications of high tax rates and their changes on output and employment.[24] It is important to model the impact of taxes on some major items of supply from the viewpoint of revenue to see the impact of changes in the rates on output, employment, and revenue. At present, the GST Council continues to rely on the analysis by the 'fitment committee' which consists of the nominated officials of the Tax Research Unit in Central Board of Indirect Taxes and Customs and some officials of the Commercial Taxes Department from some States. For a reform of this nature, it is necessary to have a strong Tax Analysis Unit in the Ministry of Finance with a small number of highly qualified specialists comprising of economists, lawyers, accountants, and administrators. In fact, this should be done without much loss of time to ensure that the Council gets quality advice in the evolving process of reforms.

One of the major constraints in undertaking detailed research is the reluctance of the GST Council to share detailed data even for research. Even the State-wise data on SGST, IGST, and compensation cess is not available in public domain. There is considerable hesitancy on the part of the Council to share the data even to the C&AG. The report of C&AG is unequivocal is stating, 'after much pursuance, CBIC has shared only the MIS reports which give aggregate statistics at Commissionerate level (for Central data) and State level (for State data)'. The independent researchers are virtually debarred from access to basic data on GST collections. In fact, even the C&AG Audit team was hampered in the detailed analysis of pan–India transactions and the report states, 'Unhindered

[24] The official estimate of reducing the tax rate on motor vehicles from 28 per cent to 18 per cent is Rs. 600 billion. This, however, is based on the collections at present.

and full access to pan-India data is crucial for meaningful audit and to draw required assurances needed, otherwise certifying revenue receipts may become difficult. The Department of Revenue's offer of providing data based on CAG's queries is not workable, as without the full data, it is neither possible to formulate queries, nor run the required algorithms on the data. The CAG sought data through the Application Programme Interface (APIs) already designed by GSTN. It needs hardly to be stated that providing such data as CAG may require is a constitutional and legal requirement'. When a constitutional body like C&AG itself has difficulties in securing the data required for conducting the audit, it is not surprising that independent researchers find it impossible to secure access to the information required to undertake quality analysis. Hopefully, the Council will wake up to the need for scientific analysis and does not try to 'shoot the messenger'.

The COVID-19 pandemic has posed the biggest challenge for the GST reform. Hailed as the example of 'cooperative federalism', in which the States were made to give up their fiscal autonomy for achieving tax harmonization on the promise of paying them compensation for any loss of revenue. The entire edifice of trust was broken when the Centre shrugged off the responsibility and presented the States with two borrowing options towards compensation, one excluding the impact of pandemic stating that it is an 'Act of God' in which the States could borrow at a concessional rate of interest from the RBI and both interest payment and repayments will be met from the compensation amount collected in future years and another where the States were required to borrow from the market and pay interest, but the repayment will be met from the compensation cess in future years. This issue is discussed in some detail in the last chapter.

6

Macroeconomics of Indian Public Finance

Deficits and Debt

The vulgar conception of public debt is the only one that is fundamentally correct and valid generally. The theory of the public debt which is accepted by most economists is at base, fallacious.

—James Buchanan

6.1. Public Debt and Future Generation: Return to the Vulgar Opinion

The classical economists who believed in the existence of full employment had envisaged a limited role for the government. For them, the flexibility in wages and interest rates ensured equilibrium in both labour and money markets to ensure full employment. In this scenario, expansion of the government by borrowing from the market would only drive up the interest rates and there will be corresponding decline in investments, employment, and income. Thus, the burden of public debt would be passed on to the future generation. The classical view was that the governments should have a limited role, should be austere, and not indulge in having deficits and accumulating debt.

It was John Maynard Keynes who showed that full employment can only happen in exceptional situations and to ensure full employment governments are required to increase expenditures to increase aggregate demand, if necessary, by borrowing when there is unemployment. They characterized the classical view as a 'vulgar conception of public debt'.

Studies in Indian Public Finance. M. Govinda Rao, Oxford University Press. © Oxford University Press 2022.
DOI: 10.1093/oso/9780192849601.003.0006

Lerner (1948) who provided a clear conceptualization of the Keynesian view made three propositions, namely: (i) The creation of public debt does not involve any transfer of the primary real burden to future generations. (ii) The analogy between individual or private debt and public debt is fallacious in all essential respects. (iii) There is a sharp and important distinction between internal and external public debt. The argument was that when the person chooses to invest in government bonds, he does it on his own volition and there is no sacrifice involved. When the bond matures, there is simply a transfer from taxpayers to bond holders. Thus, according to neoclassicals, public debt does not carry a burden on the future generation. In that respect, public and private debt are not analogous as private debt does involve a burden of repayment in the future. This is also not analogous to the external debt as the repayment has to be made to external lender and there is no corresponding transfer.

Buchanan characterized the above Keynesian view as 'the new orthodoxy' and reiterated that the 'vulgar conception of public debt is the only one that is fundamentally correct and valid generally. The theory of the public debt which is accepted by most economists is at base, fallacious' (Buchanan, 1958: 3). The main difference from the neoclassical view comes from his taking the individualistic view as against the organic view of the State and shifting of the emphasis from the 'real cost' to the 'opportunity cost'. The future generation is defined as, 'any set of individuals living in any time period following that in which the debt is created'. According to this, a person who makes investment in the bond does not undergo any sacrifice. The bond holder estimates the present value of their future income streams from the investment they make to estimate their rate of return. In contrast, the next-generation taxpayer has to service and repay the debt and they do not get any quid pro quo. They are, in fact, forced to pay for the borrowing done by the decision makers in some earlier time period. Of course, their burden is reduced if the borrowed funds are used in productive investments to yield returns required to liquidate the debt. In other words, there is an opportunity cost of the funds and when the government borrowing is not used wisely, it does not generate returns to repay the debt. Then the taxpayer in the next generation who is not a party to the decision taken by the earlier generation will have to make the sacrifice. In this sense, there is no difference between the private and public debt or internal and external debt. The 'vulgar' opinion is correct, and the 'new orthodoxy' is wrong after all!

Although, in terms of intergenerational equity, there is no difference between internal and external debt, there is a difference in terms of vulnerability and impacts in the economy. External debt will have to be serviced by foreign exchange and even if it is rolled over in the short term, it has to eventually be repaid by foreign exchange. Therefore, the ability of the government to meet its servicing and repayment obligations depends on its capacity to mobilize the required foreign exchange in time. Default in payments could result in sovereign downgrades with serious deleterious consequences. In contrast, it is easier to roll over the internal debt by borrowing from the financial system and if necessary, by borrowing from the Reserve Bank (printing currency). This could result in adverse macroeconomic consequences on aggregate output, inflation, external balance and exchange rates and microeconomic distortions arising from financial repression (to keep the borrowing rates low), and financial crowding out of private investments. While the excessive external borrowing could increase immediate vulnerability, the burden arising from excessive domestic borrowing is like administering slow poison and the effects are seen only after a period of time in terms of low growth, inflation, and external imbalance.

Even before the above arguments advanced by the 'new orthodoxy', David Ricardo had advanced his 'equivalence' theory under which the primary real burden cannot be shifted forward in time. This conclusion basically followed from the assumption that when the government borrows money, the people undertake corresponding obligation to meet the service charges from future tax revenues by writing down present values of their future income stream. Of course, unlike the arguments of the 'new orthodoxy', the primary burden of the debt fell on the taxpayer because they wrote down the value of their assets in anticipation of the future repayment obligation.

The problem with the 'equivalence theorem', however, is its assumptions. First, it would require the individuals to have perfect foresight to choose appropriate discount rates. Even if they have perfect insight and undertake full discounting by those owning income-earning assets, the argument cannot be extended to individuals who own no assets. The

Ricardian argument introduces only a slight modification of the conclusion that the primary real burden of a public debt is borne by the members of the current generation only in so far as they correctly anticipate their own tax payments as future taxpayers.

The above discussion on the primary burden of debt helps to clear a lot of confusion on the subject. When the opportunity cost of the resources pre-empted from public borrowing is considered, employing borrowed funds to any use that does not generate a comparable rate of return imposes burden on the future generation.

6.2. Why Should We Worry About Large Fiscal Deficits?

Before analysing the implications of deficits and debt, it is useful to understand various concepts of deficits. In Indian context, three important concepts of deficits are analysed. These are

(i) Revenue deficit is the excess of revenue expenditures over revenue receipts. Since revenue expenditures are largely in the nature of regular expenditures on wages and salaries, goods and services and subsidies and transfers including on interest payments, revenue receipts are expected to cover them. The deficit in the revenue account implies that this has to be financed from the borrowed funds. Using borrowed funds for non-asset creating expenditures shows lower productivity of public spending,

(ii) Fiscal deficit is the difference between total expenditures and total revenues including the non-debt capital receipts but excluding borrowing. In other words, the fiscal deficits broadly represent the volume of borrowing that the government has to undertake in a year. Of course, the actual borrowings and fiscal deficit do not exactly match as the governments also draw down the balance of various funds. Of course, these funds have to be replenished and when that is done, this is reflected in the expenditures. Since the fiscal deficits broadly represent the volume of borrowing in a year, they add to the volume of debt.

Fiscal deficit has significant macroeconomic implications which may be seen from the following identities:

$$Y = C + I + G + X - M. \quad (1)$$

Since

$$Y = C + S + T. \quad (2)$$

$$(M - X) = (I - S) + (G - T). \quad (3)$$

The first identity states that Income (Y) is the sum of Consumption (C), Investment (I) and exports (E), minus Imports (M). The second equation is also an identity showing Income as a sum of Consumption and Saving (S) minus Taxes (T). Substituting the second identity in the first will give the third identity which states that external balance (balance of payments; M-X) is equivalent to the sum of Investment-Saving imbalance (I-S) and fiscal imbalance (fiscal deficit; G-T). In other words, when the fiscal deficit increases, either there will be excess of savings over investment or balance of payment problem.

This is a simple demonstration of the macroeconomic implications of fiscal deficit. The way it happens is that when the fiscal deficit goes up, government borrowing increases. The government borrows from the financial system which is essentially from the available financial savings. This increases the interest rate and at higher interest rate, the saving increases and investment declines. The impact on the external balance works through higher aggregate demand due to public spending. A part of the higher demand spills over in terms of higher imports and with no corresponding increase in exports.

(iii) Primary deficit is equal to fiscal deficit minus interest payments. This represents the deficit incurred during the year without taking into account the liabilities from past borrowings. This concept is important to analyse the question of debt stability and sustainability.

As mentioned earlier, accumulation of debt creates a future liability for serving the debt for making interest payments and repayment of the principal. If the borrowed funds are sued to generate assets to yield returns in the future, that will help to meet the servicing liability. Otherwise, the taxes collected will have to be used for servicing it which crowds out productive expenditures. When borrowing is done even to meet debt servicing obligations, the debt will go on accumulating and the situation becomes unsustainable. To analyse the debt dynamics, most studies apply Domar (1944) condition derived from the basic debt equation as below:

$$D_t = P_t + D_{t-1}\left[(1 + i_t)/(1 + G_t)\right] \tag{4}$$

where 'D_t' denotes outstanding debt to GDP ratio in the current year, 'D_{t-1}' is the outstanding debt to GDP ratio in the previous year, P_t is the primary deficit to GDP ratio in the current year, 'i' is the nominal interest rate, and 'G' is the nominal growth rate of the economy. The equation shows that when the primary deficit is zero, the debt to GDP ratio will remain stationary if $Gt = i_t$; it will increase if $Gt < i_t$ and will decline if $Gt < i_t$. A sustainable public debt is when the debt-GDP ratio is either stationary or declines and that would require the primary deficit should be zero and the nominal growth rate of the economy exceeds the nominal interest rate on the debt. The policy implication from the above equation is that to prevent secular increase in debt it is necessary to contain the deficits and use the borrowed funds in activities that increase the growth rate of the economy.

At what level debt is sustainable? In other words, is there an optimal debt-GDP ratio for a government? This an issue on which the policymakers in the government have to make a judgement. The ideal volume of debt depends on the capacity of the government to service the debt. As mentioned above, if the borrowed funds are employed to accelerate growth, the debt-GDP ratio will not increase, and the government will have the capacity to service it. In a downturn, the economy is faced with large unemployment and excess capacity and expansionary fiscal policy supported by increase in borrowing can result in acceleration in growth and reduction in unemployment. In contrast, when the economy is in full employment, additional public spending financed by borrowed funds can add to the pressure on prices. The policy stance in such an economy should be to reduce government expenditure financed by borrowing. In other words, the fiscal policy stance should be countercyclical to ensure a stable economy.

Often, the discussion on sustainability of debt misses the consequences of forced sustainability through financial repression. While the Domar formulation gives insights into the issue of sustainability of public debt, it must be noted that when the governments are allowed to borrow from the market at rates much lower than the market rate of interest, the issue of sustainability is achieved by distorting the market. Acharya (2020), in his analysis of the quest of financial stability, has shown that fiscal dominance can be cause of several distortions in both monetary and real sectors of the economy. Government dissaving in excess of household sector's financial saving adversely impacts on monetary policy, regulation of the banking system, external balance, and exchange rates. The costs of financial repression, recapitalization of banks, laxed regulations on the financial system to accommodate government borrowing, and their impact on macroeconomic and external balances need to be taken note of.

Often, questions are raised as to why we should worry about large deficits and growing debt? Feldstein (2004) provides an insightful analogy to answer this. He states, 'Fiscal deficits are like obesity. You can see your weight rising on the scale and notice that your clothing size is increasing, but there is no sense of urgency in dealing with the problem. That is so even though the long-term consequences of being overweight include an increased risk of a sudden heart attack as well as of various chronic conditions like diabetes. Like obesity, government deficits are the result of too much self-indulgent living as the government spends more than it collects in taxes. And, also like obesity, the more severe the problem, the harder it is to correct: the overweight man has a harder time doing the exercise that could reduce his weight and the economy with a large deficit and debt is trapped by increasing interest payments that cause the deficit and debt to rise more quickly. I emphasize the analogy to stress the point that budget deficits need attention now even when their adverse effects may not be obvious'.

There are at least four reasons why the governments should watch fiscal deficits carefully. First, as mentioned earlier, fiscal deficits add to debt and increase the interest burden, thereby crowding out expenditures on productive sectors. If the borrowed funds are not used productively, there could be a vicious cycle of interest payments and repayment of debt adding to the deficits. Increased servicing of debt will account for increasing proportion of revenues and crowds out productive expenditures. Second, with increasing proportion of household sector's financial savings drawn to finance fiscal deficit, the savings available to the private sector will be less and this increases interest rates on private sector borrowings and financially crowd out private investments. Third, financing the fiscal deficits through monetization can add to inflation. In India, the sharp rise in inflation in the early 1990s was attributed to build up large fiscal deficits due to the expansionary policy followed in the second half of 1980s which led to economic crisis though the trigger for the crisis came from the Middle Eastern crisis and sharp increase in oil prices (Little and Joshi, 1996). The high inflation rate in the early part of the current millennium is also attributed to burgeoning fiscal deficit following the implementation of pay commission recommendations and increase in international price of crude oil. Despite the adoption of rule-based fiscal policy from 2004, the problem arose once again when the fiscal deficit increased sharply in 2008–2009 due to sharp increase in public spending for items like farm loan waiver, expansion of National Rural Employment Guarantee from 200 districts to the whole country and implementation of pay commission recommendations for Central government employees partly also due to the fiscal stimulus following the global financial crisis. This too was followed by a bout of inflation until 2014–2015. Finally, credit rating agencies do not take kindly to self-indulgent governments and credit rating of the country affects the cost of borrowing from abroad.

6.3. Fiscal Deficit and Debt in India

In India, the aggregate public debt of the Union and the States fore the pandemic was about 70 per cent of GDP. With the sharp increase in the fiscal deficit this year due to the COVID-19 crisis, it is estimated that even without large expenditure stimulus, the aggregate fiscal deficit in 2020–2021 estimated at about 12 per cent of GDP and debt to GDP ratio estimated at 90 per cent. The pandemic is still evolving, and its full impact is yet to unravel. How does this compare with other developing and emerging countries?

To put the choice of India's debt ceiling in perspective, it is important to compare the evolution of India's debt with that in other emerging markets.

The International comparison of deficit and debt by the IMF in its April 2020 Fiscal Monitor shows that in FY 2019, India's fiscal deficit at 7.4 per cent of GDP was the highest among emerging market economies except Venezuela (8 per cent). It was much higher than the average of emerging market economies (4.8 per cent), average of G-20 emerging economies (5.4 per cent), emerging market economies in Asia (6 per cent), Europe (0.7 per cent), and even Latin America (4.8 per cent). The outstanding debt in India at 71.9 per cent of GDP too was an outlier and among the emerging market economies, only Brazil (89.5 per cent), Argentina (86.8 per cent) and nearer home Pakistan (83.5 per cent) and Sri Lanka (86.8 per cent) had higher debt-GDP ratios. The debt-GDP ratio for the average EMIs is 53.2 per cent and only Latin American emerging market economies had an average debt to GDP ratio at 70.5 per cent which was close to India's outstanding debt.

While, generally, public spending financed by borrowing may be necessary, it is important to see that the borrowed funds are used productively to accelerate growth. Many countries follow the 'Golden Rule' that borrowing is done to finance only investment spending. According to the rule, financing of all current expenditures such as for paying salaries, interest, maintenance of capital assets, subsidies, and other transfers should be financed from current revenues and only capital expenditures should be financed from borrowing. While it is not possible to give a general rule on the optimal level of deficits and debt, borrowing can be resorted to so long as it accelerates growth and generate incomes to cover the debt servicing obligations adequately.

Excessive borrowing to finance public spending can have severe adverse implications. First, as already mentioned, it could put upward pressure on interest rates and financially crowd out private investments. Second, high volume of debt can result in high interest payments which pre-empts public spending on productive activities. Third, borrowing now will have to be repaid later through higher taxes and, therefore, involves a burden on the future generation. Fourth, high deficits could lead to balance of payment problems. For all these reasons, the credit rating agencies attach high-risk perception to countries with high fiscal deficits and debt and this can significantly enhance the international borrowing costs to the corporates. Therefore, in many countries, fiscal rules are legislated to contain the levels of deficits and debt.

In India, there have been concerns about the deficits and debt for long and the economic crisis of 1991 was mainly attributed to lax fiscal policy. As Little and Joshi (1996: 215) state, 'The crisis of 1990/91 and 1991/92 is wholly attributable to the lax fiscal policy of the preceding years. The rapid growth of debt, . . . together with political instability that delayed effective response to the gathering storm, made it impossible to finance the balance of payments deficit'. The large fiscal deficit resurfaced in 2001–2002 when the consolidated fiscal deficit was 10.3 per cent of GDP, primary deficit was close to 3 per cent, and revenue deficit was about 7 per cent. With the outstanding liabilities of the government estimated at 72.5 per cent of GDP and interest payment claiming 35 per cent of the total revenue receipts, there were serious questions on debt sustainability[1] demanding urgent intervention to restore fiscal balance in the country.

6.4. The Rule-Based Fiscal Policy Regime

Interestingly, the founding fathers of Indian Constitution did envisage that it may be necessary for the Parliament to fix the limits on the borrowing powers of the Union government. Thus, Article 292 in the Constitution, while empowering borrowing power to the Union government, subjects it to the limits fixed by the Parliament by enacting the law to that effect. However, this was never done until the Fiscal Responsibility and Budget Management (FRBM) Act was passed in 2003. In fact, since 1957, recommendations to statutorily limit the public debt by the Union government was made by the Estimates Committee, Public Accounts Committee, and the Reserve Bank of India, but it went unheeded. Even after suffering the consequences of fiscal profligacy and consequent reforms in 1991, the government's attempt to control fiscal deficit was unsuccessful and by 2001, the fiscal deficit stood elevated at 10.3 per cent of GDP, almost as much of the level in 1991–1992 (Table 6.1), with adverse macroeconomic and balance of payment consequences. In this situation, the government

[1] Buiter and Patel (1994, 2006) in their pioneering studies have drawn attention to the unsustainability of Indian public debt.

Table 6.1 Fiscal Imbalance in India.

	Centre			States			Total		
	Revenue deficit	Fiscal deficit	Primary deficit	Revenue deficit	Fiscal deficit	Primary deficit	Revenue deficit	Fiscal deficit	Primary deficit
2001–2002	4.40	6.19	1.47	2.65	4.14	1.43	7.05	10.32	2.90
2005–2006	2.50	4.73	0.37	0.19	2.33	0.16	2.69	7.26	0.79
2007–2008	1.05	3.11	−0.88	−0.86	1.49	−0.49	0.19	4.65	−1.02
2008–2009	4.54	8.20	2.59	−0.21	2.40	0.57	4.33	10.62	3.45
2009–2010	5.18	6.61	3.14	2.05	2.80	1.03	5.54	9.41	3.99
2010–2011	3.43	5.09	2.03	0.17	2.44	0.84	3.59	7.54	2.74
2011–2012	3.42	4.74	1.61	−0.26	2.00	0.49	3.17	6.76	1.99
2012–2013	3.68	4.93	1.78	−0.20	2.00	0.50	3.48	6.93	2.28
2013–2014	3.18	4.48	1.10	0.10	2.20	0.70	3.28	6.68	1.80
2014–2015	2.94	4.11	0.90	0.40	2.60	1.10	3.34	6.71	2.00
2015–2016	2.51	3.90	0.67	0.20	3.60	2.00	2.71	7.50	2.67
2016–2017	2.06	3.54	0.34	−0.10	3.00	1.30	1.96	6.54	1.64
2017–2018	2.60	3.50	0.40	0.4	3.1	1.3	3.00	6.6	1.64
2018–2019*	2.40	3.40	0.40	−0.20	2.60	0.90	2.20	6.0	1.30
2019–2020**	3.27	4.59	1.59	0.30	3.00	1.00	3.57	7.59	2.59

Note: * Revised Estimate; ** Budget estimate.

Consolidated States' revised estimate data for 2020–2021 are not available. The aggregate deficit numbers comprise of revised estimate for the Centre and budget estimate for the States.

Source: Public Finance Statistics, Ministry of Finance, Government of India and Union Budget (2020–2021) Finances of State Governments (2019–2020), Reserve Bank of India.

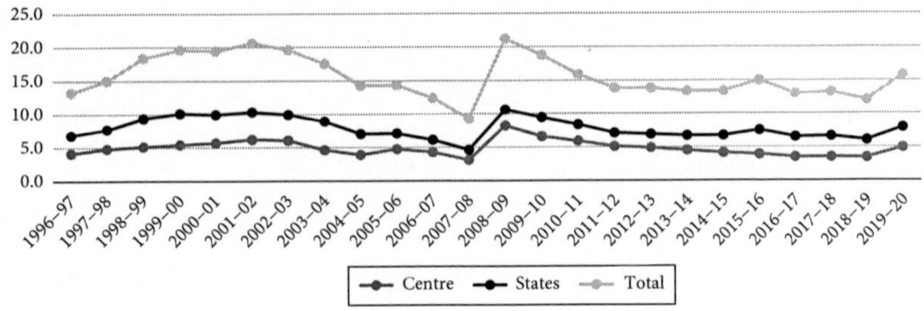

Figure 6.1 Fiscal Deficit in India: Centre, States, and Consolidated.

decided to appoint a Committee under the Chairmanship of the then Economic Affairs Secretary (E. A. S. Sharma), which prepared a blueprint for rule-based fiscal policy by progressively reducing the revenue deficit every year by 0.5 points to GDP to eliminate it by 2006–2007. Similarly, the fiscal deficit was to be progressively reduced by 0.33 point every year to contain it at 3 per cent of GDP by 2006–2007.

The enactment of FRBM Act, however, was done only after the 12th Finance Commission made a recommendation to that effect in 2003. The Commission was asked in its TOR to 'Review the state of the finances of the Union and the States and suggest a plan by which the governments, collectively and severally, may bring about a restructuring of the public finances restoring budgetary balance, achieving macro economic stability and debt reduction along with equitable growth'. It recommended that both the Union and State governments should, beginning 2004–2005, progressively reduce revenue deficits completely and the fiscal deficits at both the levels were to be reduced to 3 per cent of GDP by 2008–2009. The reasoning for fixing 3 per cent target for fiscal deficit rested on the fact that the savings-investment balance for both government and corporates are negative and they essentially depend upon the household sector's financial savings and the current account deficit. The former was around 10 per cent of GDP and the later was 1.5 per cent. After leaving 1.5 per cent of GDP borrowing space to public sector enterprises, the net borrowing space available was 10 per cent of GDP. If the corporate sector was to be provided with a borrowing space of 4 per cent, the government was left with 6 per cent, equally divided between the Union and the States (India, 2003).

To incentivize the States to adopt rule-based fiscal policy and rein in their deficits at targeted levels, the Commission recommended that on passing the fiscal responsibility legislations, the outstanding Central government debt to the States should be written off by 50 per cent. Furthermore, beginning 2004–2005, reduction in their revenue deficits by the States was to be rewarded by corresponding reduction in equivalent amounts of the remaining part of the Central debt in corresponding States.

These recommendations were accepted, and the rule-based fiscal policy started from 2004–2005 with the enactment of FRBM in 2003 at the Union level. All the States except Sikkim and West Bengal enacted the FRBM Acts for their respective States. The subsequent years saw substantial reduction in the deficits at both Central and state levels until 2007–2008. At the Central level, this was largely due to the sharp increase in revenue by about 32 per cent per year on average between 2003–2004 and 2008–2009 from both personal and corporate income taxes due to the implementation of tax information network (TIN).[2] In addition, with the progressive expansion of the base, the revenue from taxes on services increased at over 65 per cent per year. The gains from these were not only for the Centre but also the States as 30.5 per cent of the divisible pool of taxes (gross tax revenue of the Centre minus revenue from cesses and surcharges minus the cost of tax collection) was devolved to the states, besides the gains from lower interest payments on account of the writing off of Centre's debt mentioned above. Thus, by 2007–2008, the fiscal deficit of Central government was brought down to 3.1 per cent and revenue deficit was compressed to 1 per cent (Table 6.1). At the State level, there was a revenue surplus of 0.2 per cent and fiscal deficit was well below the target at 1.5 per cent.

The gains in fiscal consolidation achieved until 2007–2008 were frittered away in 2008–2009. The three important decisions taken in the election year announced in the budget, namely, farm loan waiver, extending national rural employment guarantee from 200 districts to the entire country, and the implementation of the Sixth Pay Commission, recommendations substantially increased expenditures and as the revenues failed to increase commensurately, the fiscal deficit expanded sharply.

[2] For details, see Rao (2016: 76).

In addition, with oil prices hitting the all-time high of USD 143/barrel in July 2008 combined with the government's reluctance to increase the prices of distillates in the election year, and the petroleum subsidy bill rose by almost 2.5 per cent of GDP.

In addition, the government decided to reduce excise duties and service tax as a stimulus measure to combat global financial crisis. Due to the combination of these reasons, Centre's revenue deficit increased from 1.1 per cent in 2007–2008 to 4.5 per cent in 2008–2009 and fiscal deficit increased by over five percentage points from 3.1 per cent to 8.2 per cent. The problem was further exacerbated by the decline in Centre's tax-GDP ratio by more than two percentage points to GDP from 11.8 per cent in 2007–2008 to 9.6 per cent in 2010–2011. Consequently, the consolidated revenue and fiscal deficits in 2008–2009 increased to 4.4 per cent and 10.6 per cent, respectively.

The 13th Finance Commission was asked to review the state of finances of the Union and State governments and 'Suggest measures for maintaining a stable and sustainable fiscal environment consistent with equitable growth' (India, 2009: 12). The Commission's recommendations covered the period from 2009–2010 to 2014–2015. The fiscal road map in its recommendations required the Centre to bring down the revenue deficit from 4.8 per cent in 2009–2010 to create a surplus of 0.5 per cent in the terminal year of its recommendations (2014–2015). The fiscal deficit was to be reduced from 6.8 per cent to 3 per cent during the same period and with non-debt capital receipts were targeted at 1 per cent in the terminal year and with 3 per cent fiscal deficit, the capital expenditure was targeted at 4.5 per cent. Based on the recommended targets and the assumption about the growth of GDP, the outstanding debt was supposed to come down from 54.2 per cent in 2009–2010 to 44.8 per cent in 2014–2015. The Commission also recommended that the Union Finance Ministry should appoint a committee to monitor the progress of fiscal adjustment which should eventually be transformed into a Fiscal council. The Council would be reporting to the Finance Ministry.

As far as the States were concerned, the target of 3 per cent GSDP worked out to 2.4 per cent of GDP of the country as GSDP then was estimated at factor cost and the deficit estimates did not include Union Territories. The aggregate debt to GDP ratio of the States was to be brought down from 27.1 per cent in 2009–2010 to 24.3 per cent in 2014–2015. The facility to avail the incentive of writing off of Central loans on enacting the fiscal responsibility legislation and for reducing the revenue deficits in subsequent years was extended to Sikkim and West Bengal, the two States that did not avail the incentive given by the previous Commission. While most of the States had complied with the targets of phasing out revenue deficits and reducing their fiscal deficit to 3 per cent of GSDP by 2008–2009, three states of Kerala, Punjab, and West Bengal continued to have sizeable revenue deficits in 2007–2008 and to avoid abrupt cut in capital expenditures on enforcing 3 per cent fiscal deficit target, they were given slightly relaxed targets for each year to reach phase out the revenue deficits and reach the target of 3 per cent of GSDP in fiscal deficits by 2014–2015.

The serious slippage in the targets in 2008–2009 described above has continued to be a bane. The subsequent years have seen slippages in targets, repeated shifting of dates to achieve the targets, inventing a new concept of 'effective revenue deficit' to reduce the burden of revenue deficit reduction required, and resorting creative accounting through off budget liabilities, advance collection of taxes, and postponement of bills. In 2014–2015, the last year of the 13th Finance Commissions recommendation period, the fiscal deficit at the Centre was 4.1 per cent as against the 3 per cent target and revenue deficit slipped badly to 2.9 per cent as against the 0.5 per cent surplus projected by the Commission. Thus, not only the Centre was not able to adhere to the targets but also there were increasing attempts to obfuscate the numbers resulting in increased opacity in the budgets contrary to the recommendation by the 13th Finance Commission's assertion that the FRBM process should be made more 'comprehensive and transparent and sensitive to exogenous shocks'.

The 14th Finance Commission was also asked to review the state of finances of the Union and State governments keeping in view the road map recommended by the previous Commission and suggest measures for maintaining a stable and sustainable fiscal environment consistent with equitable growth including suggestions to ament the Fiscal Responsibility and Budget Management (FRBM) Acts currently in force. The Commission recommended that the Union government should compress its fiscal deficit to 3 per cent of GDP by 2016–2017 and thereafter maintain it at that level. It also recommended that improvement in macroeconomic conditions and tax reforms (implementation of GST) would enhance the tax revenues and would enable the government to reduce the revenue deficit to 0.93 per cent by 2019–2020. For the States, the Commission recommended that the fiscal deficit target would be 3 per cent of GSDP (2.74 per cent of GDP) and in the aggregate, they were to generate a revenue surplus of 1.88 per cent of GDP. The Commission recommended an additional borrowing space of 25 basis points to those States with debt to GSDP ratio of less than 25 per cent and another 25 basis points to those States with interest payments less than 10 per cent of their revenue receipts. The outstanding debt was to be reduced from 64.53 per cent of GDP in 2015–2016 to 58.24 per cent in 2019–2020 with the ratio for the Union government going down from 43.6 per cent to 36.3 per cent and for the States a marginal increase from 21.9 per cent to 22.38 per cent.

The sharp decline in oil prices in the mid-2014 helped the new Government, which came to power in May 2014, not only to ease the pressure on the current account but also substantially reduce both oil and fertilizer subsidies. Despite this, the government could not reduce the fiscal and revenue deficits to the targeted levels. The decline in the international price of crude helped the government to garner more excise duties. The attempt to contain the deficits was seen in mainly compressing capital expenditures. Despite this, the Union government could never achieve the targets recommended by the Finance Commission. A new FRBM Review Committee was appointed in 2016 to revise the road map for consolidation. The TOR of the Committee included (i) the review of FRBM targets; (ii) to examine whether it is appropriate to have a range of FRBM target instead of a single target; (iii) feasibility of linking fiscal expansion and contraction to credit expansion and contraction to make FRBM targets counter cyclical. The Commission (India, 2017) recommended that debt should be the target and fiscal deficit should be the anchor to achieve the target and the target was set at 60 per cent of GDP to be achieved by 2023–2024. The Union government was to reduce its debt to GDP ratio to 40 per cent and the States to 20 per cent. Considering that the financial savings of the households was just about 7.6 per cent of GDP, and assuming a current account deficit of 2.3 per cent of GDP, the total fiscal deficit was estimated at 10 per cent of GDP. This was to be shared equally between the public and private sectors.

The Committee did not favour range of estimates nor did it recommend countercyclical targets. As far as the Centre is concerned, to achieve the target of containing debt-GDP ratio at 40 per cent by 2013–2014, the fiscal deficit target was set at 3 per cent of GDP for the first 3 years and thereafter this was to be reduced to 2.5 per cent of GDP. Further, the Committee recommended that the revenue deficit should be reduced by 0.25 per cent of GDP in each of the years to contain it at 0.8 per cent in 2013 so that the ratio of revenue deficit to fiscal deficit could be reduced from the prevailing 66 per cent to 32 per cent. Like the 13th Finance Commission, the Committee recommended the setting up of a Fiscal Council to monitor the progress in the implementation of FRBM targets which will submit reports to it from time to time. However, unlike the 14th Finance Commission which recommended the setting up of an independent fiscal council by the Parliament and reporting it by amending the FRBM Act, the Council recommended by the FRBM Review Committee was to be appointed by the Finance Ministry and would be reporting to it.

The FRBM Review Committee further recommended that the government may deviate from the target when (i) there are overriding considerations such as natural calamity and war; (ii) the government has undertaken far reaching reforms with fiscal implications; and (iii) there is a sharp decline in the output of at least 3 percentage points for four successive quarters. Symmetric approach was to be adopted when there is a case of increases in output.

The Union Finance Minister in his 2018–2019 budget speech accepted the key recommendations of the Committee and made significant amendments to the FRBM framework through the Finance Act of 2018. The important amendments are (i) fiscal deficit, the key operational target is to be brought down to 3 per cent of GDP by the end of 2020–2021; (ii) abandon the targets on revenue deficit altogether and inclusion of primary deficit as a key fiscal indicator; (iii) achieving the general government debt target of 60 per cent of GDP and Central government target of 40 per cent of GDP by 2024–2025; the concept of Central government debt is to include all outstanding liabilities incurred on the security of consolidated fund of India and public accounts and other financial liabilities of all body corporates and entities owned and operated by the Central government which the government is required to service and repay; (iv) desisting from giving additional guarantees to any loan on the security of the consolidated fund in excess of 1 per cent of GDP in any financial year; (v) escape clauses for breaching the deficit targets by a maximum of half a per cent of GDP for reasons of such as national security, act of war, national calamity, collapse of agriculture, structural reforms in the economy, and decline in output growth; (vi) the fiscal deficit to be reduced at least by one-quarter per cent of GDP in a year when there is an increase in the output in a quarter by at least three percentage points above the average of the previous four quarters; (vii) half-yearly review as against the prevailing quarterly review and preparation of monthly statement of accounts. The amendment, however, did not include the recommendations of the Committee relating to the revenue deficit nor did it consider the recommendation in the establishment of the Fiscal Council.

With the outbreak of the coronavirus pandemic, the entire process of debt consolidation and deficit correction has taken the beating. The pandemic is still evolving, and it is not yet clear how much the economy will contract, how long it will take for the economy to revive, what would be the reduction in revenues at Central and State levels, and how much of stimulus has to be given to save the lives and livelihoods of people and to revive the economy. The advance estimate puts the contraction of real GDP in 2020–2021 at 7.7 per cent and nominal GDP at 4.2 per cent. The revised estimate of fiscal deficit for the year is 9.5 per cent and when the States' deficit is considered, the aggregate fiscal deficit could work out to 14 per cent of GDP and the total debt to GDP ratio can touch 85–90 per cent. This would mean that a new credible adjustment path will have to be worked out once the crisis created by the pandemic subsides. The government will be faced with a challenging and painful task of fiscal adjustment in a credible manner. Unlike the situation that prevailed in 2008–2009 when the global financial crisis struck, the economy and its fiscal situation is much weaker now and contraction will be unprecedented. It is extremely important to chart out a credible adjustment path to revive the economy immediately as the crisis subsides.

6.5. New Institutional Framework for Comprehensiveness, Credibility, and Transparency

The foregoing discussion shows that Indian public finances, particularly the finances of the Union government, have been under severe pressure since the last Finance Commission made its recommendations. While the incentive-based process initiated with the recommendation of the 12th Finance Commission has helped to rein in the States' deficits, the experience of fiscal adjustment at the Union government raises questions. This has called for introducing an institutional mechanism to undertake independent review and monitor the adjustment process by the Parliament and its committees, accurately costing the various policies and programmes initiated by the government and raise the level of budget debates both inside and outside the Parliament.

The State governments, with a few exceptions, have been able to conform to the fiscal targets set by the 13th Finance Commission although the deficits in the power sector threaten to destabilize the finances of some of the states. The incentive-based fiscal adjustment process recommended by the 12th Finance Commission has helped to put the state finances in general on a sustainable path and States on the whole have adhered to the fiscal targets set by the 13th Finance Commission as well. Of course, some states like Kerala, Punjab, and West Bengal for which separate adjustment path was recommended by the 13th Finance Commission, continue to face varying degrees of fiscal pressures. Also, there are questions on the quality of adjustments in some States as often the targets have been achieved by compressing capital expenditures. Further, in the case of some States, the power sector continues to bleed as the fiscal targets set by the States based on the recommendations of the Finance Commissions are not comprehensive. Despite these shortcomings, on the whole, State finances have conformed to the revenue and fiscal deficit targets.

The fiscal health of the Union government continues to be worrisome. Although the fast growth of tax revenues helped to achieve substantial fiscal consolidation until 2007–2008, the significant fiscal expansion introduced in the 2008–2009 budget along with the inability of the government to increase the prices commensurate with the sharp increase in the crude oil prices in mid-2008 resulted in the severe escalation in both revenue and fiscal deficits. Further, the deceleration in the growth of the economy in the wake of global financial crisis and the attempt to provide fiscal stimulus by reducing the rates of excise duty and service tax resulted in lower buoyancy in revenues and this added to the problem. In the event, despite attempts by the Union government to contain the deficits, there have been large slippages in conforming to the targets set by the 13th Finance Commission and these have put severe pressure on the macroeconomic policy space.

The experience with the rule-based fiscal policy discussed in the last chapter brings out some important shortcomings of the system. First, while the overall borrowing limit is implemented by the Union government, they do not have much leeway to expand their deficit beyond what is permitted by the Union government. In contrast, the Union government does not face such a constraint and Parliamentary control in terms of monitoring the FRBM needs to be strengthened. Second, with actual revenue and expenditures available in public domain with almost a year's lag, reliability of forecasts is extremely important. As mentioned in the previous chapter, the pressure to achieve fiscal targets has adverse impact on the budget management practices. Inability to realize the ambitious revenue targets set in the budgets have resulted in unplanned compressions of expenditures. Invariably, capital expenditures got squeezed with adverse growth implications and adding to the time and cost runs of projects. Third, in its effort to show that the targets are achieved, the government can take resort to various kinds of off-budget financing and creative accounting which can seriously erode the credibility of the budgets.

Transparency in budgeting requires that costs of all new programmes and policy announcements—both in the short and in the long term—are properly estimated and included in the budget. In Indian context, schemes are announced without making proper estimate of the expenditure involved. This is true of the more recent programmes like Sarva Shiksha Abhiyan and food security. There are also various pre-election announcements (like loan waivers) which need to be costed in an objective and scientific manner. Similarly, loan waiver programmes are announced before elections or introduced in the budget without working out the financial implications. The estimates put out on the revenue forgone on account of various tax concessions need to be made on a much more scientific manner. Despite recommendations by the Finance

Commissions to make an estimate of asset and liability positions of the government, not much seems to have been done. There is no estimate of contingent liabilities arising from various public private partnership projects.

Although the rule-based fiscal policy has raised the awareness for containing deficits and debt and has helped to contain the deficits until 2008–2009, the slippages from the targets set in the MTFPs have been fairly common thereafter. Even the targets set in MTFPs have deviated from the Finance Commission targets. Furthermore, there have been repeated postponement of the targets, resorting to off-budget liabilities to show lower deficits, non-settlement of bill payments to contractors and commercial entities facilitated by the cash accounting system to show lower deficits and manipulation of the disinvestment figures with one public enterprise purchasing another and remitting the money to the government. Besides, a considerable part of adjustment that has been made by reducing capital and maintenance expenditures, thereby reducing the productivity of public expenditures. As noted earlier, the central government never achieved the target of phasing and put revenue deficits, contrary to what the Finance Commissions had emphasized. In fact, to ease the target, the Central government initially 'invented' a concept of 'effective revenue deficit', and in the 2019–2020 amendment to the FRBM Act, the reference to reducing revenue deficit was abandoned altogether.

A budget, to be credible, should be comprehensive, realistic, and transparent. Over the years, with various obfuscations made to show lower deficits, the credibility of the budget has been lost. The Report of the Comptroller and Auditor General on the compliance of FRBM Act, 2003, for 2016–2017 brings out the details of the off-budget liabilities incurred to meet both revenue and capital expenditures. Special banking arrangements for covering fertilizer subsidy and arrears, borrowing from National Small Savings Fund (NSSF) in the Public Accounts to cover deferring fertilizer subsidy, and its arrears of Food Corporation of India (FCI) are the main off-budget items in the revenue account. In the capital account, long-term borrowing by NABARD under the Long-Term Irrigation Fund (LTIF) is essentially a liability on the government. There are also off-budget financing of railway projects through borrowings of the Indian Railway Finance Corporation (IRFC) and financing of power projects through the Power Finance Corporation (PFC). The report states that when the borrowing from Public Accounts is included, the outstanding liabilities of the Centre relative to GDP work out to 50.5 per cent as against the projection of 47.1 per cent in the Medium-Term Fiscal Plan (MTFP) and 45.5 per cent shown in the Consolidated Fund. In addition, there were misclassification of revenue expenditures and non-transfer of earmarked cesses to the public account underestimating the revenue deficit in the budget. There are also cases of the Life Insurance Corporation of India buying out IDBI Bank which required recapitalization and PFC buying out Rural Electrification Corporation (REC) and remitting the money to the government as disinvestment proceeds.

From the above discussion, it can be surmised that even though the FRBMA has helped the governments at both Central and State levels to exercise restraint, their success in containing deficits at targeted level has been limited. In fact, there have been a number of other adverse repercussions form the way the adjustment processes have been carried out. One of them relates to the problems arising from overestimation of revenues. The problems begin with the budget forecasts. In its attempt to show lower deficits, the tax revenues are overestimated in the budgets. In fact, in 6 years of the last 10 years from 2000–2001 to 2019–2020, there were overestimations of various magnitudes. The scatter diagram shows that on average, the extent of overestimation has been increasing over the years (Figure 6.2). Furthermore, obfuscations and creative accounting to show lower deficits have made the budgets opaque and enormously complicated. Extensive use of off-budget borrowings obscures the real

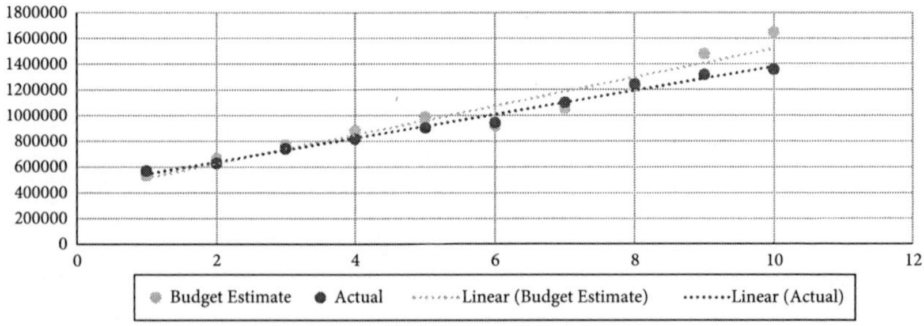

Figure 6.2 Tax Revenue of the Central Government: Budget Estimates and Actuals.

Source: Estimated from Union Budget Documents.

picture. Considerable overlap between the finances of public enterprises and the consolidated fund causes increases in off-budget liabilities. Lack of comprehensiveness in the targets is also seen from the fact that the governments follow cash accounting systems where the reported deficits accurately reflect the actual situation. As these are deliberate actions by the government to manipulate the deficit estimates, there are serious questions of credibility of the budgets.

Taking targets rather than realistic forecasts in revenue projections based on empirical trends poses several problems in fiscal management. First, failure to achieve targeted revenues results in cutting expenditures during the course of the year and most often, given the sociology of fiscal politics, the axe falls on expenditures on creation and maintenance of capital works. Second, overestimation creates expenditure management problems for both the Union and State governments as 41 per cent of the divisible pool of Central taxes is shared with the States based on the 15th Finance Commission's recommendations. The States prepare their budgets and base their estimate of tax devolution on the Central tax forecasts. Third, the overestimation in revenues can lead to 'tax terrorism'. Often, search and seizure operations are initiated in allegedly 'suspicious' cases resulting in harassment to the taxpayers. The Commissionerates are given the targets by the Central Boards, and to show better performance, they invariably reassess many cases and make unreasonable demands resulting in disputes. The taxpayer is required to pay 20 per cent of the disputed tax demanded, and while this helps to increase the collections, it also ends up with prolonged litigations. A report of C&AG in 2018 on Direct Taxes brought out that almost 65 per cent of the cases in the Income Tax Tribunals, 79 per cent of the cases in High Courts, and 71 per cent of the cases in the Supreme Court are decided in favour of the taxpayers requiring the tax department to pay huge amount of interest payments on the disputed tax collected.

Often, the governments initiate various schemes and also make various policy pronouncements during the course of the year after the budget is presented and they do not have the time to make a proper assessment of the present and future costs and benefits of these schemes. It is also well known that even those pronouncements included in the budget do not undergo rigorous cost–benefit analysis. Consequently, too many projects are taken up and without adequate funds being allocated they result in enormous time and cost overruns. As the projects take long periods to complete due to inadequate allocations, the intended objectives are not achieved in a time-bound manner and productivity of public spending remains at a low level. Not surprisingly, the 14th Finance Commission made a specific recommendation that, 'The Union and the State Governments provide a statutory ceiling of the sanction of new capital works to an appropriate multiple of the annual budget provision'. The issue of scientifically assessing the costs and benefits is not confined to capital works alone. It is also important to assess the desirability and viability of various policies, programmes, and schemes and make a comparison with alternative policy and programme options for ensuring efficient budget management.

Clear examples of not making assessment of present and future liabilities can be seen in the adoption of policies such as 'one rank–one pension' or announcements made from time to time on various schemes and policies. The decision of the elected government in adopting such schemes is not in question. What is necessary is to understand what it entails in terms of present and future costs to the exchequer. This can be the case with rights like the Right to Education, Right to food security, or various centrally sponsored schemes. Whenever a scheme is announced, it is important to clearly define its scope, design, duration of the scheme, implementation strategy, the costs involved for each of the years of its duration, and the funding strategy if this has to be financed from outside the consolidated funds. In reality, many of the policy pronouncements are created for political expediency without estimating the costs involved and when it is implemented, the scope of the pronouncement is 'adjusted' to minimize the liabilities in the current year. The most common example is the announcement of farm loan waivers in election manifestos and when the party is elected, narrowing its scope of application to minimize the liabilities.

6.6. Independent Fiscal Institutions: Worldwide Experience

Worldwide experience shows that political economy considerations play an important role in the persistence of deficits and pro-cyclicality biases in fiscal policy. The deficit bias is associated with the myopic view of the policy makers who indulge in proliferating expenditures, particularly by expanding subsidies and transfers and cutting taxes to get re-elected on the eve of elections (Alesina and Tabelini, 1990). This is due to the lack of transparency, and fiscal illusion obscures the true budget constraint and poor understanding of the long-term implications of deficits. Often, this is facilitated by lack of transparency and creative accounting and off-budget financing schemes (von Hagen, 2010). The problem can also arise when the political interests dominate fiscal decisions and *ex ante* considerations in national interest are not found to be desirable *ex post*. This could result in a government leaving the successor government with a larger debt burden and constrain the fiscal space.

Creating an independent fiscal institution to monitor the conduct of fiscal policy and reporting to the Parliament is an important innovation to alter policymakers' incentives to pursue sustainable fiscal policy. With clear commitments on fiscal adjustment path and transparent medium-term fiscal framework (Kumar and Ter-Minassian, 2007) the new institutional framework strengthens discipline in the calibration of rule-based fiscal policy. In cases where political commitment is not strong, numerical fiscal targets can be helpful in raising the awareness, but this could turn out to be mechanical and may not address the quality of adjustment and it may not be possible to stipulate countercyclical numerical rules. Therefore, to make the system comprehensive and transparent, and to depoliticize fiscal policy calibration, an independent fiscal institution is appointed. The institution helps to make the assumptions clear and transparent and report the findings of non-partisan and scientific analysis of the policies including their costs and benefits in public domain. The institution can also be required to monitor the medium-term fiscal plans and fiscal rules to impart comprehensiveness, transparency, and accountability.

Fiscal councils or IFIs with a statutory (or executive) mandate to promote stable and sustainable public finances. Hagemann (2011: 76) defines a fiscal council as, 'A publicly funded entity staffed by non-elected professionals mandated to provide non-partisan oversight of fiscal performance and/or advice and guidance—from either a positive or normative perspective—on key aspects of fiscal policy'. These institutions assist in calibrating sustainable fiscal policy by making independent, objective, and scientific analysis of fiscal policies for achieving the objectives of macroeconomic stability and sustainability. First, unbiased report to the

Parliament helps to raise the level of debate and brings in greater transparency and accountability. Second, costing of various policies and programmes helps to promote transparency and discourages populist shifts in fiscal policy and improve accountability. Third, scientific estimate of the cost of programmes and assessment of forecasts help to raise public awareness about their fiscal implications and make them clearly understand the nature of the budget constraint.

Increasing number of countries have opted to appoint independent fiscal institutions and their numbers have surged particularly after the global financial crisis. In 1960, the Netherlands was the only country with an active fiscal council, but by 1990, Denmark, Germany, the United States, and Belgium also adopted similar institutions. The numbers increased particularly after the global financial crisis and, by March 2014, there were 31 countries with such institutions. The most recent countries to join the list are Chile and Spain (in March 2014). Although most of the countries adopting fiscal councils are advanced economies, there is a growing interest among developing and emerging market economies.

While the common agenda of these institutions has been to promote sound fiscal policies as watchdogs, there is considerable diversity in their structure and the functions they are assigned to perform. The important tasks they are assigned to perform include (i) independent analysis, review and monitoring, and evaluating of government's fiscal policies and programmes; (ii) developing or reviewing macroeconomic and/or budgetary projections; (iii) costing of budget and policy proposals, programmes including the proposals in the election manifestos; and (iv) advising the policymakers on various policy options. Over the years, the task of monitoring the compliance with fiscal rules and costing the policies and programmes has become a major task of these councils.

The concept of 'independence' in the case of the fiscal council is different from the one used in the case of the Central Bank. In the case of the fiscal council, independence does not imply legal separation but simply refers to operational autonomy necessary for non-partisanship approach in performing its tasks. The Councils are required to benchmark their assessments against the policy objectives of the executive. It cannot set the objectives unlike in the case of the independent Central Banks. While the fiscal council has the oversight objective, its functions are different from that of the auditor (comptroller and auditor general). The fiscal council plays an ex-ante role of planning and policy formulation, whereas the focus of the audit is ex-post evaluations. The fiscal council follows a macroeconomic approach, whereas the auditor follows legal or microeconomic approaches.

The OECD (2013) has documented the important principles needed for successful fiscal councils under nine broad heads and these are (i) local ownership; (ii) independence and non-partisanship; (iii) mandate; (iv) resources; (v) relationship with legislature; (vi) access to information; (vii) transparency; (viii) communication; and (ix) external evaluation. These principles are important to ensure autonomy, unbiasedness, transparency, effectiveness, and accountability. For fiscal council can be successful only when there is a broad national commitment and ownership and consensus across the political spectrum. While the international experience with different models of fiscal councils can be helpful, the structure, role, and functions of the councils should be designed keeping in view the particular conditions and needs and capacity constraints in the country (Kopitz, 2011).

Independence and non-partisanship of the council are extremely important preconditions for a successful IFI. In fact, a majority of the IFIs enjoy legal protection against partisanship (IMF, 2013). Merit and technical competence are the keys to a successful IFIs. The IFI should earn its respect from the professional excellence of its reports. The leaders of the IFI should be selected on the basis of their technical competence without connection or political affiliation. Term lengths of the leadership should be clearly specified. Non-renewal of terms of the leaders is one of the methods to safeguard independence. The leadership of the IFI should have full freedom to hire or dismiss the staff along the lines of civil service. Operational independence of the institution critically depends on the assurance on funding and the funds allocated should be commensurate with their remit. The appropriations to IFIs should be treated in the same manner as those of other independent bodies such as audit offices.

The budget allocation to the IFIs depends upon its remit. International experience shows wide variation. The fiscal council in Sweden is required to only make the assessment of fiscal policy of the government which it undertakes with a staff of five persons and a cost of USD 1 billion. On the other extreme, the Congressional Budget Office in the United States has a much wider remit and has a staff of 240 and incurs a cost of

USD 240 billion every year (IMF, 2013). Clarity in the mandate including the types of reports to be prepared and placed in the legislature is important. It should also have authority to produce studies and reports at its own initiative.

Regardless of whether the IFI is under the statutory authority of the legislature or the executive, it should be made accountable to the legislature. This can be done by sending all the reports of the IFI to the legislature, appearance of the IFI leadership before the legislative budget committees, legislative scrutiny of the IFI budget, and the role for the budget committee in the appointment of IFI leadership. It is also important to clearly establish the role of the IFI in servicing requests from various legislative committees and individual members of the legislature.

Access to information is an important pre-requisite for undertaking scientific analysis and evaluation. It is important to guarantee the access to information through legislation and reaffirm it through protocols and memorandum of understanding. IFIs should have full access to information in a timely manner, including the methodology and assumptions implicit in the preparation of the budget and various proposals included in the budget.

In the interest of transparency, all IFI reports should be published and made available to the public free of cost. Such of those reports which are required to be placed in the legislature should be put in public domain after they are placed. The IFI should develop effective communication channels with the media. There should also be a mechanism for external evaluation of the work of the IFI to be conducted by local or international experts.

The important question is the effectiveness of the IFI in improving fiscal management. It is difficult to make a clear statistical analysis as the existence of IFIs is associated with fiscal rules and it is difficult to disentangle the effects. Nevertheless, based on broad correlations, the study (IMF, 2013) draws some interesting conclusions. The econometric analysis shows that certain characteristics of IFIs are associated with stronger fiscal performances, particularly the existence of IFIs is associated with stronger primary balances. The result is particularly strong in countries with legal guarantees on the independence of the IFIs. It is also seen that in countries where the fiscal rules and IFIs complement each other, the beneficial effects are stronger. The analysis shows that IFI are likely to raise awareness of the people and raise public debate on fiscal policy. Similarly, the IFIs entrusted to monitor fiscal rules tend to attract greater press coverage and impact fiscal outcomes. The study also shows that countries with IFI tend to have more accurate macroeconomic and budgetary forecasts.

Hagemann (2011) makes a detailed review of the country-specific studies on the effectiveness of IFIs in improving fiscal performances. The case studies of Belgium, Chile, and the United Kingdom show that fiscal councils contributed to improved fiscal performances. In Belgium, he concludes that the government is legally required to adopt the macroeconomic forecasts of the Federal Planning Bureau, and this has significantly helped to reduce bias in these estimates. In Chile, the existence of two independent bodies on Trend GDP and reference copper price has greatly helped to improve budget forecasts. In the United Kingdom, the Office of Budget Responsibility played an important role in restoring fiscal sustainability when the new government came to power after 2010. The cross-country evidence shows that fiscal councils exert a strong influence on fiscal performances, particularly when they have formal guarantees of independence.

The 13th Finance Commission, while recommending the revised road map for fiscal consolidation, underlined the need for making the FRBM process more transparent and comprehensive and sensitive to exogenous shocks and introduction of mechanisms to improve monitoring and compliance. In the case of the states, the Commission noted that while the incentive-linked conditions were effective in improving the fiscal health, the independent review provided in the FRBM legislations of many state governments significantly contributed to improving credibility and transparency of the actions taken by these state governments. Therefore, the Commission recommended the setting up of a committee to conduct an independent review of FRBM compliance including the fiscal impact of policy decisions on the FRBM road map to be presented along with the annual budget and medium-term strategy. The Commission recommended that the committee should act as an autonomous body reporting to the Ministry of finance and should, over time, change into a full-fledged Fiscal Council (India, 2009: para 9.65). The Commission concluded, 'As the size and complexity of the Indian economy expands, it is imperative that such an institution be developed to assist the government in addressing its fiscal tasks in a professional, transparent and effective manner' (para 9.66). The FRBM Review Committee too recognized the need for an independent monitor but reiterated the same recommendation. It must be recognized that what is required is an independent institution and any council appointed by the Finance Ministry and reporting to it ceases to be independent.

It is in this context that the recommendation of the 14th Finance Commission that the FRBM Act should be amended to enable the Parliament to appoint a Fiscal Council to monitor the fiscal management in the country assumes significance. The Commission felt that it is necessary to establish an independent institution to undertake ex-ante evaluation of the fiscal implications of the budget proposals. The 'review' by the C&AG provided for in the amendment to FRBM Act under a new Section (7A) would only be an ex-post review and does not help in transparency or concurrent monitoring. Therefore, it is recommended that the FRBM Act should be amended by inserting a new Section, mandating the establishment of an independent fiscal council to undertake ex-ante assessment of the fiscal policy implications of budget proposals and their consistency with fiscal policy and Rules (India, 2014: para 14.101).

6.7. Concluding Remarks

The problem of high deficits and debt continues to threaten fiscal stability and sustainability in India. While the first 4 years from 2004 to 2005 when the FRBM process was implemented held a tremendous promise mainly due to significant increase in the Union tax revenues, the subsequent period has seen slippages, changes in the originally set targets, creative accounting to show better than actual performances. The budget has ceased to be comprehensive, transparent, and accountable. Various types of obfuscations are done year after year to show lower deficits through creative accounting and off-budget borrowings. Even the efforts to contain deficits had adverse impact as expenditure reduction was mainly by compressing capital expenditures.

With the outbreak of the coronavirus pandemic, the entire process of debt reduction has taken the beating. Pandemic time is not the time to bother about deficits and debt because saving lives and livelihoods and fast tracking the recovery process is the priority and the government will have to loosen the purse strings even while faced with severe revenue contraction. However, as normalcy returns, the government will have to work out a new fiscal consolidation road map and implement it in a credible manner. To increase the credibility of the budgets, the government should make the deficit and debt numbers comprehensive and transparent, set the targets for deficit and debt reduction in the next years after normalcy returns, and lay down the road map for achieving them. It is also important to embark on a phased adoption of accrual accounting system from the present cash accounting.

An important way to increase credibility is to set up a Fiscal Council appointed by the Parliament and reporting to it. The analysis of fiscal adjustment in India shows that there is a need for such institution. The independent fiscal institution can help to improve the quality of budget estimates, achieve better compliance of the fiscal targets set in MTFP, and enable more scientific costing of the policies and programmes to evaluate their costs and benefits. Such institutions have improved the fiscal performances in a number of countries and growing number of countries have opted to appoint them. Setting up an IFI could help in altering the incentives of policymakers towards calibrating sustainable fiscal policy.

However, it is important to note that even as the fiscal council can help to improve fiscal performance, it cannot be a 'silver bullet'. The effectiveness of IFI will ultimately depend upon the political commitment of the executive. No government likes to be criticized on its conduct of fiscal (or any other) policy. Safeguarding the independence of the IFI is a difficult challenge particularly as the government may find the institution inconvenient. It is not surprising that in Hungary, the Fiscal Council established by the government in 2009 was looked at with suspicion by the new government elected to power in 2010. Displeased with the Council's critical assessment of the new government' medium-term budget strategy spelt out in the 2011 budget, the government took a series of measures to weaken the Council by disbanding the office, changing the composition, and weakening the remit to render it a part-time body with no particular task to perform.

Despite this, in most countries the experience has been favourable and, therefore, it is yet another step in creating checks and balances in the system by enhancing credibility and transparency in calibrating fiscal policy. The time for creating such an institution is opportune as COVID-19 threatens to throw fiscal situation completely out of gear. The sharp increase in deficit and debt has risks of rating downgrade and the appointment of a Fiscal Council could bring some comfort in avoiding it. While the government will have to loosen its purse to save lives and livelihoods threatened by the Coronavirus pandemic, the restoration in the confidence of the markets, general public, and the credit rating agencies will crucially depend upon the workable adjustment path and the credible mechanisms and institutions to ensure compliance with the path. Creation of such an independent institution will help to restore credibility. Of course, the government will have to ensure that the Fiscal Council is really independent, and the Council will have to earn its respect and credibility through high-quality work assigned to it. Thus, both bipartisan political commitment to fiscal discipline and competence and independent working of the Council are critical.

7
Evolving Landscape of Indian Fiscal Federalism

The federal system was created with the intention of combining the different advantage which result from the magnitude and the littleness of nations.

—Alexis de Tocqueville in Democracy in America

7.1. Public Finance in a Multilevel Fiscal System

Fiscal federalism is a multilevel fiscal system designed to provide efficient levels of public services. The decentralized provision of public services caters to the diversified preferences of people while binding them together and enables reaping economies of scale. Federalism creates a unified common market, enables reaping economies of scale in the provision of national public goods, helps to provide public services according to diversified preferences of the people, ensures greater accountability due to closeness of the people to the service provider, and permits efficiency gains in the service provision due to intergovernmental (yardstick) competition. In political terms, this implies building a strong national polity by combining the subnational entities while providing adequate political space to them. The case for federalism is made also on the grounds of enhancing freedom and greater participation (Elster, 1994). In emotional terms, federalism also enables recognizing and accommodating multiple identities based on language, religion, ethnicity, and culture (Arora and Verney, 1995). It can also be construed as an outcome of bargaining to ensure security and stability

Studies in Indian Public Finance. M. Govinda Rao, Oxford University Press. © Oxford University Press 2022.
DOI: 10.1093/oso/9780192849601.003.0007

(Riker, 1964). The realization of these advantages depends on the way in which the different units combine and extent of cooperation and harmony in the functioning of the federal system.

In the case of India, federalism is not an option but an imperative. Inhabited by over 1.38 billion people characterized by wide social, ethnic, religious, linguistic, and economic diversities, India cannot survive as a democratic republic without providing political space to the diverse groups to exercise their voice. The challenge of accommodating multiple identities in a single State cannot be met in a unitary system. Thus, democracy and federalism are the two important pillars on which integrity, stability, and development of the country are rooted. At the same time, ensuring cohesion of diverse groups continues to be a formidable challenge requiring a lot of compromise. Extreme centralization restricts the freedom and extreme decentralization can create chaos. The problem of cohesion and achieving an optimal degree of decentralization is a major challenge.

This chapter attempts to review public finances in the Indian multilevel system of governance. A large country with marked linguistic, ethnic, religious, social, and economic diversities cannot be governed in a centralized system. Economically, it is important to ensure provision of public services according to the diversified preferences while reaping the economies of scale with respect to national public goods and creating a unified market across the country. Politically, the multilevel system serves to build a strong polity with political space given to subnational units. It helps to enhance freedom and greater participation in the political processes through both voice and exit. The multilevel system accommodates multiple identities in a single State and serves to strengthen emotional bond of the people of the country both to their state and the nation. A federal system enhances the participation of the people in the political process. While the general aspects of decentralization and federalism have a wide canvass, this chapter focuses on the analysis of Indian fiscal federalism. The chapter attempts to review the functioning to highlight its successes, understand its failures, and identify areas requiring reforms in both policies and institutions to enable the Indian fiscal federalism to meet the emerging challenges from diversity, globalizing economic environment, information revolution, and technological changes.

There are several reviews and commentaries on Indian fiscal federalism—both in official reports and by independent scholars.[1] While these may provide useful background material for understanding the salient features of Indian fiscal federalism, it is important to adopt an analytical framework rather than drawing conclusions based on opinions and judgements. The theories of fiscal federalism are rich and vibrant, and they provide useful lessons for adopting a framework for analysis. This chapter attempts to analyse the trends and issues in Indian fiscal federalism by drawing the lessons from the first- and the second-generation theories.

7.2. The First- and the Second-Generation Theories

(a) Normative Theories of Fiscal Federalism

An important implementable rule of fiscal decentralization is clear assignment of functions (Bahl, 2002). Assigning functions is like assigning property rights. Without clear assignment of functions, there is neither incentive nor accountability. Second, finances should follow functions and the subnational governments should have the capacity to vary the public services as demanded by their residents. Assignment of revenue sources is necessary for a strong linkage between the decision to spend and the decision to raise revenues. Third, the people who benefit from public services should be made to pay for them. Fourth, there should be a mechanism to deal with overlapping functions. In a multilevel system, even when the assignments are made carefully, as the benefit spans of various public services do not perfectly map the jurisdictional boundaries, spillovers are unavoidable. Voluntary bargains may fail to resolve these externalities and therefore there must be mechanisms to resolve them. Thus, proper assignment of functions and sources of finance, consequences arising from their overlap, and the mechanism to match their functions and finances both vertically among different levels of government and horizontally among different governmental units constitute the

[1] See Rao and Chelliah (1996), Bagchi (2000), Rao and Sen (1996), Rao and Singh (2005), and Reddy and Reddy (2019).

subject matter of fiscal federalism. From this perspective, fiscal federalism is simply an efficient organization of multilevel public sector. As stated by Oates, 'The term *federalism* for the economist is not to be understood in a narrow constitutional sense. In economic terms all governmental systems are more or less federal: even in a formally unitary system' (italics in the original; Oates, 1977: 4).[2] Similarly, Bird (2000: 135) states, 'In the traditional world of *fiscal federalism* in principle everything—boundaries, assignments of finances and functions, the level and nature of transfers and so forth—is malleable'.[3]

The above formulation, however, blurs the difference between decentralization and federalism. According to Watts (1996), the structure can take the form of 'Decentralized Unions' which are basically unitary states in which subnational units have greater or lesser degree of policy autonomy devolved to them by the Central government or *formal federations* which combine a strong Central government with subcentral tiers having their own powers. Indeed, there can be considerable devolution of powers to subnational governments even in formal unitary systems. However, the formal federal systems, besides having devolved assignment systems to subnational levels, also ensure a continuity. Although it is difficult to get instances of classical federalism conceptualized by Wheare (1964) in which, the participating governments are 'coordinate and independent', the assignment system must be determined independently and should have a measure of permanence. There should an effective system of checks and balances to ensure a measure of permanence. In confederal systems, the assignments are done by lower-level governments (States), whereas in decentralized systems, powers are assigned by senior-level governments. As argued by Breton (2000), the distinguishing feature of decentralization and federalism is that, under the latter, the powers of lower-level governments cannot be extinguished by higher-level governments. Thus, checks and balances to safeguard the system is an inherent part of the federal system, whereas decentralization does not necessarily

[2] Not surprisingly as Breton (1981: 253) states, 'Political scientists who know better, have in their more generous moments treated economists as poor souls with a model in hand in need of an application'.

[3] Bird (2000) makes a distinction between fiscal federalism and federal finance. In his formulation, under fiscal federalism everything—boundaries, assignments, and the transfers—is malleable, under federal finance these must be taken to be fixed at some earlier (constitutional) stage and not open to further change under normal circumstances.

entail that. In other words, all federal systems are decentralized whereas all decentralized systems are not federal.

The first-generation theories assume that fiscal federalism is designed to be optimal and the objective is to maximize welfare. Welfare is maximized by the people by exercising the options of either 'exit' or 'voice'. Tiebout (1956) demonstrates this with the 'exit' model. When there are a large number of jurisdictions with varying public service-tax mixes, and assuming that people have footloose mobility, they 'vote on their feet' to move to the localities that provide the fiscal package matching their preferences. Even when the assumption of 'footloose' mobility is relaxed, Oates (1969) shows the superiority of decentralized system as fiscal differentials can be capitalized into property values.

The models demonstrating the welfare gains using the 'voice' models are best characterized by the 'decentralization theorem' developed by Oates (1968) based on the earlier works of Breton (1965) and Olson (1965). The theorem states, 'In the absence of cost savings from the centralized provision of a (local public) good and of inter-jurisdictional externalities, the level of welfare will always be at least as high (and typically higher) if Pareto-efficient levels of consumption are provided in each jurisdiction than *any single, uniform* level of consumption is maintained across all jurisdictions' (italics added; Oates, 1972: 54). This contention rests on two basic assumptions. First, governments are benevolent and provide public services to match varying preferences of people to enhance their welfare. Second, centralized provision necessarily results in uniform level of public outputs in all jurisdictions. As noted by Breton (1996: 185), 'If Central governments could perform the difficult task of estimating marginal spillover flows and designing the appropriate grants program, a division of functions is not only unnecessary but wasteful'. However, transaction costs and political constraints may prevent the Central planner from generating an optimal pattern of local public services (Oates, 1999).

An extension of the traditional theory is the assumption that solutions to fiscal federalism must be found in 'co-operative federalism'. As argued by Coase (1960), clear assignment works like the assignment of property rights. Efficient provision of public services in their respective domains and internalizing externalities and spillovers require bargaining between different governmental units. When there are some overlapping assignments, 'Coasian bargains' can resolve many issues arising from spillover of costs and benefits. This is the essence of 'cooperative federalism' (Inman and Rubinfeld, 1997a, 1997b). However, cooperative federalism is possible only in cases where there are incentives to bargain for mutual gains, there is a measure of equality in the bargaining strength, and there is an effective referee and monitor to ensure efficient bargaining processes. Besides, there are transaction costs of bargaining.

(b) Political Economy Approaches to Fiscal Federalism

This branch of literature on fiscal federalism draws heavily from the developments in public choice and industrial organization (information) theories—it does not assume an altruistic government and motivated public officials for common good in the Samuelson–Musgrave tradition (Besley and Coate, 2003). Instead, it assumes that participants in the political processes seek to maximize their own gain rather than the welfare of the society (Oates, 2005). In other words, the new literature recognizes the importance of motivations or incentives of the bureaucrats and politicians. The models employing the public choice approach (the second-generation theories or SGT) underline efficiency gains in terms of better 'accountability' at decentralized levels versus better coordination of policies to internalize spillovers (Seabright, 1996).

There are three distinct set of theories under the second-generation theories. The first is the application of developments in industrial organization theory to fiscal federalism, particularly modelling the multilevel fiscal arrangements in terms of the principal–agent framework (Levaggi, 2002; Tommasi, 2003). The second strand focuses on the problems arising from the soft budget constraints and derives motivation from the fiscal crisis precipitated by exploitation of 'fiscal commons' leading to perverse behaviour of subnational governments, particularly in Latin America (Prud'homme, 1995; Tanzi, 2001). Finally, the third strand employs more formal political economy approaches based on a legislative structure and electoral process to analyse different kinds of fiscal outcomes under centralized and decentralized politics. Among others, this strand examines the outcomes from 'market promoting federalism' (MPF) (Weingast, 2009), 'yardstick competition' (or laboratory federalism), and 'competitive federalism' (Breton, 1996, 2002, 2006; Salmon, 2006).

7.3. Lessons from the Theories

As mentioned above, an important precondition for efficient multi-level fiscal system is clarity in the assignment system. The assignment should be clear and when there is overlapping, there should be systems and institutions to minimize the transaction cost of intergovernmental bargaining, conflict resolution, and promotion of intergovernmental cooperation. Clarity in assignments does not imply mere assignment of revenue and expenditure powers; it is also necessary to ensure that the functions of different functionaries within a level are unambiguous. In a democratic polity, it is necessary to make the elected representatives responsible for decision-making and bureaucrats to implement the decisions taken by the executive.

The functions should be assigned according to comparative advantage and the financial powers should follow the functions assigned to avoid giving subnational governments unfunded mandates. It is important to ensure that the subnational governments are not overwhelmed by transfer dependency. Ensuring a strong 'Wicksellian link'—the linkage between revenue and expenditure decisions at the margin requires that the subnational governments should have adequate revenue powers. Accountability requires that subnational services should be paid for by the residents of the jurisdiction. The analysis of appropriate revenue handles at subnational levels shows that user charges should cover the cost of most private goods provided by them; the cost of public services benefiting the jurisdiction should be collected by way of taxes on the residents; and those with spillovers should be partly paid for by taxes on the residents and partly through intergovernmental transfers. The subnational governments can levy taxes on immobile bases. Taxing mobile bases by subnational governments could prove to be ineffective in raising revenues besides transferring the burden to non-residents.[4]

A major advantage of a multilevel fiscal system is the large common market, but the benefit can accrue only when all impediments to mobility and trading in labour, capital, and commodities are eliminated. Ensuring a common market is at the heart of creating dynamism in fiscal federalism. The literature on MPF shows that it is important to avoid soft

[4] For a detailed analysis of appropriate tax handles, see Bird and Slack (2007) and for the analysis in the context of Australian federation, see Bird and Smart (2009).

budget constraint at subnational levels to ensure efficient and market friendly policies. This requires an efficient assignment system, policies to promote responsible fiscal behaviour, and measures to strengthen and deepen the markets, particularly the land and capital markets.

There can be gains from intergovernmental competition. Competition can lead to efficiency gains in public service provision; it can also motivate innovations and productivity increases in public service delivery. However, to reap the gains, it is important to ensure that there is a measure of competitive equality and predatory competition is prevented. Unequal competition could be destabilizing and can, in the extreme, break up the federation. This is particularly important in the context of globalization as the States with more developed markets and infrastructure can reap higher benefits from access to domestic and international markets and grow faster than those with less developed markets and infrastructure. To ensure a measure of competitive equality of jurisdictions, it is necessary to ensure that the combined impact of regional policies and intergovernmental transfers should ensure provision of comparable levels of public services at comparable tax effort.

The analysis brings out the need for strong systems and institutions to promote and regulate efficient competition. One method to deal with the problems of predatory competition is centralization, but that is tantamount to 'throwing the baby with the bath water'. The argument for decentralization in the first instance is to create a system to take advantage of lower information and transaction costs in public service delivery and, therefore, this cannot be a viable solution. The solution has to be found within the decentralized framework to create institutions to bargain and resolve inter-State and Centre-State conflicts.

Some of the important features of strong institutions for creating hard budget constraints emerge in a well-developed market economy. Efficient credit markets and a mature banking system and well-developed debt market with developed credit rating institutions are important preconditions for the Centre to keep itself away from bail outs. Similarly, well-developed land and property markets and efficient mobility of factors and products can prevent public decisions that impede the development of markets. These will promote intergovernmental competition and minimize incentives for bail outs. It is important to discourage protectionist policies at subnational levels. Equally important is the need to have strong fiscal institutions. Effective local system of taxation, to match revenue–expenditure decisions at the margin, and the efficient system of intergovernmental transfers which do not involve perverse incentives are extremely important to ensure a hard budget constraint. Legislatively imposed constraints on deficits and requirement to balance the current budgets will place a limit on fiscal expansion and ensure more productive public spending. Limitations placed on borrowings can also help to contain perverse incentives for fiscal expansion. It is also necessary to have effectively enforceable bankruptcy laws that specify the fiscal crisis and the way that needs to be handled.

While the theories of fiscal federalism discussed provide great insights into the way the federal fiscal systems should function, they essentially address the issues of advanced market economies. There are a variety of reasons to re-examine and modify the mainstream fiscal federalism analysis to multilevel fiscal systems in developing and transitional countries (Rao, 2006). This is because developing countries have a dominant primary sector, coexistence of a large traditional sector, and a small modern sector which links itself well with the market. It has segmented labour markets, low level of savings and investment, large part of the savings in physical rather than financial assets. There is imperfect mobility of labour, competition with significant trade distortions, and scarcity of foreign exchange (Newbery, 1987). Secondly, most of these economies have adopted centralized planning in a multilevel system. Even as most countries have chosen to make a transition from centralized planning to market-based resource allocation, the vestiges of planning continue to influence resource allocation outcomes. These factors influence the fiscal federalism outcomes and, therefore, need to be analysed in greater detail. In most such economies, several impediments to the movement of factors and products continue. Similarly, as a part of planning system, controls on prices, outputs, credit allocations, and financial repression continue in many countries in transition, and this alters the allocation of resources and determines incomes across different regions in unintended ways (Rao, 1997, 2006). As Stated by Oates (1999: 1145), 'While the existing literature on fiscal federalism can provide some general guidance, … my sense is that most of us working in the field feel more than a little uneasy when proffering advice on many of the decisions that must be made on vertical fiscal and political structure. We have much to learn'.

7.4. Evolution of Indian Federalism

Article 1 of the Indian Constitution states, 'India, that is Bharat, shall be a Union of States'. The word 'federalism' does not find any place in the Constitution, but it has all the features of a federal system, though with significant centripetal bias. The seventh schedule in the Constitution divides the legislative powers of the Parliament and State legislatures in terms of the Union, State, and Concurrent Lists. The Union and State lists demarcate the functions and sources of finance between the Union and the States, and the Concurrent List details the joint responsibilities of the States with the Union government. Thus, the Constitution exhibits the features of a federation. However, unlike a classical federation in which confederating units join to form a common market evolving into an economic and political union, Indian federation was formed mainly from the unification of the principalities in British India and after independence, accession of the remaining princely States to the Union. The 1.38 billion people in the federation are spread over 28 States and 9 centrally administered territories (two with their own elected governments). Separate legislative, executive, and judicial arms of government are constituted at both Union and State levels. Like most other federations, as the States' power to raise revenues is not commensurate with expenditure responsibilities, the Constitution provides for the setting up of an independent expert body, the Finance Commission, by the President of India every 5 years (or earlier) to review the finances of the Union and the States and recommend devolution of taxes and grants-in-aid for the ensuing 5 years. The Commission is required to make recommendations on the division of the Union taxes among the Centre and States and the shares of individual states. The Commission is also required to recommend the grants-in-aid to be given to each State.[5]

[5] A number of other tasks are entrusted to the Finance Commissions, and these include (i) measures to augment the consolidated funds of the States to supplement the resources of rural and urban local bodies based on the recommendations of the State Finance Commissions

Historical factors have played an important role in the adoption of a federal Constitution with strong unitary features. During the British rule, administrative and fiscal centralization was a colonial imperative. Although there were strong arguments for decentralization at the time of achieving independence, and even though the Cabinet Mission sent by the imperial government before granting independence envisaged limited powers for the Union in a three-tiered federal structure, the constitution that was eventually adopted by the Indian Republic closely followed the Government of India Act, 1935, with pronounced centripetal bias. The shift probably occurred for two reasons: First, once the Muslim majority areas opted out of India to form a separate country, the principal rationale for a loose federal structure no longer existed. Second, a strong Centre was found desirable to safeguard against fissiparous tendencies among constituent units (India, 1968; Chelliah, 1991) particularly, the erstwhile princely States.

The Indian Constitution adopted in 1950 was erected on the foundation provided by the Government of India Act, 1935. As mentioned above, the Seventh Schedule of the Constitution divided the legislative domains of the Union and States in terms of Union, State, and Concurrent Lists. The matters of national importance were assigned to the Union government (List I) and those of regional importance were assigned to States (List II). Those matters relevant to both the Union and States were listed in the Concurrent List (List III) with the former having precedence in the event of a disagreement. The residuary powers were reserved for the Union government.

India evolved as a two-tier federation until the 73rd and 74th Constitutional amendments were promulgated in 1992 providing the recognition of the third tier of government below the State level in rural and urban areas. Consequent to the amendments, Articles 243 A-O for rural local bodies (Panchayats) and 243 P-ZG for urban local bodies (nagar panchayats, municipalities, and municipal corporations) were inserted in to the Constitution. The amendment also listed some functions under Schedule 11 and Schedule 12, respectively, for rural and urban local bodies, which the legislature of the respective State may devolve to enable them to function as institutions of self-government. Thus, even as local governments were given recognition through the 73rd and 74th

and (ii) any other matter entrusted to the Commission by the President of India in the interest of sound finance.

amendments to the Constitution, the functions of the local bodies are to be decided by the respective state governments at their discretion and the overall responsibility for the local governments is entirely assigned to the State governments under Entry 5 of the State List. The local bodies do not have independent revenue powers either. Article 243-H entrusts the State legislatures to authorize the levy, collect, and appropriate such taxes or tolls and duties subject to the limits specified by the respective state government. There is also a provision for the States to assign the taxes collected by it to the local bodies at its discretion. Also, the Governor of the State is required to appoint a State Finance Commission, an expert body, to review the finances of the financial position of the rural and urban local bodies and recommend to the Governor, the devolution of State revenues as well as grants in aid to them for the ensuing 5 years. By and large, with the States continuing to exercise control over the local bodies' in political administrative as well as fiscal spheres, lacking in independent revenue sources and with several shortfalls in the functioning of State Finance Commissions, the decentralization below the State level is still a work in progress and much needs to be done to make them effective.

7.5. Centralization in Indian Federalism

As mentioned earlier, history and compulsions of the time resulted in imparting a heavy centripetal bias to the Indian Constitution. The Constitution borrowed heavily from the Government of India Act, 1935. Not surprisingly, there are several pronounced unitary features in the Indian Constitution which raise serious questions on genuineness of the federal character of the country. This has led some to characterize India as a quasi-federal country. The important centralizing Articles of the Constitution are

(i) Article 3 allows the Union government to mutilate and divide the States merely referring the bill providing for such alteration or annihilation to the Legislature of the States concerned for expressing their views.

(ii) Article 249 empowers the Rajya Sabha (Council of States) to temporarily transfer any item in the State List of 7th Schedule to the

Union List with two-thirds of the members present and voting if it is thought to be expedient in the national interest to do so.

(iii) The residuary powers not listed in the Seventh Schedule in any of the Lists are assigned to the Union government.

(iv) Article 250 empowers the Parliament to make laws for the whole or any part of the territory of India with respect to any matters enumerated in the State List when emergency is proclaimed.[6]

(v) Article 354 empowers the Union government to suspend the provisions of Articles 268 to 279 which deal with the distribution of revenues between the Union and the States while the proclamation of emergency is in operation. The Constitution also envisages the possibility of financial emergency in the States and, in such circumstances, restricts financial authority of the States.

(vi) The Constitution lays down the primacy of Central laws in the event of a conflict between a State legislation and a Parliamentary law in the case of items covered in the Concurrent List.

(vii) Under Article 356, the President, if he/she is satisfied that a situation has arisen in which the government of a State cannot be carried on in accordance with the provisions of the Constitution, can dismiss the duly elected government and place the administration of the State under the Presidential rule.

The centripetal bias inherent in the Constitution got exacerbated over the years due to the development strategy followed and Central government exercising control over the resources. The most important factor that has caused centralization in economic decisions was the item placed in the Concurrent List, 'economic and social planning'. The adoption of centralized planning in a mixed economy framework constrained the roles of both the market and the State governments in the allocation of resources. Allocating resources according to plan priorities called for introduction of several controls and regulations on both financial and real sectors of the economy. On the real sectors, various controls had to be exercised on both prices and output and in several sectors, administered

[6] Article 352 provides that if the President is satisfied that there is a grave danger for security of India or in any part of the country is threatened by external aggression or internal disturbance, he can proclaim emergency. When emergency is proclaimed, the fundamental rights under Article 19 remain suspended.

pricing mechanism virtually replaced the market and, in fact, constrained the development of the market altogether. Even after market reforms were introduced in 1991, the vestiges of planned development and centralization inherent in the system have continued.

An important fall out of the planning process was that the States had to prepare their plans and allocate resources in harmony with the overall priorities and programmes decided by the Central Planning Commission. The entire process of resource allocation in the country had to be aligned to the planned development strategy. The practice of getting the approvals for the State Plans from the Planning Commission continued even after the planned development strategy was given up and market-based reforms were introduced in 1991. This was done using the leverage of giving plan assistance to the States and through the process of giving approval to State Plans. The plan assistance comprised of both grants and loans. In the initial years, the shares of individual States in plan assistance as well as their grant-loan components were discretionary, but later the National Development Council (NDC) approved a formula when Dr. D. R. Gadgil was the Deputy Chairman of the Planning Commission (known as the Gadgil formula). Under this formula, 30 per cent of the total plan assistance was earmarked to special category States with 90 per cent given as grants and 10 per cent as loans. The remaining 70 per cent was divided among the general category States according to the formula with 30 per cent of the assistance given as grants and the rest as loans.

Another important factor that led to significant centralization was the nationalization of financial institutions. The nationalization of Imperial Bank of India to create the State Bank of India in 1947 and the Life Insurance Corporation of India in 1956 was to ensure allocation of resources according to plan priorities. The subsequent nationalization of 14 major private commercial banks in 1969 and 6 more private banks were nationalized in 1980. These actions vested the virtual control over the entire financial system with the Central government.

In a number of areas, centralization was achieved by the Central government intruding into the States' domain either by transferring the subjects in the State List to the Concurrent List (e.g. education and forestry) or expanding the scope of Entry 52 in the Union List to assume control over one sector after another or by creating several 'institutions of national importance' to intrude into the areas in the State List or by influencing the pattern of spending on items in the State List through Central Sector and Centrally Sponsored Schemes (which are specific purpose conditional transfers). Secondly, interpretation of Article 282 of the Constitution as a miscellaneous provision and making overwhelming proportion of the transfers for Central sector and Centrally Sponsored Schemes has virtually undermined the relevance of the Constitutional scheme of making transfers based on the recommendations of the Finance Commission, namely, tax devolution under Article 270 and grants under Article 275 which is based on the recommendation of the Finance Commissions.

This development has led to several undesirable consequences on both public service delivery and systems of accountability. First, the role of the Finance Commission, the Constitutional body meant to recommend transfers, has substantially eroded as increasing proportions of the Central transfers to States have become discretionary. Second, from 2003, the transfers for many Central schemes were given directly to local bodies and various other implementing agencies bypassing the States until the decision was reversed in 2014 to route these grants through the consolidated funds of the States. This, besides violating the principle of accountability made it difficult to take a holistic view of delivering various public services. Third, the entire budgeting system was segregated into plan and non-plan with each of the spending agencies of the Centre and States taking a partial view of spending on various public services. Although the Central government stopped this after 2014 subsequent to the abolition of the Planning Commission, many of the States continue this practice. This results in distortions by underproviding maintenance expenditures, misclassification of expenditures to shore up the plan size, and even more importantly, poor systems of expenditure management.

7.6. Changing Landscape of Indian Fiscal Federalism

There have been important political and economic factors, often conflicting developments, that have changed the federal fiscal landscape in the country. The realization that sustained development of the country required a course correction to enable greater role to the market resulted in the initiation of reforms in 1991. The liberalizing economic reforms, on the one hand, changed the role of the government vis-à-vis the market and, on the other, significantly altered the roles of the Union and State governments. This has unleashed creative energies to steady acceleration in economic growth from an average of 3.5 per cent during the first 40 years after Independence to 5.8 per cent in the next 20 years and 7.5 per cent since 2000–2001.

Despite the acceleration in the growth, there is growing awareness that the economic performance of the country has been far below its potential. The most important reason for this is that the vestiges of planning have continued to persist in terms of both directed public sector resource allocation and administrative controls over prices and outputs. Furthermore, after the initial burst, the reforms have been moving at a crawling pace mainly because of the difficulties in building consensus in a democratic polity and due to the influence of special interest groups. Indeed, there is tyranny of status quo in reforms for those who gain from the reforms are ungrateful and those who loose are vengeful.

One of the most important reasons for the gap between the potential and actual growth performance is the lack of coordination between the Union and the States. The Seventh Schedule to the Indian Constitution assigns tax powers either to the Union or the State governments, but as the separation is only in the legal and in economic sense, there is considerable overlap. Thus, the taxes on agricultural incomes and wealth are assigned to the States whereas taxes on non-agricultural incomes and wealth can be levied only by the Union government. This makes the levy of comprehensive income tax difficult and results in low compliance as many evade the tax through misclassification. Similarly, until the GST was implemented, there was considerable overlap in domestic trade taxes as the Centre levied the excise duty collected on manufactured goods and the States levied the sales taxes on the excise duty paid value of the goods.

The most important development after 2014 was the abolition of the Planning Commission and establishment of National Institution for Transforming India (NITI Aayog) in its place. The Prime Minister, in his Independence Day speech on 15 August 2014, declared that the Planning Commission has outlived its usefulness and declared its abolition. In early 2015, the NITI Aayog was appointed with the mandate to function as a Think Tank of the government and coordinate the functioning of different governmental department and facilitate intergovernmental cooperation and promote and regulate healthy intergovernmental competition.

Of course, despite the need to reform itself after market-based reforms were introduced in 1991, the institution continued with the old practice of working on inter-sectoral consistency framework for economic planning and allocation of resources. With economic liberalization, public sector lost its pre-eminence in resource allocation and allocation of private investment according to plan priorities was infeasible. The Commission should have transformed itself into planning for infrastructure with the States and the private sector through public–private partnerships. It was also necessary to rethink on the role of the State in a market economy where the focus should have been to strengthen regulation of the private sector to prevent predatory competition and ensure fair competition wherever market failure argument did not warrant ownership.

Unfortunately, the Commission continued to function in the traditional manner of preparing plans, asking the States to prepare their plans and approve their plans annually and not many will shed tears on the abolition of the Planning Commission. In fact, the outgoing Prime Minister himself had called for redefining its role to suit changing realities. The planning exercise that was followed had hardly any relevance for the market economy. It did very little to plan and implement even public sector investments for infrastructure and its role in promoting public–private partnership was mostly seen as obstructive. The whole exercise of giving approvals to State plans smacked dispensing patronage. The proliferation of various centrally sponsored schemes with 'one size fits all' design and conditionality contributed to severe distortions in public spending. Often, the Planning Commission came up with discretionary transfers to states to meet non-plan revenue deficits negating the norms set by the Finance Commissions. The presence of a member of the Planning Commission as a part-time member of the Finance Commission did very little to correct this anomaly.

The Cabinet Resolution appointing the NITI Aayog lists 13 different tasks to it which may be grouped under four major heads namely: (i) fostering cooperative federalism by providing structured support to States on a continuous basis; (ii) formulation of strategic vision and long-term policies and programme framework both for the macroeconomy and for different sectors; (iii) acting as a knowledge and innovation hub and provide research inputs by undertaking and accessing globally available research; and (iv) providing a platform for interdepartmental coordination. Each of these functions may be discussed in some detail.[7]

The effectiveness of NITI, however, will depend on how well it charts out the course for itself. Despite the claims of marked departure from the past, the institution has to function in the prevailing milieu and deal with the burden of legacy. The important question is whether the Aayog will have the influence when it does not have the power to give grants and when it does not have the powers to make plan allocations to different ministries and departments.

The legacy issues do not end merely with the abolition of Planning Commission. There are parallel institutions in the States, and it is important to transform them to meet the new requirements. Similarly, the Constitution requires the establishment of district planning committees and metropolitan planning committees and their role in the new environment needs to be specified. Although the Cabinet Resolution states that NITI Aayog will facilitate grassroots planning, how exactly this will be carried forward needs to be seen. The success of an institution in fostering cooperative federalism, however, will depend on the trust of and cooperation from the States. So far, the experience has not been very encouraging, and it remains to be seen how the institution will shape up in meeting the challenges.

There is a larger issue of the need for an institution for intergovernmental bargaining and conflict resolution. In an economy with overlapping jurisdictions between the Union and the States and when the parities in power are different at the Union and individual State levels, it is not easy to achieve a cooperative solution even when both the parties to the bargain gain. Moreover, there is considerable transaction cost due to bargaining and coordination and it is important to have an institutional mechanism to minimize it. The NDC could have shaped up into such an institution, but with infrequent meetings, it merely became a forum to vent the political disagreements made through speeches by the

[7] For a more detailed analysis of NITI Aayog, see Rao (2015).

Chief Ministers of the States. The Commission on Centre–State relations Chaired by Justice Sarkaria recommended the constitution of an independent Inter-State Council to deal with the issue of bargaining, coordination, and conflict resolution between the Union and States. However, the Government implemented the recommendation by constituting the Commission within the Union Home Ministry which ceased to be an independent institution and lost its importance as well as independence.

7.7. Emerging Environment in Union–State Relations

The new policy and political developments have important bearings on the stability of Indian fiscal federalism. On the policy front, with liberalizing reforms, market-based allocation has the potential to aggravate interregional disparities. The sharp differences in the standards of infrastructure and basic public services endow differential competing powers to different States and in a market-based allocation of resources this could accentuate the already high inter-State differences in incomes and poverty. In this environment, the stability of federalism requires the transfer system to offset the revenue and cost disabilities to ensure a measure of competitive equality to poorer States.

Secondly, in an environment in which the parties in power at the Union are different from those in the States, political factors could influence the transfer system. The empirical studies in India have shown that the State governments ruled by the coalition partners or parties friendly to the Central coalition tend to get favourable allocation of non-Finance Commission transfers (Rao and Singh, 2005). In such an environment, besides equity, objectivity in the transfer system is violated.

The liberalizing reforms and, more recently, the abolition of the Planning Commission have had important effects on the role of the private sector as well as the State governments. In the globalizing environment, the States are required to provide competitive levels of infrastructure and enabling environment to enable the private sector to compete internationally. Similarly, in the new environment, the Finance Commission will have to effectively offset revenue and cost disabilities of the States to enable them to provide comparable levels of public services at comparable tax rates in an objective manner. In this section, we explore these challenges in some detail.

Development of infrastructure is not the only responsibility of the States for creating a healthy environment for private sector growth. Equally important are improvements in governance to ensure speedy issuance of clearances, construction permits, power connections, ease of paying taxes, flexibility in the labour market conditions, speedy enforcement of contracts and adjudication of disputes, and effective regulations to ensure healthy competitive environment. In the new environment, inter-State competition to attract capital can result in the race to the bottom in both levying taxes and environmental regulation. It is also important that competitive federalism requires a measure of competitive equality and cost–benefit appropriability (Breton, 1987, 1996). The ranking of States in terms of the Ease of Doing Business introduced by the Department of Industrial Policy and Promotion (DIPP) based on 340 action points is a welcome move. This has set the competition among the States, but to what extent this will result in investment decisions needs to be seen. Such rankings can be effective if there is a measure of competitive equality in the standards of physical and social infrastructure in the states and this requires an effective fiscal transfer system to enable to provide comparable levels of public services at comparable tax rates.

The most important requirement for the successful working of a federation is the institutional mechanism for intergovernmental coordination, bargaining, and conflict resolution. Absence of such a mechanism is a major vacuum in Indian federation. This is necessary to foster the spirit of trust and cooperation between the Union and the States and among the States *inter se*, enable health intergovernmental bargaining and resolve conflicts and regulate intergovernmental competition. With the end of single party rule in both the Union and States and emergence of coalition governments at the Union level with regional parties being pivotal members, formal institutional mechanism for intergovernmental bargaining and conflict resolution has become necessary to minimize the coordination and other transaction costs of multilevel decision-making. In other words, bargaining, coordination, and conflict resolution in a multilevel system are important and at present, there is no institution undertaking this task in India. Indeed, this has resulted in either no coordination/

conflict resolution or ad hoc arrangements. Article 263 provides a basis for creating such an independent institution and the Government set up the Inter-State Council for the purpose. However, instead of setting it up as an independent neutral institution, the Government of India constituted the Inter-State Council under the Union Home Ministry. Similarly, with the establishment of the Planning Commission under a Cabinet Resolution in 1950, the National Development Council was constituted to facilitate collaborative planning exercise. The Council comprised members of the Union Cabinet, Deputy Chairman and Members of the Planning Commission, and the Chief Ministers of the States. However, rather than being a cementing institution and a neutral referee, the Council became a speech-making body. The meetings became a forum for voicing the opinions and grievances. The meetings too became infrequent and since 2005 there were just two meetings of the Council. With the abolition of the Planning Commission, the NDC too has seen its last. However, one of the mandates of NITI Aayog established in the place of the Planning Commission is to promote cooperative federalism and enable healthy intergovernmental competition. While the jury on its functioning is still out, it is important to make this a Constitutional body rather than based on the Cabinet Resolution. The NITI Ayog can become an important body for intergovernmental bargaining and conflict resolution if it is made a Constitutional body and the Inter-State Council is placed under it. This could then undertake an important task of promoting trust and cooperation between the Union and the States and among the States *inter se*, regulate intergovernmental competition to avoid predatory competition and race to the bottom and promote harmonious development in the country.

Another important shortcoming of Indian federalism is the failure to decentralize below the State level. Some of the States are larger than many countries and, therefore, decentralization is necessary to ensure effective delivery of public services in response to the diversified requirements of people and effective participation in the political processes. Indeed, everyone wants decentralization, but only up to their level. This is amply demonstrated by the States with very few exceptions, which in spite of the amendments to the Constitution to devolve powers to urban and rural local governments have failed to do so. Inability to achieve substate decentralization is one of the most important shortcomings of Indian federation.

An important development in the Indian fiscal federalism is the creation of GST Council to administer the new tax by amending the Constitution. The GST Council is a unique institution with representation from both the Union government and each of the States and Union Territories with legislatures. The Union Finance Minister is the Chairman of the Council and the Minister of State for revenue is a member. Each State is required to nominate its Finance Minister or any other Minister as a member of the Council. The decisions in the Council on the structure and operation of the tax are taken by voting. The Union government has one-third weightage in the votes and each of the States and Union Territories has equal shares in the remaining two-thirds. Any decision can be taken only when they are voted with at least 75 per cent of votes. By and large, it has been claimed that the decisions are taken on consensus but focus on consensus could result in the tyranny of status quo. Furthermore, the fear of losing revenue prevents taking serious reform initiatives.

The COVID-19 pandemic has brought out a clear cleavage in the functioning of GST Council. The contraction in the economy and the subsequent sharp decline in the GST revenue collection has required significant increase in the compensation to the States. However, there was a sharp decline in the revenue from compensation cess as well and the Union government proposed two alternative options. In the first, although the shortfall in States' revenues is estimated at Rs. 3 trillion, and the collections from compensation cess estimated at Rs. 650 billion, total compensation payable was estimated at Rs. 2.35 trillion. In the first proposal, the loss on account of the pandemic was separated as an 'Act of God' and the States could take the remaining shortfall of Rs. 970 billion, which could be availed by the States as a loan to be contracted with the RBI at a subsidized rate of interest and both the interest payment and loan repayment would be done from the future collections of the cess. In the second proposal, the States can borrow the entire shortfall of Rs. 2.35 trillion in the market and the interest payments will have to be made by them. The principal amount would be repaid from the future collections of the compensation cess. The compensation cess which was meant to be levied during the transition period of 5 years will be extended to facilitate the repayment of the loans. This has raised severe strains in the relations between the Union and States ruled by opposition parties.

7.8. Concluding Remarks

Indian fiscal federalism has had to adapt to the changes in economic and political environment in the country. The economic liberalization has altered not only the roles of the government and market but also has warranted changes in the relative responsibilities of the Union and the States. As remarked by Chelliah (1991), centralized planning is a negation of federalism. Thus, until 1991, the States had limited role in resource allocation even in the subjects assigned to them in the Constitution. Even after economic reforms were initiated, the practice of giving approvals to the State plans by the Central Planning Commission continued until the Planning Commission itself was disbanded in 2014.

Indian Constitution, based on the pre-independent Government of India Act, 1935, has a heavy centripetal bias. The planned development strategy cemented the centralization in economic decisions further. The fiscal instruments shaped by the development strategy have only increased the dependence of the States on the Union government for providing public services mandated to them in the Constitution. There are other problems associated with overlapping assignments between the Union and the States and among the States *inter se*. Political developments with coalition of parties coming to power at the Centre and parties in power in States different from that of the Centre have brought out the need for an effective institution for bargaining and conflict resolution. The absence of an effective institution for intergovernmental bargaining and conflict resolution is a major vacuum in Indian federalism. Considering the asymmetric distribution of power between the Union and States, the absence of such an institution results in forcing the centralized solutions on the States which is not in the long-term interest of harmony and cohesion.

There have been a number of notable developments in Indian fiscal federalism. First, the attempt to create the third tier of governance is yet to gather roots even after three decades after the Constitutional amendments and in the interest of participatory governance and development, this should be addressed without much loss of time. Second, as mentioned above, it is important to have an effective institution for intergovernmental bargaining and conflict resolution. Third, the abolition of the Planning Commission and creation of NITI Aayog in its place is yet to create an environment to foster harmonious intergovernmental relationships. Fourth, the GST Council is a unique institution to levy and administer domestic consumption taxes, but its success depends on both the Union and the States honouring the commitments made to the States when they were persuaded to join in tax harmonization process by sacrificing their fiscal autonomy. The attempt to renege the agreement to pay compensation for the loss of revenues to the States in the wake of a sharp contraction in the revenue arising from the most severe lockdown has created a lot of trust deficit. This will have to be overcome to steer the tax in its transition phase. Fifth, there has been an increasing tendency by the Union government to intervene in the State subjects through Central Sector and Centrally Sponsored Schemes. As a result, the Finance Commission which is supposed to resolve fiscal imbalances does not have control over the total volume of resource transfers nor its distribution across States.

The above discussion makes it clear that Indian fiscal federalism is still a work in progress requiring reforms in both decentralization policies and federal institutions. The existing institutions will have to be made to work as intended by the founding fathers of the Constitution. If indeed, changes are warranted for accelerating development, enhancing welfare, and increasing people's participation in the developmental process, they should be brought about. Sustained development requires the participation of diverse groups in a harmonious manner. It is important to nation-wide product and factor markets which requires creation of nation-wide markets for goods and services as well as capital and labour unhindered by impediments. Similarly, for reasons of both efficiency in service delivery and accountability, it is important to foster the spirit of cooperation and achieve efficiency gains through intergovernmental competition.

8
Intergovernmental Transfers in India

> The mere acceptance of the equity principle establishes a firm basis for the claim that the citizens of low income States within a national economy possess the 'right' that their States receive sums sufficient to enable these citizens to be placed in positions of fiscal equality with their equals in other States.
>
> —James Buchanan. Federalism and Fiscal Equity, *American Economic Review*, Vol 40 (1950), p. 594

8.1. Intergovernmental Transfers: Some Theoretical Issues

The assignment system in the normative framework of fiscal federalism necessarily results in vertical imbalances. Assignment, according to comparative advantage, implies that all broad-based taxes are assigned to the Centre and most expenditure functions are assigned to subnational levels. Thus, redistribution and stabilization functions are considered to be mainly the functions of Central government and therefore, all broad-based and redistributive taxes, money supply function, and borrowing powers are predominantly assigned to the Centre. At the same time, to cater to diversified preferences in the provision of public services, the allocation function which involves spending is predominantly assigned to subnational governments. In this scheme, vertical imbalance is unavoidable, and the intergovernmental transfer system has to resolve the imbalance. At the same time, it is important to match the revenue and expenditure decisions at the margin for subnational governments for reasons of efficiency and accountability. The efficient system of tax assignment envisages that tax powers should

Studies in Indian Public Finance. M. Govinda Rao, Oxford University Press. © Oxford University Press 2022.
DOI: 10.1093/oso/9780192849601.003.0008

be assigned to subnational levels up to the point where the marginal efficiency loss due to tax disharmony is matched with marginal efficiency gain from fiscal autonomy. Even with such an assignment system, vertical imbalance is a feature seen in all federation.

The rationale for horizontal transfers is advanced on horizontal equity grounds—to offset the fiscal disabilities arising from lower revenue capacity and higher unit cost of providing public services. Differences in the capacity to raise revenues and unit cost of providing public services among subnational jurisdictions violate horizontal equity as they create different 'fiscal residuum' (per capita expenditures minus per capita taxes) or net fiscal benefits (Buchanan, 1950). The problem is exacerbated when there are origin-based taxes and similar other factors altering the net fiscal benefits in different subnational jurisdictions (Boadway and Flatters, 1982). If there is perfect mobility of people across jurisdictions, fiscal differentials will be equalized automatically as people migrate from places where the net fiscal benefits are lower to those where they are higher. Even when there is no perfect mobility, if the property market is reasonably well developed, fiscal differentials will be capitalized into property values (Oates, 1969). In general and particularly in developing countries, there is neither perfect mobility nor a developed property market and the only way left is to offset these fiscal disabilities arising from low revenue capacity and high unit cost of providing public services through intergovernmental transfers. Such transfers have to be necessarily unconditional—to enable every State to provide comparable levels of public services at comparable tax rates.

Efficiency consequence of equalizing transfers has been a matter of considerable debate in the literature. The debate on the issue of whether the horizontal equalization transfers are efficiency enhancing or involve efficiency cost is an issue that has remained unresolved. Buchanan (1950) and in the later formulation based on horizontal equity argument by Boadway and Flatters (1982) argue that equalizing transfers are growth enhancing. Similarly, the competitive federalism literature recommend transfers to create a level playing field by enabling poorer jurisdictions to compete effectively with fiscally stronger ones (Breton, 1987). Buchanan's claim is that equitable transfers are also efficiency enhancing because, as capital–labour ratio in these regions is lower, the productivity of capital is high and transfer of capital to poorer regions would lead to higher productivity and incomes.

However, the view that equitable transfers to poorer regions are growth enhancing is not shared by many. The contrarian view is that there is a clear trade-off between equalization and growth. Scott (1950, 1964) argues that income levels in poorer regions are low mainly because of lower productivity and transfer of capital to these regions will entail lower productivity and incomes and there is clearly a trade-off between equity and efficiency. Despite a large volume of literature, the issue as to whether or not there is equity—growth trade-off in the case of equalizing transfers remains theoretically unresolved and remains an empirical issue. The transfers can help to realize the growth potential of the locality by creating the necessary infrastructure or it may actually be used to impart skills to labour, enhance productivity, and accelerate mobility of labour from poorer regions. In any case, the practice of giving equalizing transfers is in the realm of history, tradition, and political economy and countries such as Australia, Canada, India, and Germany have been giving such transfers, whereas the United States does not.

There is a case for transfers also to ensure that people are provided with minimum standards basic services with significant inter-jurisdictional externalities. The efficiency reason for intergovernmental transfers arises from spillovers. The assignment system, however well done, does not match with the geographical boundaries of the jurisdictions and spillovers have to be resolved thorough the transfer system. There are also services which must be available at minimum specified standards to all, and these include minimum standards of education, healthcare, water supply, and sanitation. Martin Feldstein calls them 'categorical equity' goods (1975) as these services have nation-wide externalities and yet subnational governments have a comparative advantage in providing them. In respect of all these services which overlap jurisdictions and involve significant externalities, it is necessary to ensure minimum levels for reasons of efficiency.

Ensuring minimum levels of public services for externality or merit good reasons is best done with a system of open-ended matching grants. The extent of matching by the higher-level government is supposed to reflect the degree of externality and open-endedness is necessary to provide incentives of expansion of the service at the margin. In practice, however, the matching ratios do not have any relationship with the extent of externality and in most cases, multiplicity of shared cost programmes and the resource constraint at the Central level results in making such programmes closed ended, but such programmes do not provide the incentive for expansion at the margin. In many cases, both the matching ratios and the volume of transfers are determined not on the basis of the externalities but simply for political reasons.

Using a collective choice framework, Bradford and Oates (1974) showed that lump sum grants to a group of persons would have identical allocative and distributional effects to the transfers directly given to individuals in the group. In other words, the lump sum grants to a group of persons would be simply a 'veil' for a central tax cut to individuals in the group. However, empirical analysis has not provided any support to this 'veil hypothesis'. In contrast, empirical analyses show that lump sum grants result in the expansion of public spending and this has come to be known as 'flypaper effect'. There is a large body of literature in the United States that tries to explain this empirical fact (Gramlich, 1977). Indeed, in a situation where subnational governments raise very little revenues through taxes like in the case of local governments in India, the possibility of substituting own taxes to transfers simply does not exist and the hypothesis itself does not make much sense.

In the actual design of the transfer system, there are serious operational questions which cannot be resolved easily. The first has to deal with the proper combination of conditional and unconditional transfers. The second issue has to deal with the extent of horizontal and vertical distribution. There is no unambiguous way to measure the degree of vertical imbalance and the extent of violation of horizontal equity. As regards specific purpose transfers are concerned, it is impossible to measure the degree of externalities to work out optimal cost sharing arrangements or matching ratios. Ironically, the very argument for decentralization is based on asymmetric information or the inability of the Central government to estimate the correct degree of spillovers, but, designing specific purpose transfers requires that the matching ratios will have to be determined according to the degree of externalities! Finally, even if some approximations on fiscal disabilities and matching ratios are made, there are many non-economic objectives including political objectives and the actual transfer system differs from the ideal. It is useful to understand the deviations from the ideal to reform the transfer system.

Are intergovernmental transfers a good idea? Despite the rationale for transfers detailed above, the review of literature shows that transfers tend to soften the budget constraint of subnational governments. It shows that intergovernmental grants promote fiscal irresponsibility and macroeconomic instability (Prud'homme, 1995). It is also argued that equalization may actually impede the development of backward regions by preventing the interregional mobility of resources, particularly labour (both emigration and immigration) in response to cost differentials (McKinnon, 1997). They create 'transfer dependency' (Rodden et al., 2003), which undermines fiscal discipline. Even in the case of matching transfers, in which matching ratios should be worked out according to the extent of spillover, Inman's (1988) study in the United States found that in actual practice, the matching ratios never correspond to the extent of spillovers, and the federal share is invariably much higher than the spillovers involved. Even more serious are the objections raised on equalizing transfers given in many federations (the notable exception being the United States). It is argued that the transfers given to offset fiscal disadvantages can interfere with the normal process of income convergence seen in the process of economic growth which occurs due to migration of labour and capital in undesirable ways.

The above analysis casts serious doubts on the efficacy of intergovernmental transfers in serving the long-term interests of a federation. Nevertheless, transfers are a part of every federation because perfect matching of revenue powers with expenditure responsibilities is not possible. Nevertheless, the literature provides guidance on a number of issues relating to transfers. First, the role of transfers should not be large as to create transfer dependency. There has to be matching of revenue and expenditure decisions at the margin so that decisions on additional spending are matched by financing it through taxation (Bird and Vaillancourt, 1998). Second, the system of grants must be transparent and predictable and should not have incentives to freeride. Surely, designing and implementing the transfer system is the most important issue in fiscal federalism.

Mismatch between revenue capacity and expenditure need at subnational levels is an inherent feature of all federations. The assignment of revenues and expenditures according to the principle of comparative advantage results in the Central governments having access to most broad-based taxes and subnational governments having responsibilities to provide most of economic and social services but inadequate revenue handles to provide them. Furthermore, there are wide differences among the States in the capacity to raise revenues as the size of the tax base varies widely. The variations in the tax base among the States result in variations in the standards of public services delivered even when the States make uniform effort at raising revenues. Variations in public services can also arise when there are significant differences in the unit cost of providing them. These variations violate the principle of 'horizontal equity' or 'equal treatment of equals' (Buchanan, 1950; Boadway and Flatters, 1982). These vertical and horizontal fiscal imbalances will have to be resolved through a system of intergovernmental transfers from the Centre to the States. In addition to these factors, in centrally planned economies with decentralized fiscal systems, controls on prices and outputs and regional policies (central allocation of investments) can create invisible transfers, often negating the objectives of explicit Central transfers (Rao, 1997, 2006).

While intergovernmental transfers are inevitable in all federations, it is important to understand that they soften the budget constraint by loosening the link between revenue raising and expenditure decisions. Efficiency considerations require that public services should be paid for by the people who benefit from them and there should be a strong linkage between revenue raising and expenditure decisions. Intergovernmental transfers tend to soften the budget constraints of the States and adversely impact on efficiency. While the Central transfers to States are inevitable in federations, it is important to design the transfer system carefully to ensure that they do not have adverse effects on incentives and lead to laxity in tax effort and expenditure economy. Ensuring incentive compatibility is at the heart of designing an efficient transfer system.

8.2. Rationale for Intergovernmental Transfers in India

Indian economic growth has shown a steady acceleration from just about 3.5 per cent per year during 1950–1980 to 5.8 per cent during 1980–2000 and further to 7.4 per cent since 2001–2002. Although it decelerated after the global financial crisis in 2008, India is one of the countries which turned around fast and is presently the fastest growing emerging economies. Most observers consider even this to be well below the potential and further reforms to liberalize the economy would help to reach the potential. Nevertheless, the performance seen in recent times shrugs the image of the country as a laggard.

Despite the impressive growth performance, its regional spread has been uneven, and even as some of the low-income States have been trying to catch up with their more advanced counterparts, interstate disparities have shown an increase, particularly after the market-based reforms were initiated in 1991. The States with better physical and social infrastructure and market friendly governance were able to grow faster (Panagariya et al., 2014). This has led to significant divergence of incomes among the States with coefficient of variation in per capita incomes increasing from 0.33 in 1991–1992 to 0.47 in 2000–2001 and marginally reducing to 0.40 in 2014–2015. Ironically, most of the low-income States are natural resource rich which implies that physical and social infrastructure has been a binding constraint in their development (Rao and Mandal, 2009).

It is important to accelerate growth and development in low-income States for reasons of both inclusiveness and stability of Indian federation for a variety of reasons. Overwhelming proportion of the poor is concentrated in low-income States and, therefore, accelerating growth in these States is an important prerequisite for creating income earning opportunities to them. The working age population (15–64 years) in India is presently 63.4 per cent and given the staggering demographic profile in low-income States, the high proportion of working age population will continue for a longer period as the fertility rate in these states remains high.

While in developed federations, high mobility of population can take surplus labour to capital rich jurisdictions to overcome adverse effects of uneven development, in countries like India the restrictions on mobility caused by linguistic, cultural, and various institutional factors make it important to ensure an even spread of physical and social infrastructures. Furthermore, acute interstate inequalities in the levels of living can be a source of instability and unrest.

Regional differences in social and physical infrastructures can be mitigated either through regional policies or through intergovernmental transfers. In a small country, the Central government can identify the diverse needs for public services and accordingly allocate resources to achieve the required balance. In a large, diverse federation, this has to be mainly achieved through intergovernmental transfers as the lower level jurisdictions are better placed to provide public services according to the diversified preferences of the people. In almost all the federations, therefore, the policy of intergovernmental transfers plays an important role in ensuring equitable access to public services (Ahmad, 1997) even as they tend to soften the budget constraints at subnational levels.

The rationale for intergovernmental transfers is to offset the fiscal disabilities of subnational jurisdictions. For reasons of redistribution and stabilization which is predominantly (not exclusively) a Central function, all broad-based and redistributive taxes, money supply function, and borrowing powers are exclusively or predominantly assigned to the Centre. At the same time, most expenditure functions are assigned to the States due to their comparative advantage in providing public services according to the diversified preferences of the people in different jurisdictions. In this scheme, vertical imbalance is unavoidable and intergovernmental transfer system has to resolve the imbalance. At the same time, it is important to match the revenue and expenditure decisions at the margin for subnational governments for reasons of efficiency and accountability. The efficient system of tax assignment envisages that tax powers should be assigned to subnational levels up to the point where the marginal efficiency loss due to tax disharmony is matched with marginal efficiency gain from fiscal autonomy. Even with such an assignment system, vertical imbalance is a feature seen in all federations.

In addition to vertical fiscal imbalances, horizontal imbalances arise due to the differences in the ability to raise revenues and unit cost of providing public services. Such revenue and cost disabilities across States violate horizontal equity across States (Buchanan, 1950). The problem is exacerbated when there are origin-based taxes and similar other factors alter the net fiscal benefits in different subnational jurisdictions (Boadway and Flatters, 1982). When there is perfect mobility of people across jurisdictions, *ceteris paribus*, fiscal differentials tend to be equalized as people migrate. Even when there is no perfect mobility, if the property market is reasonably well developed, fiscal differentials will be capitalized into property values (Oates, 1969). However, in developing countries, there is neither perfect mobility nor a developed property market and the only way left is to offset these fiscal disabilities arising from low revenue capacity and high unit cost of providing public services through intergovernmental transfers. Such transfers have to be unconditional—to *enable* every State to provide a standard level of public service at a normative tax rate.

There is also a case for transfers to *ensure* that people, irrespective of the jurisdiction they live in receive prescribed minimum standards of meritorious public services or those with high degree of spillovers such as elementary education, basic healthcare, water supply and sanitation, and anti-poverty interventions. Such transfers must be purpose-specific but linked to providing the specified minimum standards. The States may be asked to make matching contributions to avoid substituting these transfers to own expenditures. Given the varied levels of service provision prevailing in different states, it is possible to design the transfer system with varying matching requirements (Feldstein, 1975).

8.3. Fiscal Transfer System in India

India is a large and diverse developing country. The Constitution describes India as a 'Union of States'. It is the largest democratic federal republic, inhabited by 1.3 billion people spread over 28 States and 9 Union Territories covering an area of 3.29 million square kilometres. The country has a three-tier federal structure with governments at Union, States, and local levels. There are 28 States and 7 centrally administered territories (Delhi and Pondicherry). Below the State level, in urban areas, there are 96 municipal corporations, 1494 municipalities, and 2092 smaller municipalities (called *Nagar Panchayats*). There are 247,033 rural local bodies or *panchayats*, of which 515 are at the district level, 5930 at the block level, and 240,588 at the village level. However, the devolution of powers to the third level is uneven among States and their participation in public service delivery is negligible.

There are wide variations in the size and economic structure among the States. In 2011, Uttar Pradesh, at 200 million people is the largest State, and Sikkim, with 0.6 million, is the smallest. The per capita Gross State Domestic Product (GSDP) among the general category States in 2014–2015 was the highest in Haryana at Rs. 165,728 (excluding the small State of Goa which had the per capita GSDP of Rs. 304,666) and the lowest in Bihar, at Rs. 33,954.

The Seventh Schedule to the Constitution specifies legislative, executive, and judicial functions in terms of Union,[1] State, and Concurrent lists. Most broad-based taxes are assigned to the Union government and States are given the predominant responsibility of providing social services such as education, healthcare, water supply and sanitation and urban development and co-equal responsibility of providing economic services. The assignment system results in a significant vertical fiscal imbalance. The Founding fathers of the Constitution were aware of the problem and provided for the sharing of central taxes with the States and giving grants to them from the consolidated fund of the Centre based on the recommendations of the independent Finance Commissions appointed by the President of India every 5 years. The task of the Commission includes recommending the devolution of Central taxes to the States, laying down the principles of distribution and shares of individual States. The Commission is also required to recommend grants and address any other matters entrusted to it in the interest of sound finance in the Presidential Terms of Reference.[2]

Table 8.1 presents the shares of the Central and State governments in raising revenues and implementing expenditures. It is seen that total revenue collected in the country is about 20.5 per cent of GDP and of this 37.5 per cent is raised by the States. The States, however, incur over 60 per cent of the total public expenditures. Thus, the States' total expenditure is 18.3 per cent of GDP of which they raise about 8 per cent of GDP from own sources and receive transfers amounting to about 7 per cent of GDP. The remaining expenditure is financed from borrowing.

There is considerable variation among the States on their fiscal dependence on the Union government. There are 17 relatively homogenous

[1] The terms 'Union' and 'Centre' are used interchangeably in this paper.

[2] The Commission is also required to recommend measures to assist the augment the consolidated funds of the States to supplement the resources of the third-level government.

Table 8.1 States' Share in Total Revenues and Expenditures.

Years	Total revenue (Union + States)	Total expenditure (Union + States)	States' share in revenues (per cent)			States' share in expenditures (per cent)		
	Per cent of GDP	Per cent of GDP	Tax revenue	Non-tax revenue	Total revenue	Rev expenditure	Capital expenditure	Total expenditure
1990–1991	17.4	26.7	34.4	44.9	35.9	55.2	44.5	53.6
2000–2001	16.7	25.8	38.2	40.8	39.1	56.0	57.0	56.5
2005–2006	18.9	24.9	37.7	34.7	36.8	55.2	59.4	56.7
2007–2008	20.2	24.4	31.9	38.5	32.9	53.5	53.1	54.7
2008–2009	18.7	25.7	33.9	40.5	34.7	49.3	64.2	53.8
2009–2010	18.2	27.2	37.6	39.6	37.5	51.2	61.5	54.3
2010–2011	19.9	26.4	37.6	23.8	35.0	51.3	53.7	53.1
2011–2012	18.4	26.8	38.9	38.3	34.0	53.7	60.9	55.8
2012–2013	19.1	26.1	39.2	40.8	39.0	54.9	59.6	54.9
2013–2014	20.4	27.6	40.3	35.7	37.3	56.0	62.4	56.9
2014–2015	20.5	27.3	39.0	37.3	37.3	62.2	56.9	60.7

Source: Indian Public Finance Statistics, Ministry of Finance, Government of India.

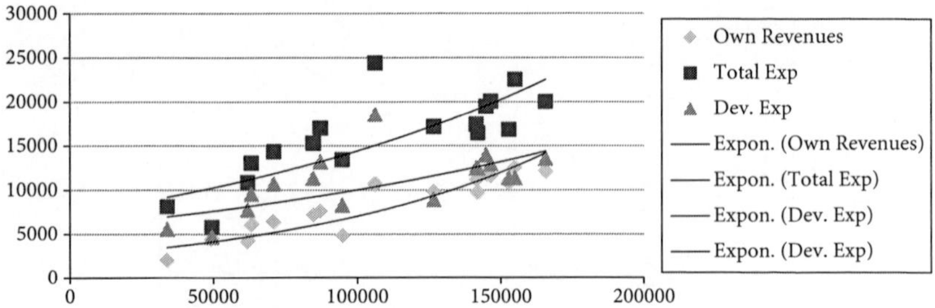

Figure 8.1 Per Capita Revenues and Expenditures of the States According to Per Capita GSDP.

general-category States, but even these have wide differences in size, revenue-raising capacities and efforts, per capita developmental and total expenditure levels, and fiscal dependence on the Union government (Table 8.2). Per capita own revenues of the States closely follow variations in per capita GSDP with the correlation coefficient of 0.940 broadly reflecting their revenue capacities (Figure 8.1). Per capita expenditures of the States—both developmental expenditures (expenditures on social and economic services) and total expenditures, also have a positive and significant correlation with per capita GSDP (0.786 and 0.614). This shows that even after the Central transfers, low-income States with low revenue capacity spend significant lower per capita expenditures on social and economic services.

Some important features of the State finances may be summarized here. First, interstate disparities in per capita incomes (GSDP) are not only high but also have been increasing over the years. In 2014–2015, among the General Category States, at Rs. 165,728, Haryana, the State with the highest per capita income (leaving out a small state of Goa), had five times the per capita income in Bihar, the lowest income State. As mentioned earlier, the coefficient of per capita incomes in the States has steadily increased from 0.30 in 1981–1982 to 0.35 in 1991–1992 and further to 0.40 in 2014–2015 (Panagariya et al., 2014). Second, not surprisingly, per capita revenues vary with per capita incomes predominantly due to variations in revenue capacity. The tax-GSDP ratios do not show a clear trend and, therefore, the variations in tax-GSDP ratios are due to both variations in taxable capacity and effort. Third, although per capita transfers are higher in the States with lower per capita incomes, it fails to

Table 8.2 Interstate Differences in Per Capita Income and Fiscal Variables (2014–2015).

States	Per capita GSDP	Per capita revenue	Tax-GSDP ratio	General purpose transfers	Transfer-specific purpose	Total transfers	Total expenditure	Dev. expenditure
	Rupees	Rupees	Rupees	Rupees	Rupees	Rupees	Rupees	Rupees
Andhra Pradesh	106263	10687	8.00	5376	2017	7393	24410	18588
Bihar	33954	2026	5.55	3872	1223	5095	8136	5579
Chhattisgarh	87354	7629	6.65	4830	1584	6414	17005	13202
Gujarat	141405	11187	6.85	2067	1263	3329	17446	12486
Goa								
Haryana	165728	12095	6.25	1836	1371	3207	20030	13579
Jharkhand	62091	4199	4.77	3343	1484	4827	10903	7772
Karnataka	144869	11788	7.63	2488	2121	4609	19482	13987
Kerala	155005	12512	6.69	2942	1600	4542	22549	11376
Madhya Pradesh	63323	6135	7.55	3732	1718	5450	13073	9564
Maharashtra	152853	10887	6.42	1795	1426	3221	16822	11383
Odisha	71184	6411	6.40	4392	2295	6686	14356	10740
Punjab	126606	9787	6.95	2371	1266	3637	17153	8932
Rajasthan	84837	7193	6.32	5251	213	5463	15291	11355
Tamil Nadu	146503	11668	7.20	2839	1910	4749	20062	12995
Telangana	141979	9719	5.61	2752	1411	4163	16461	12469

Continued

Table 8.2 *Continued*

States	Per capita GSDP	Per capita revenue	Tax-GSDP ratio	General purpose transfers	Transfer-specific purpose	Total transfers	Total expenditure	Dev. expenditure
Uttar Pradesh	49450	4460	7.11	3557	1150	4707	5802	4667
West Bengal	94711	4853	4.92	3385	1993	5378	13465	8290
All Gen. Cat. States	95802	7895	6.63	3498	1531	5030	14082	9807
Special Category States								
Arunachal Pradesh	110217	6185.6	2.82	30159.6	25094.3	55253.8	34257	58102
Assam	60621	3630.2	4.77	5325.3	2728.7	8054.0	7700	13156
Himachal Pradesh	147330	11323.6	1.59	11189.5	2675.3	13864.8	17186	31423
Jammu & Kashmir	77559	6278.4	2.68	12231.7	3348.4	15580.2	13060	26032
Manipur	58442	2269.2	1.13	18021.7	5616.2	23637.8	13087	27855
Meghalaya	75156	4005.2	0.10	11587.6	4482.9	16070.5	13211	23018
Mizoram	93136	4297.2	0.06	30945.2	11331.7	42276.9	32982	55607
Nagaland	89607	3207.8	0.37	15122.5	18900.5	34023.0	32907	37886
Sikkim	240274	19361.1	0.51	40251.8	10876.0	51127.9	33186	74434
Tripura	77358	3572.1	0.54	13905.4	6615.7	20521.1	11961	26793
Uttarakhand	153076	8929.2	0.91	7408.8	2795.0	10203.8	12361	24667
All Spl. Cat. States	84572	5604.4	0.97	9836.3	4243.8	14080.1	12449	22738
All States	95802	7419	6.58	3757.99	1641.16	5399.15	9977	14637

Source: Finance Accounts of the State Governments, C&AG, Government of India.

offset the revenue disabilities of the poorer States fully and more affluent States end up spending significantly higher per capita expenditures than those with their poorer counterparts (Figure 8.1). It is not surprising that the low-income States with poorer infrastructure deficits are unable to catch up with their more affluent counterparts.

8.4. General Purpose Transfers

As mentioned above, Article 280 of the Constitution mandates the President to appoint a Finance Commission every 5 years. The Commission has a Chairman and four other members whose qualification for appointment is laid down in the Finance Commissions (Miscellaneous Provisions) Act, 1951. The terms of reference (TOR) of the Commission are (i) the distribution of the net proceeds of Union taxes between the Union and States and among the States *inter-se*; (ii) grant in aid of revenues to be given to the States; (iii) measures to augment the consolidated funds of the States to supplement the resources of rural and urban local governments in the States based on the recommendations of the State Finance Commissions; and (iv) any other matter referred to the Commission by the President in the interest of sound finance. Under the last item, a number of tasks have been assigned to the Commission in the past such as setting the fiscal rules and targets for the Union and States, measures to be taken for sustainable development and the protection of ecology and environment, rescheduling and writing off of States' loans, examination of public expenditure management systems, review disaster management systems, strategic approach to public enterprise reform, and incentivizing the States to undertake tax reforms.

However, with the creation of the Planning Commission under a Cabinet Resolution, the role of the Finance Commission was constrained from the third Finance Commission as the role of the Planning Commission in allocating resources gained in importance. The Finance Commission recognized the rising importance of the Planning Commission and recommended that 25 per cent of the Plan grants may be given by it, but the note of dissent of the member-Secretary of the Commission that the plan revenue expenditure requirements and grants for the purpose should be entirely left to be decided by the Planning Commission was accepted by the Government. From the Fourth to the 13th Finance Commission, the TOR itself confined the Finance Commission to making recommendations on the transfers to cover only the non-plan revenue expenditure requirements of the States and giving plan grants was left to the Planning Commission. The grants were given based on a formula decided by the NDC (Gadgil formula). Of the total assistance, 30 per cent was earmarked to the special category States and the general category States were given assistance by way of loans and grants in the ratio 70:30 based on a formula and the ratio for special category States was 10:90. This practice, however, was discontinued as the TOR of the 14th Finance Commission required it consider the entire revenue accounts of the States without making a distinction between plan and non-plan.

The practice of channelling plan grants to the States under 282 construing it to be a miscellaneous provision has been questioned by some Constitutional experts (Tamil Nadu, 1971; NIPFP, 1993). In the Constitutional scheme of things, all grants are supposed to be given under Article 275 which has to be based on the recommendation of the Finance Commission. According to K. K. Venugopal (NIPFP, 1993), Article 275 empowers the Union Parliament to pay such capital and recurring sums as may be necessary to enable the States to meet the cost of such schemes of development undertaken by the State with the approval of Government of India. This implies that Article 275 empowers the government to give grants for revenue and capital purposes as well as general and specific purposes and, therefore, there is no need for any other provision. Furthermore Article 282 is not a miscellaneous provision for, it states, 'The Union or a State may make any grants for any public purpose, notwithstanding that the purpose is not one with respect to which Parliament or the Legislature of the State as the case may be may make laws'. According to Venugopal, the Article simply empowers both the Union and the State governments to make grants to the other for any public purpose even when that is not within their respective jurisdiction (NIPFP, 1993 p. 210).

According to K. K. Venugopal (NIPFP, 1993), the Constitution does not necessarily envisage the Finance Commission to be a temporary body. According to Article 280, the President is required to appoint a Finance Commission every 5 years or earlier as may be required and the Commission can continue until the next Commission is appointed and there is no need for the Commission to wind up after it gave the recommendation. A continuing Commission with a permanent secretariat would bring to bear a great deal of information and data expertise in the staff and the Commission can oversee the implementation after the recommendations are accepted.

The change in the design of the transfers came about when the TOR of the 14th Finance Commission did not restrict it to assess only the non-plan expenditure requirements of the States and the Commission made recommendations to meet the entire revenue expenditure requirements of the States without making a distinction between plan and non-plan. However, the Commission decided to recommend only general purpose transfers and avoided recommending any specific purpose grants. However, while making recommendations, it left adequate fiscal space to the Union government and recommended specific purpose grants.

After the 14th Finance Commission made the recommendations, the entire architecture of the transfer system changed. A clear distinction has emerged in respect of general purpose and specific purpose transfers in Indian fiscal federalism after the report of the 14th Finance Commission was implemented. All general purpose transfers are now recommended by the Finance Commission and all specific purpose transfers are given by the respective Central ministries. Although the 14th Finance Commission made a recommendation that the design and implementation of specific purpose transfers should be decided by a committee comprising of the representatives of Central and State governments as well as domain experts (India, 2014, Chapter 12), the Central government has continued the practice of taking decisions on these transfers at the relevant Central ministry level.

The 14th Finance Commission was also concerned with the intrusion of the Central government in States' domain through the proliferation of specific purpose transfers through Central sector and Centrally Sponsored Schemes. Its analysis showed that between 2005 and 2012, the Central government's spending on State subjects increased from 14 to 20 per cent and its spending on Concurrent Subjects increased from 13 to 17 per cent. Taking into account the need to cover plan revenue expenditure requirements and to provide the fiscal space to the States to cover the expenditures under the State List to reduce the Central governments intrusion into State subjects, the Commission increased the share of the States in the divisible pool of taxes[3] from 32 per cent recommended during the 13th Finance Commission to 42 per cent. Thus, according to the Commission's reasoning, the increase was partly on account of the inclusion of plan expenditure requirements of the States which was given by the Planning Commission based on the Gadgil formula and partly to provide greater flexibility to the States by giving them untied transfers. The Commission adopted a formula for distribution comprising of a mix of variables representing revenue and cost disabilities. It gave 50 per cent weightage to distance from the highest per capita income, 27.5 per cent weightage to population, 15 per cent weightage to the area, and 7.5 per cent weightage to the forest area.

The 14th Finance Commission's recommendations substantially altered the landscape of federal fiscal transfers. While there was a no significant change in the total transfers to the States in 2015–2016 over 2014–2015, the share of general purpose transfers rose significantly from 55.5 per cent to 71 per cent (Table 8.3, Figure 8.2). In other words, the sharp increase in tax devolution by the 14th Finance Commission resulted in the share of general purpose transfers going up significantly, but this was countered by the Central government reducing the specific purpose transfers (Chakraborty and Gupta, 2016). Thus, about one percentage point increase in general purpose transfer was offset by equivalent reduction in the allocation to Central Schemes.

8.5. Specific Purpose Transfers

In addition to the tax devolution and grants given to the States based on the recommendations of the Finance Commissions, the Central government gives specific purpose grants for various purposes through the respective ministries. The objective of specific purpose transfers, as mentioned earlier, is to *ensure* minimum standards of services in respect of

[3] Divisible pool of taxes comprises of total central taxes (excluding the revenue from earmarked taxes) minus the revenue from cesses and surcharges and cost of collecting the taxes.

Table 8.3 Trends in General and Specific Purpose Current Transfers.

	Gen purpose transfers	Specific purpose transfers	Total current transfers	Share of general purpose in total current transfers
2011–2012	3.63	1.97	5.60	64.78
2012–2013	3.61	1.63	5.24	68.89
2013–2014	3.48	1.76	5.24	66.39
2014–2015	3.41	2.74	6.15	55.49
2015–2016	4.32	1.74	6.06	71.23
2016–2017(RE)	4.69	1.84	6.53	71.81
2017–2018(BE)	4.61	1.80	6.41	71.93

Source: Budget Documents of the Union Government.

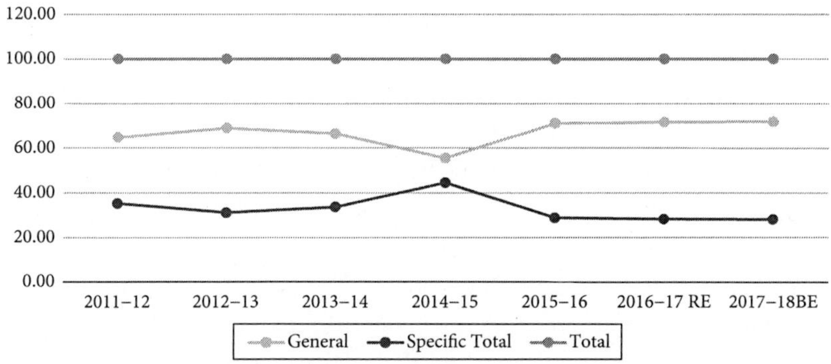

Figure 8.2 Share of General Purpose and Specific Purpose Transfers.
Source: Estimated from Union Budgets, Government of India.

those services that are considered meritorious or those services with significant interstate spillovers. However, in Indian context, this has been used as a patronizing instrument to serve political objectives of the ruling parties at the Centre to woo the electorate by expanding its reach to spend on the State subjects.

In 2012, there were 147 such schemes initiated by various Central ministries and many of them were directly implemented by numerous implementing agencies specifically created for the purpose and the grants were given to them directly bypassing the States. In 2014, these schemes were consolidated into 66 schemes based on the recommendation of a committee chaired by a Member of the Planning Commission (B. K. Chaturvedi). Also, the Central government stopped the practice of sending the grants directly to implementing agencies and channeling the funds through the States' consolidated funds after the Expert Committee on Efficient Management of Public Expenditure recommended it (India, 2011a). After the 14th Finance Commission made the recommendation to increase the tax devolution to 42 per cent of the divisible pool, the Central government appointed a committee of selected Chief Ministers of the States with the Chief Minister of Madhya Pradesh as the Convener to further consolidate and rationalize the schemes. The Committee consolidated them into 28 umbrella schemes and classified them into 'Core of the core', 'Core', and 'Optional' with matching requirements from the States stipulated at 30 per cent, 40 per cent, and 50 per cent, respectively.

There are six 'core of the core' schemes including the MGNREGA and 22 'core' schemes. In addition to these, there are 45 Central Sector schemes implemented in States to for specified purposes. The total amount of funds spent on all Central Sector and Centrally Sponsored Schemes in 2016–2017 amounted to 1.8 per cent of GDP constituting about 28 per cent of total transfers. Of these, only five schemes—National Rural Employment Guarantee, National Health Mission, Elementary Education, Rural Roads, and Housing schemes constituted 66 per cent of specific purpose transfers.

The analysis of the various components of transfers shows that the general purpose transfers are most equalizing with the elasticity coefficient of (–) 0.452 (significant at 1 per cent level) and the specific purpose transfers are the least equalizing with the elasticity coefficient of 0.162 which is not significant. The overall transfer system is equalizing with the elasticity coefficient of (–) 0.267. This is shown in Figure 8.3. The index of own revenues of the States (with all-State average specified at 100) increases steeply with per capita incomes. The index of total revenues (including transfers) too shows a positive slope with per capita incomes but is flatter than the former reflecting the extent of equalization. Thus, it is seen that (i) the Finance Commission transfers are equalizing but offset the fiscal disabilities of the States only partially; (ii) the Central schemes are not equalizing at all; and (iii) even after the fiscal transfers are considered, per capita revenues accruing to the States are positively correlated with per capita incomes of the States. The resources in low-income States enable them to incur much lower levels of spending than their richer counterparts.

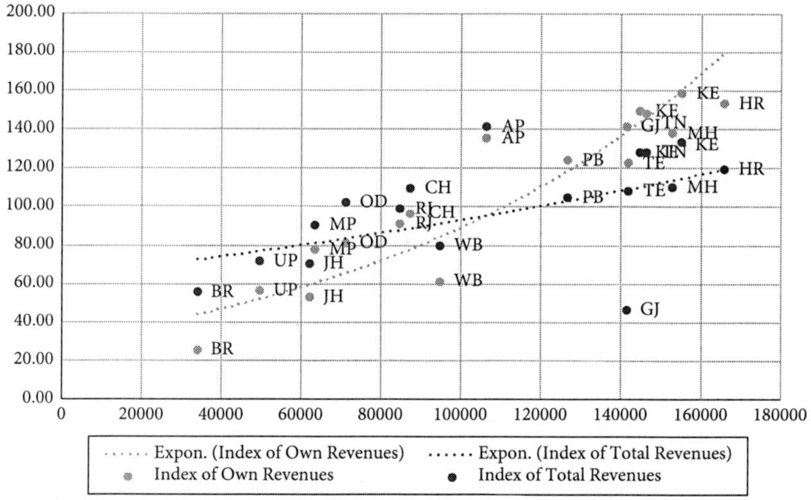

Figure 8.3 Equalizing Impact of Intergovernmental Transfers in India.
Note: The vertical axis represents index of own revenues and total revenues with the States' average set at 100. The differences in the slopes represent the extent of equalization in the transfer system.

The lower levels of per capita expenditures in States with lower per capita incomes is clearly brought out in Table 8.4, where per capita expenditures under various categories are regressed on per capita incomes in the States for the year 2014–2015 in a double-log function. It is seen that total as well as almost all expenditure categories except capital expenditures show a positive and significant relationship. In the case of total State expenditures, per capita expenditures are higher by 0.65 per cent when per capita incomes are higher by 1 per cent. The relevant elasticity is 0.69 in the case of current expenditures; 0.65 in the case of expenditures on social services, and 0.43 in the case of economic services. Within social services, the elasticity is 0.64 in the case of education and 0.72 in the case of healthcare.

The analysis shows that despite equalizing transfers, public expenditures are much higher in more developed States. This trend leads to increasing inequalities in infrastructure levels and human development causing divergence of incomes across Indian States. The matter is particularly concerning in the case of education and healthcare where the elasticities are high, and given the staggered demographic profile in poorer States, the requirement for public spending in these States is much

Table 8.4 Elasticities of Per Capita Expenditures with Respect to Per Capita GSDPs in the States.

Expenditure category	Constant (a)	Regression coefficient (b)	Adj. R^2
1. Revenue Expenditures	1.5486 (1.2189)	0.6906 (6.2535)*	0.70
2. Capital Expenditures	2.6142 (0.8169)	0.4248 (1.5202)	0.077
3. Expenditures on Economic and Social Services	2.9471 (2.0104)	0.5488 (4.3063)*	0.52
4. Expenditure on Social Services	1.1281 (0.8551)	0.6511 (5.6781)*	0.66
5. Expenditure on Economic Services	3.5793 (1.8422)	0.4274 (2.5307)*	0.25
6. Expenditures on Education	0.4324 (0.2499	0.6420 4.2681)*	0.52
7. Expenditures on Public Health	−1.6654 – (1.0743)	0.7185 (5.3322)*	0.63
8. Total Expenditures	2.0866 (1.6440)	0.6562 (5.9465)*	0.68

Estimated Equation is Per Capita Expenditure = Log a + b log Per Capita income + ∈.
Note: * denotes significant at 1 per cent level.

higher, but these States continue to spend lower per capita expenditures due to their lower taxable capacity and inability of the transfer system to offset their fiscal disabilities. While these figures confirm the fact that the transfer system could offset the fiscal disabilities of poorer States only partially and inequalities in per capita expenditure on social and economic services continue to persist.

Considering the wide variations in per capita GSDP among the States with the richest State having more than five times the per capita GSDP of the poorest, completely offsetting the fiscal disabilities to enable the low-income States to equalize their per capita expenditures may simply not be politically feasible in India. First, presently the Union government does not have fiscal space to meet its own obligations and cannot be expected to make any significant increase in the transfers. Second, there are significant deficiencies in the standards of physical and social infrastructures provided even by high-income States and they too need to spend large amounts on the developmental heads. Therefore, there is a clamour for higher transfers from all the States. Third, there are arguments that equitable transfers may reduce the overall growth of the economy which, in the long run, may prove inimical to the interests of the poorer States themselves. Therefore, the general purpose transfers, which are supposed to enable all the States to provide comparable levels of public services at comparable tax rates, can do this only to a limited extent.

It is in this context that the role of specific purpose transfers becomes critical. In particular, equalization in specific meritorious services such as education and healthcare, rural roads, and anti-poverty interventions can help in augmenting the services in these areas. However, as pointed out above, in Indian context, the Central government has adopted 28 schemes under Centrally Sponsored Schemes and another 45 Central Sector schemes competing for assistance. With too many schemes for equalization and with limited fiscal space available for giving grants, this has meant thin spread of resources without much impact on service levels. Most of these schemes are in the areas specified in the State List and truly belong to the domain of the States and if the latter are not able to provide these services adequately, they should be enabled to provide them through general purpose transfers rather than through conditional transfers. Of course, specific purpose grants should be given to augmenting services with high degree of interstate externalities or those which are considered highly meritorious, but these will have to be a few to make a difference in the service levels.

In terms of assistance, as mentioned earlier, the grants for the five schemes constitute 66 per cent of total grants under Central schemes and it is useful to examine in some detail the design and implementation of these schemes. The case studies of schemes for rural employment, elementary education, and healthcare schemes reveal some important shortcomings in both the design and implementation mechanisms.

A close examination of the grants for these schemes brings out some revealing aspects. In the case of elementary education, for example, each State is required to prepare the action plan for 42 different interventions including teachers' salary, textbooks, teachers' training uniforms, transport, residential schools, and libraries (Appendix 8.A2). The work plan for the year after consolidation for all States is approved by a committee chaired by the Union Education Secretary. The first instalment is given after the budget is approved and the second tranche is given only after fulfilling the formalities on spending including the furnishing of 'utilization certificates'. Invariably, by the time they have to release the second instalment, there are budget cuts or new developments would have taken place requiring additional allocation to some other sectors or the government was not able to raise the budgeted volume of revenues. In the event, often, the final grant given is significantly lower than the originally approved amount. The detailed analysis of National Health Mission and MGNREGA presented in the Appendices 8.A1 and 8.A2 too suffer from the same malice.

The above brief description brings out a number of shortcomings in the schemes. First, there are too many schemes and within each scheme, too many sub-schemes with different objectives. This results in the thin spread of resources, and it is not possible to clearly specify the target in terms minimum standards of services to be achieved.

Second, the grants for the schemes are not determined on the basis of the shortfall in the prescribed standard of services. Both the total and individual State allocations are based on incremental plans prepared by the respective State governments and approved by the Committee. Inability to link the transfers with service levels makes it difficult to judge them based on achieving minimum standards. The focus is on spending money rather than ensuring services.

Third, designing the grants is not linked to meet the shortfall in services from the prescribed levels and results in significant misallocation. It is not necessarily the educationally backward State or the State with poor health indicators that gets more education or health grants. The telling case is of rural employment guarantee. The volume of grants depends on the ability of the bureaucracy in preparing the plans and fulfilling the formalities including furnishing of the utilization certificate. As may be seen from Figure 8.4, the per capita spending on rural poor is lower in States with higher rural poverty ratio!

Fourth, the uniform matching ratio across States makes it difficult for the low-income States to utilize the grants allocated to them fully. In a situation in which the general purpose transfers are not able to offset the fiscal disabilities of the low-income States satisfactorily, they will not have the fiscal space to provide matching requirements. In the event, Kerala, one of the most advanced States in elementary education and healthcare

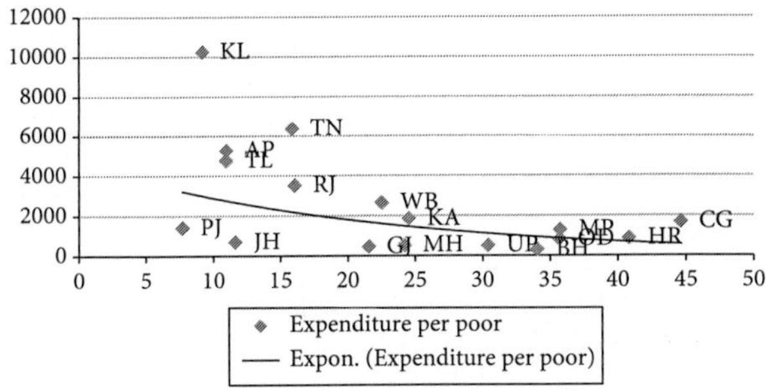

Figure 8.4 Rural Poverty Expenditure per Poor According to Poverty Ratio.
Source: Ministry of Rural Development and Panchayati Raj, Government of India.

comparable to many advanced economies also avails the grant by making the same matching contribution, while Bihar which is educationally the most backward State does not get adequate grants as it finds hard to contribute its share at the same matching ratio. Introduction of varying matching ratio depending on the shortfall in services levels could improve the design of the grant system.

Fifth, there is considerable difference between the approved allocation and actual grants given. In 2014–2015, for example, only 71 per cent of the allocated funds were disbursed in the case of rural employment guarantee scheme and the extent of difference varied between 38 per cent in Bihar, the poorest state, and 91 per cent in West Bengal, a middle-income state. This creates uncertainty in implementing schemes and invariably the States with greater shortfall in services levels suffer the most. A careful analysis shows that the shortfall from the approved is generally higher in the States with lower incomes.

Sixth, the analysis of grants for healthcare shows that the States are able to substitute grants to their own spending so that the incremental spending on the services is much less than the grant amount. In the case of healthcare, for example, econometric analysis relating to changes in health expenditures with changes in own revenues, general purpose transfers, and specific purpose transfers shows a significant substitution of expenditures on account of specific purpose grants (Rao and Choudhury, 2012).

Seventh, approval of the schemes with various components and requirement to adhere to the originally approved composition often leads

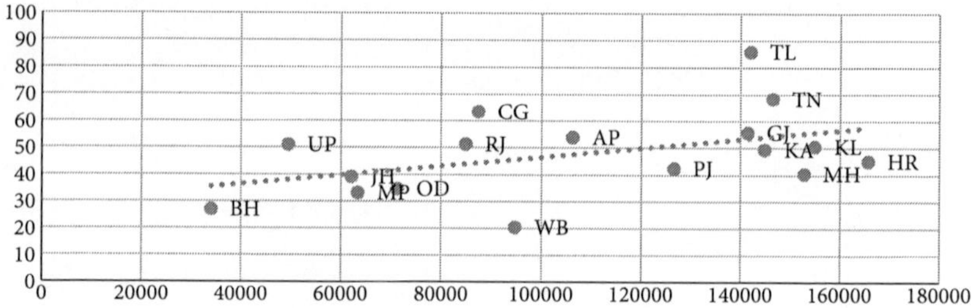

Figure 8.5 Release as a Per Cent of Allocation According to Per Capita GSDP.

to micromanagement, proliferation of bureaucracy, and inefficiency. In the case of education, for example, the States have to prepare the budgets and the Centre has to monitor in terms of 28 different interventions. In the case of healthcare, the Action Agenda report of the NITI Aayog referred to 2000 budget heads in which the grants are given. Although after the consolidation of the schemes, the volume of flexi funds has been increased to 10 per cent of the grant in some cases, most schemes suffer from micromanagement, inadequate allocation to different activities, and wastage therefrom.

This foregoing analysis indicates that the design and implementation of both general and each of the specific purpose transfers need to be analysed in detail. This will help in making recommendations to enhance effectiveness in equitable and incentive compatible provision of public services by the states. A detailed analysis of general purpose transfers in the form of tax devolution and Article 275 grants recommended by the Finance Commission and three important specific purpose transfers, namely, SSA, NHM, and MGNREGA will be undertaken in the final report to make specific recommendations on improving their effectiveness. The Finance Commission transfers are decided by the Finance Commission and the government itself does not have a say in changing the formula. However, the analysis can help in providing guidelines to the Commission while drafting its terms of reference to incorporate improvement in the formula. As regards Centrally Sponsored Schemes are concerned, the analysis will help in improving the design and implementation of the schemes. This will also help in analysing other important schemes to ensure equalization with incentives.

8.6. Concluding Remarks

Considering the high degree of vertical and horizontal imbalances in India, fiscal transfers from the Union to the States are critical. Unlike in many developed federations when the tax base differentials are not very significant, India has large and growing horizontal fiscal imbalances besides a high degree of vertical imbalances arising from the assignment of tax powers and expenditure responsibilities in the Constitution. Therefore, design and implementation of general and specific purpose transfers is critical in Indian federation from the viewpoint of not only ensuring horizontal equity, balanced regional development, and overall stability and integrity of the federation. This becomes even more important when the fact that there are significant hindrances to mobility of population and, therefore, it is necessary to take capital to the people and not wait for the people to move towards capital.

Analytically, general purpose transfers are made to offset fiscal disabilities of the States so that all the States are enabled to provide comparable levels of public services at comparable tax rates. However, given the large variations in fiscal disabilities in Indian States with per capita income in the highest income State is five times that of the lowest income State, it becomes difficult to design the general purpose transfers to fully offset the revenue and cost disabilities. Even the richest State suffers from physical and social infrastructure deficits and, therefore, seeks transfers and this poses constraints on the extent of targeting and equalization through instruments like tax devolution. This brings in the importance of specific purpose transfer to ensure minimum standards of services considered meritorious or those with significant interstate externalities.

In India, after the recent changes in the institutional architecture, all general purpose transfers are given on the recommendations of the Finance Commission. The latest is the 14th Finance Commission whose recommendations have been implemented since 2015–2016. The second source of grants is from various Central ministries which are scheme based. There are at present 28 Centrally Sponsored Schemes and another 45 central Sector schemes for which grants are given by various Central Ministries.

The analysis of intergovernmental transfers shows that the tax devolution and grants given on the recommendations of the Finance

Commission have a strong equalizing element, whereas those given by various Central Ministries do not. Even the former is able to offset the revenue disabilities of low-income States only partially. The consequence of this is that the higher income States are able to incur significantly lager per capita expenditures on all major social and economic services as well as in the aggregate. This tends to accentuate inequalities in social and economic infrastructures among the States leading to increasing divergence in developmental outcomes.

There are a number of problems with the design and implementation of specific purpose transfers. First, there are too many schemes, often each with multiple objectives resulting in the thin spread of resources and inability to design the transfer system to achieve minimum standards of specified services. Second, these are not linked to service-level outcomes but tend to be incremental. Thus, the transfers are not designed to achieve the basic purpose of ensuring minimum standards of services. Third, the large number of specific purpose transfer schemes taken up for equalization results in the thin spread of resources with hardly any impact on service levels. Fourth, the grants are not linked to improving service levels and it is not necessarily the States with larger shortfall in services receiving higher grants. Thus, educationally backward States do not get larger grants for education and states with lowest health standards do not get higher per capita grants for health. The analysis shows that the States with higher concentration of the rural poor get lower per poor grants for rural employment. Fifth, there is considerable difference between the originally approved allocation and final release of funds under various schemes. In the case of rural employment, the shortfall was 20 per cent in 2014–2015. The variation between allocation and release is different in different States and, generally, the difference is larger in the case of low-income States. The inability of the Centre to provide the funds allocated in the beginning of the year creates considerable uncertainty in the use of funds. Sixth, a part of the reason for the grater shortfall in low-income States is perhaps the uniform matching requirements. The low fiscal space available in these states makes it difficult to provide the matching contributions to fully utilize the funds allocated to them. Seventh, the requirement to seek grants under several different interventions within a scheme results in lack of flexibility to the recipient in the use of funds. Finally, in some schemes like healthcare, the States were able to substitute grants for their own spending with the result that there has not been a commensurate increase in spending on healthcare after the grants are received.

The Central government may not be able to influence much as far as the Finance Commission's recommendations are concerned as this is an independent body-making assessments of Union and State finances and recommending tax devolution and grants. At the same time, while providing guidelines to the Commission in the Terms of Reference, it can specify the need to design the devolution system to incentivize, tax effort, and expenditure efficiency in its recommendations. However, the Centre can certainly do well to rationalize the centrally sponsoring schemes. In the case of specific purpose transfers, the Centre has to determine the design itself. Here, it is important to limit the number of schemes and fund them adequately to make a difference to service level. It is important to link them to shortfall in specified services so that the overall objective of ensuring minimum standards is achieved. The design should result in increased outlay on the aided services. There is certainly a case for having differential matching requirements with states contribution increasing as the shortfall in services reduces. The 14th Finance Commission has made the recommendation that the number of transfers should be minimized and the design and implementation mechanism for each scheme should be decided by a committee comprising of Union and State government representatives and domain experts.

Appendix 8.A1. Analysis of Centrally Sponsored Scheme on National Health Mission

A1.1. Introduction

The National Health Mission (NHM) is a specific purpose grant given to the States and Union Territories to augment their healthcare system to provide 'accessible, affordable, accountable, effective and qualitative' healthcare. Initially started as the National Rural Health Mission (NRHM) by consolidating various programmes on health in 2006, the programme was expanded also to address health concerns of the urban poor living in listed and unlisted slums in 2013. The chapter on health in the 12th Plan document provides a broad framework for implementation of the programme during 2012–2017 and beyond.

The objective of the programme is to provide assistance to the States to ensure universal access to equitable, affordable, and quality healthcare services, accountable and responsive to people's needs with effective inter-sectoral convergent action to address wider social determinants of health. The core values of the programme are to (i) safeguard the health of the poor, vulnerable, and disadvantaged persons; (ii) strengthen public health systems as a basis for universal access and social protection against rising costs; (iii) build the environment of trust between the people and health service providers; (iv) empower the communities to become active participants in attaining the highest possible levels of health and; (v) improve efficiency and optimize the use of resources. These are supposed to be achieved by building integrated network of primary, secondary, and a substantial part of tertiary healthcare facilities and achieve inter-sectoral coordination to address food security, nutrition, access to safe drinking water and sanitation, education of female children, occupational and environmental health determinants such as women's rights and employment, and different forms of marginalization and vulnerability. The programme proposes to incentivize the States and Union territories to undertake health sector reforms to achieve greater efficiency and equity. It also proposes to prioritize services to address the health of women and children and the prevention and control of communicable and non-communicable diseases. Finally, it proposes to reduce the out-of-pocket expenditure of the households on healthcare.

The NHM support to States/UTs has five key components. (i) The National Rural Health Mission—Reproductive and Child Health (NRHM-RCH) Flexible Pool extends financial assistance to two components namely (a) Reproductive, Maternal, Newborn, Child and Adolescent Services (RMNCH + A) which is a continuum care approach covering all stages of life and (b) health System Strengthening under NRHM which is meant to augment infrastructure, human resources, programme management, and patient transport services. (ii) National Urban Health Mission (NUHM) provides financial assistance to effectively address the health concerns of the urban poor living in listed and unlisted slums. (iii) Control of Communicable Diseases includes programme assistance to control communicable diseases such as tuberculosis, vector-borne diseases, leprosy in addition to Integrated Disease Surveillance Project. (iv) Control of non-communicable diseases provides financial assistance to States to meet the challenges of controlling non-communicable diseases such as cancer, diabetes, cardiovascular diseases and stroke, National Programme for Control of Blindness, National Mental Health Programme, National Tobacco Control Programme, and National Programme for Health Care of Elderly. (v) Infrastructure maintenance is the assistance given to States to meet the salary on Family Welfare Schemes.

A1.2. Financing Issues

When the NRHM programme was initiated, it was entirely funded by the Central government. However, during the 11th Plan period (2007–2008 to 2011–2012), the Central contribution was 85 per cent and the States were required to contribute 15 per cent. Later, during the 3 years of the 12th Plan (2012–2013 to 2014–2015), the ratio of Central and State contributions to the programme was 75:25 for the general category States and 90:10 for the special category States. However, after the 14th Finance Commission increased the tax devolution to 42 per cent (as against 32 per cent by the previous Commission) of the divisible pool, the funding pattern was changed based on the recommendation of the NITI Aayog's Committee of Chief Ministers convened by the Chief Minister of Madhya Pradesh to 60:40 in the case of general category States and 90:10 in the case of special category States.

For allocating funds to individual States, the Union Ministry of Health and Family Welfare works out the resource envelops for each of the States for the year and conveys it. The envelops are determined on the basis area and population weighted by and the socio-economic backwardness and the health lag indicators in the States. Ten per cent of the funds is given to the states that demonstrates that they are able to efficiently absorb the funds provided as seen from the progress in key areas of institutional reform identified in the MOU with the States. For the NRHM—RCH Flexible pool, population weights for States are predetermined. The large Empowered Action Group (EAG) State (Madhya Pradesh, Bihar, Rajasthan, and Odisha) are assigned with the weight of 1.3. The two EAG States of Jharkhand and Chhattisgarh are assigned the weight of 1.5, the eight north-eastern States including Sikkim are assigned the weight of 3.2, the small Union Territories (excluding Delhi and Pondicherry) are assigned the weight of 3, and the remaining States are given the weight of 1. The allocation for NUHM is done on the basis of urban population and slum population by giving 50 per cent weightage to each of the two factors.

Based on the resource envelop communicated to them, the States are required to prepare their annual Programme Implementation Plans (PIPs) based on the State's context and felt needs. These are appraised and approved by the National Programme Coordination Committee (NPCC) chaired by the Secretary, Ministry of Health and Family Welfare and the States are required to implement the plan as approved plan.

A1.3. Analysis of Transfers under NHM

As mentioned earlier, the basic purpose of specific purpose transfers is to ensure minimum standards of healthcare throughout the country. This requires the government to define the minimum standard, work out the cost of ensuring the minimum in different states and design the transfer system to ensure that every State spends the minimum prescribed expenditures to achieve the prescribed standards. However, it must be recognized that equalizing health expenditures in a State is only a necessary condition to ensuring minimum standards of healthcare for there are a number of social determinants of health and some of them may even be outside the control of the governments. The analysis of the design and implementation of the schemes bring out a number of policy issues of the programme which need to be revisited and has to be made effective. These are discussed in the following.

(i) Designing the transfer system to achieve the objective of equalizing expenditures is extremely important. As mentioned above, it is important to define the standards and cost them. This implies that there should be clarity in the objectives. It is impossible to judge the effectiveness of the programme when multiple objectives are specified. Specifying too many objectives spreads the resources thinly across many activities besides increasing the difficulties in monitoring. In a shared cost programme, it is important that the implementing level of government should be allowed to plan and implement the programme and allocating resources across several activities within the health sector will increase bureaucratic role without ensuring efficient resource allocation. Such a micromanagement of the programme betrays the lack of trust with the States. As reported in the Action Agenda document of the NITI Aayog, there are as many as 2000 budget heads. It would be useful to set the targets in terms of infrastructure created such as the number of health centres and sub-centres, the number of health professionals, and availability of medicines as per the norms and institute an accountability system where the health system is made accountable to the people. Specifying the targets in terms of the above and providing expenditures to these would help to link the outlays to the creation of health facilities making it easy to fix accountability.

(ii) At present, the resource envelop is worked out and communicated to each State government. As pointed out above, the envelope is determined for five different components and a predominant part of this is determined on the basis of population weighted according to health lags and area. It is not clear how the weights indicating the health lags are determined. However, the weights assigned to the EAG States at 1.3 or 1.5 and for North-eastern and Himalayan Hill States at 3.2 as compared to the other States at 1 indicate that these are based on broad judgements rather than the actual position on health lags. In other words, it is hard to find significant and positive correlation between the grants given and the health status in the States. Kerala, the State with the best IMR, gets the third-highest grant allocation as well as release. This is clearly seen from Table 8.A1.1 (Figure 8.A1.1) where the per capita NHM grant allocation as well as release to States is shown against Infant Mortality Rate according to NFHS IV. Similarly, Uttar Pradesh, the State with the highest IMR, the grants allocated as well as released are much lower than many other States with much lower IMR. Thus, both the allocation and release of funds to the States are not to ensure minimum standards of services.

(iii) The analysis shows that the actual release of funds was lower than the original allocation in all the States. The largest shortfall was in Jharkhand followed

Table 8.A1.1 NHM Grants: State-Wise Allocation and Release (2014–2015).

States	IMR	Allocation	Release	Release as a ratio of allocation
Andhra Pradesh	35	147.52	111.81	75.8
Bihar	48	129.50	117.69	90.9
Chhattisgarh	54	227.77	189.33	83.1
Gujarat	34	165.88	148.39	89.5
Haryana	33	147.48	124.25	84.3
Jharkhand	44	165.91	109.85	66.2
Karnataka	28	146.29	126.57	86.5
Kerala	6	176.30	158.18	89.7
Madhya Pradesh	51	176.00	157.36	89.4
Maharashtra	24	140.68	125.57	89.3
Odisha	40	177.53	158.00	89.0
Punjab	29	150.06	134.55	89.7
Rajasthan	41	177.06	161.93	91.5
Tamil Nadu	21	158.21	141.00	89.1
Telangana	28	139.24	106.55	76.5
Uttar Pradesh	64	148.23	125.91	84.9
West Bengal	27	151.39	131.95	87.2

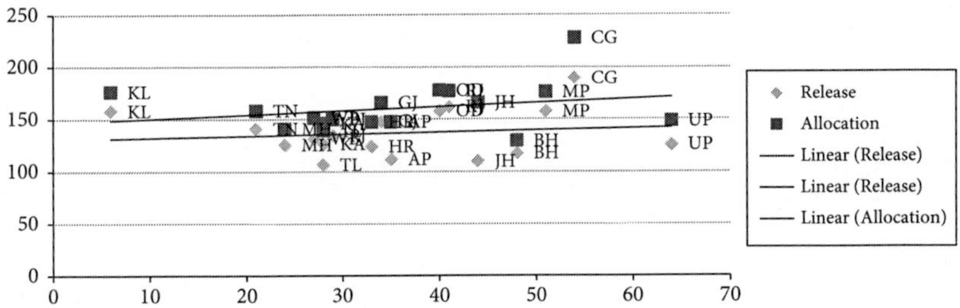

Figure 8.A1.1 Distribution of Central Grants According to Infant Mortality Rate 2014–2015.

by Andhra Pradesh and Telangana. Among the low-income States, besides Jharkhand, the shortfall was more than 15 per cent in Chhattisgarh and Uttar Pradesh.

(iv) The fact that there was shortfall in the actual release from the original allocation implies that this was substantially due to the budget cut. This is revealed by the fact that the actual expenditure on NHM in 2014–2015 was lower than the budget estimate by 20 per cent. Cutting the expenditure arbitrarily defeats the purpose of ensuring minimum levels of expenditure.

(v) It has been mentioned that one of the reasons for the shortfall in the actual release of expenditures from the original allocation is the inability to provide the utilization certificates and fulfil other compliances in time. At the same time, as the Union Ministry of Health and Family Welfare wants to utilize the funds, the funds allocated to those states which do not fulfil the compliances are distributed to those that fulfil them. This defeats the purpose of equalization. The issue must be addressed by building capacity in non-complying states and perhaps introducing multi-year budgeting so that these States avail the funds and use them in an efficient manner to get the desired outcomes.

(vi) The important objective of requiring the States to make matching contributions is to ensure that the funds given by the Central government for augmenting health services add to the overall health expenditures and that the states do not substitute these funds to their own spending. However, an econometric analysis carried out in a recent study by regressing changes in expenditures on changes in NHM transfers, own revenues, general purpose transfers, and priority assigned to the health sector (as shown is the share of health expenditure in total expenditure) in a fixed effects model for the period 2013–2015 shows that specific purpose transfers showed that every rupee of per capita specific purpose transfers reduces the spending by the State by 0.36 paise when the impact of own revenues and general purpose transfers are accounted for (Table 8.A1.2). While this is definitely an improvement over the previous estimate by Rao and Choudhury (2012), it still shows that the States do substitute some portion of transfers by cutting down non-aided portion of health expenditures and this needs to be corrected to additionality in expenditures.

A1.4. Reform Issues

The foregoing analysis shows that the scheme has been less than optimal in achieving the objectives it has set forth. The basic objective of ensuring a prescribed minimum stand of health services cannot be achieved with the present design and implementation mechanism. Therefore, the scheme needs to be revisited, making it more effective. Important reform issues to make the scheme more effective are discussed in the following:

(i) As mentioned earlier, it is necessary to define the objective of the scheme clearly. This implies that it is necessary to avoid multiple objectives and focus on a single objective of ensuring minimum levels of health infrastructure

Table 8.A1.2 Regression Results-Dependent Variable: Changes in States' Own Expenditure on Health (Dep Variable: Changes in Per Capita Expenditure on Health-NHM).

#	Independent variable	Coefficient of variation (and standard error)			
		Rao and Choudhury (2012)			New analysis
		1991–2007 (Model I)	1991–2000 (Model II)	2001–2007 (Model III)	2012–2015 (Model IV)
1	Changes-Specific Purpose Transfers from Union Government on Health Δ (PC_CGH) it = {(PC_CGH) it – (PC_CGH) it–1}	−0.952*** (0.074)	−0.777*** (0.114)	−1.059*** (0.109)	**−0.360***** **(0.137)**
2	Changes State's Own Revenues Δ (PC_SOR) it = {(PC_SOR) it – (PC_SOR) it–1}	0.012*** (0.003)	0.015*** (0.004)	0.1545*** (0.006)	**0.012** **(0.020)**
3	Changes State's Priority for Health (as % of spending) Δ (SPH) it = {(G hi/G bi)t – (G hi/G bi) t–1}	17.649*** (1.828)	15.03*** (2.038)	19.487*** (4.231)	**38.644***** **(12.069)**
4	Changes in General Purpose Transfers (Unconditional) from Union Government Δ (PC_GPGC) it	0.019*** (0.007)	0.014 (0.011)	0.013 (0.01)	**0.017**** **(0.008)**
5	Constant	18.252*** (3.561)	17.17*** (3.885)	3.552 (5.035)	**58.204***** **(17.542)**
6	State-specific fixed-effects	Yes	Yes	Yes	**Yes**
7	Time-specific fixed-effects	Yes	Yes	Yes	**Yes**
8	Number of states	14	14	14	**11**
9	Number of observations	224	126	84	**55**
10	R^2	0.69	0.62	0.77	**0.29**

Estimated equation is Δ (PC_OHE)it = α + β Δ (PC_CGH)it + γ Δ (PC_SOR)it + ψ Δ (SPH)it + τ Δ(PC_GPGC)it + υ (State Dummies) + σ (Year Dummies) + εit.

Source: Pavan Srinath et al. (2017), *Public Expenditure on Health in India 2005–2006 to 2015–2016*, Takshashila Institution, Bangalore.

across the country. It is necessary to avoid multiple objectives and linking transfers to several interventions. The objective should be to ensure a prescribed minimum health infrastructure for primary and secondary healthcare including physical infrastructure, health professionals, and drugs. A significant portion of the tertiary healthcare and some portion of secondary healthcare must be provided by the States themselves.

(ii) Once the focus shifts to ensuring minimum standards of services, it is not necessary to have multiple interventions and give grants under a large number of budget heads. The NITI Aayog document states that there are as many as 2000 budget heads for NHM transfers. Such micromanagement and minute division of transfers hugely enhances the transaction cost and spreads the resources thinly across several interventions which will prevent making appreciable impact on the health infrastructure. When the nature of the intervention is decided by the States themselves, it is important to trust them and provide them flexibility to ensure the type of infrastructure and strengthening of services they intend to provide. According to the Constitution, 'Public Health' is a State subject, and it is appropriate to trust them and empower them to provide a mix of infrastructure as perceived by them to be appropriate.

(iii) The resource envelop allocation to the States should be made purely on the basis of shortfalls in infrastructure as per the specified norms. The present system of allocating funds on the basis of area and population weighted according to health lags to a considerable extent arbitrary and does not allocate resources according to varying standards of health infrastructure. As the objective of any specific purpose transfer is to ensure minimum standards of services, it is necessary to define what is the minimum standard sought to be equalized and make allocations accordingly.

(iv) The difference between original allocation and ultimate release creates difficulties in implementing the planned activities by the recipients of the grants. The difference largely arises on account of cuts in the Central budget for the schemes or inability of the recipient state governments to fulfil the compliances including the timely provision of utilization certificates. Simplification of the transfers in the lines indicated in (ii) above should considerably reduce the compliance requirements by the States. In addition, as some infrastructure facilities in the health sector may require longer time period to complete, multi-year budgeting may be thought of as a solution.

(v) Creation of infrastructure facilities by itself may not improve the health outcomes. It is important to institute a system of incentives and accountability. This does not fall in the realm of design of the transfer system but implementation. To a considerable extent, this has to do with the system of governance in the State.

(vi) The matching requirements from the States for NHM have been changed after the NITI Aayog Committee of Chief Ministers convened by the Chief Minister of Madhya Pradesh recommended the marching ratio between the Centre and states at 60:40 for the General Category States (GCS) and 90:10 for the Special category States. Given the large number of schemes and significant interstate variations in the health infrastructure including human resources between the States and the need to bring up the States lagging in the services to the minimum level, it may be appropriate to design the scheme requiring varying matching requirements. The GCS may be grouped into three categories depending on their taxable capacity as high-, moderate-, and low-capacity States and the matching ratio for the states may be fixed at 50 per cent, 40 per cent, and 30 per cent. This way, low-capacity States will find it easier to contribute their marching requirements and avail the Central transfers.

(vii) It is important to ensure that the grants given to the States add to the expenditure on healthcare and the States are not allowed to substitute their own spending by transfers. This would require adding a condition to availing the grants. This could be done either by stipulating that the expenditure excluding the transfers on health does not fall short of the projected health expenditures excluding the transfer for the year or by stipulating that the share of health expenditure in total budgetary expenditure increases by the volume of grants received.

Appendix 8.A2 Analysis of Centrally Sponsored Scheme on Sarva Shiksha Abhiyan

A2.1. The Scheme

Sarva Shiksha Abhiyan (SSA) is a Centrally Sponsored Scheme implemented in partnership with the States to achieve universalization in elementary education in the country. The scheme was conceptualized and introduced based on the experience gained from the erstwhile programmes, namely, Operation Black Board (OBB), Shiksha Karmi Project (SKP), and District Primary Education Programme (DPEP). The National Mission for SSA was initiated in January 2001. The objectives of the scheme are to ensure universal access and retention, inclusiveness by bridging gender and social category gaps in education, enhancement in the learning levels of children. These are sought to be achieved through as many as 42 interventions such as opening of new schools, construction of schools and additional classrooms, toilets and drinking water, provisioning of teachers, periodic teacher training and academic resource support, textbooks and support for learning achievement.

The enactment of the Right of Children for Free and Compulsory Education (RTE) Act in 2009 and consequent insertion of Article 21A in the Constitution states that, 'the State shall provide free and compulsory education to all children in such manner as the Stare may, by law, determine'. Thus, the Act mandates that every child in the 6–14 age group is entitled to have free and compulsory education in a neighbourhood school till the completion of elementary education. The framework for implementation of SSA has accordingly been amended in September 2010 to align with the provisions of the RTE Act. An important provision of the Act is the requirement of admitting 25 per cent of the seats in private schools for the children belonging to the weaker sections and disadvantaged groups in class 1 or pre-primary class with the government required to reimburse the fees of these children. The Act also inter alia (i) the provision for a non-admitted child to be admitted to an age appropriate class; (ii) specifies the responsibilities of different levels of government in implementation; (iii) lays down the norms and standards relating to pupil–teacher ratio, buildings, infrastructure, school-working days, and teacher working hours; (iv) rational deployment of teachers to maintain the pupil–teacher ratio in every school and not the block or the district as a whole; (v) the norms for pupil–teacher ratios, buildings and infrastructure, prohibits physical punishment and mental harassment of students, prescribes screening procedure for admission of children, parents charging capitation fees, private tuition by teachers and running of schools without recognition; (vi) development of curriculum in consonance with the values enshrined in the Constitution; and (vii) provides for 25 per cent admission of children belonging to weaker sections and disadvantaged groups in class 1 or pre-primary class and reimbursement of fees towards expenditure incurred by them for admission of economically weaker section (EWS) of students in private unaided schools with effect from 2014 to 2015.

The objectives of the programme of universalizing elementary education, closing the gender and social groups' gaps, and improving the quality of education are sought to be achieved through 42 interventions grouped under 8 different components. These include access and retention, quality, gender, equity, Section 12 (1) (C) of RTE Act reimbursement of expenditure for 25 per cent of admissions in private schools, infrastructure development, programme management, and other issues. This is a shared cost programme between the Central and State governments. During the period 2010–2014, the sharing ratio between the Centre and States was 65:35 for general category States and 90:10 for Special Category States. After 2015–2016, this was changed to 60:40 in the case of general category States and 90:10 in the case of Special Category States has continued.

The shares of different States and Union Territories in total grants are determined on the basis of the approved Annual Work Plan and Budget (AWP&B). Each State and Union Territory submits it AWP&B to the Project Appraisal Board Chaired by the Secretary in the Ministry of Human Resource Development as per the financial norms of the scheme, which includes the shares of the Centre and the States.

The share of the Central government is released in three instalments in different months—ad-hoc, first and second instalments to ensure uniform flow of funds. The release is done after the required documents such as provisional/audited utilization certificate, state share statement, outstanding advances, and pace of expenditure implementation. The Central share is released to the States and the latter in turn release the funds to State Implementing Societies (SIS). The Central share is divided into General and Capital heads from which the SC, ST, and General components are segregated. SISs function under the supervision of the respective State governments. They release the funds received by them to Government schools, Government-aided schools, and private schools identified by the State government for giving grants.

A2.2. Analysis of Grants

As mentioned earlier, there are as many as 42 interventions within the SSA with multiple objectives and the States have to prepare their plans for each of the interventions. Multiple objectives make defining the minimum standards difficult. For example, while enrolment ratio can be defined, it is not possible to clearly define and set minimum standards for the quality of education to be achieved through the transfer system. The focus then shifts to inputs such as teacher–student ratio or physical infrastructures provided rather than learning outcomes. At the end, the Right to Education ends up with attendance at schools rather than educating the young.

There are a number of issues of both design and implementation of the scheme. As may be seen from Figure 8.A2.1, the expenditure per child in the school-going age (6–13) in the States is positively related to per capita GSDP with a correlation coefficient of 0.688. This shows that SSA has not had a significant impact on equalizing per child expenditures and the States with low revenue capacity continue to suffer from poor educational standards as compared to their more affluent counterparts. In addition to lower expenditures, the poor implementation results in lower teacher–student ratio, employment of untrained teachers, absenteeism of teachers, and inability to provide teaching accessories. Thus, the basic objective of equalizing standards of elementary education gets defeated.

As mentioned above, preparation of plans for SSA is done on incremental basis and not on the basis of the shortfall in standards of elementary education. In the event, the grants are given not on the basis of the shortfall in the standards of the service but on the basis of the ability of the State to prepare its plans. The distribution of grant per child in the age group 6–13 in the States arranged according to per capita GSDP shows very little relationship between the two variables (Figure 8.A2.2). This is a matter of concern as in low income—highly populated states with higher proportion of the children in the school-going age, the low per child expenditures will accentuate educational inequality.

The shortcoming in the design of the grants under SSA is reinforced when we look at Figures 8.A2.4. It is seen that the SSA grant in 2014–2015 in the States is shown against the ratio of out-of-school children taken from the *Statistics on School Education 2011–12* published by the Ministry of Human Resource Development. If out-of-school is taken as a measure of educational standard, the graph shows that there is hardly any relationship between the grants given and educational standards in the States (Correlation coefficient: 0.112). Similarly, per child grant to States according to dropout ratio too shows virtually no relationship between the two variables with a correlation coefficient of (–) 0.0698 (Figure 8.A2.3).

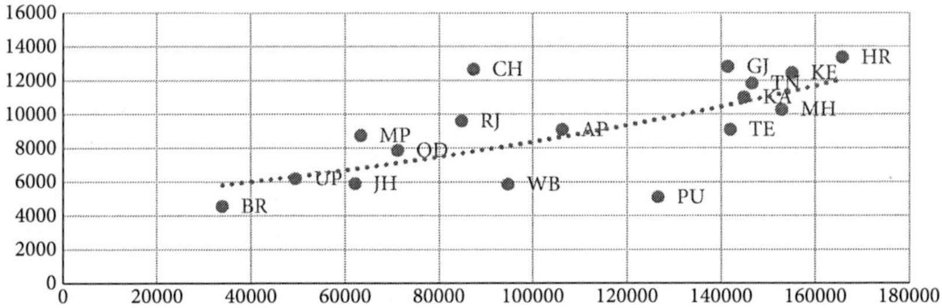

Figure 8.A2.1 Expenditure per Child in the Age Group 6–13 in States According to Per Capita GSDP.

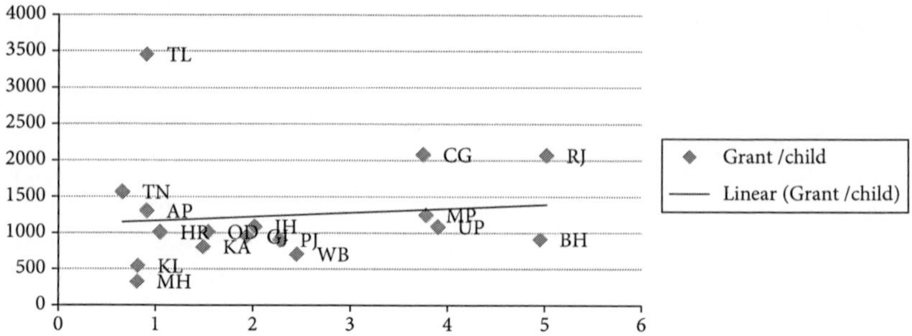

Figure 8.A2.2 Per Capita Expenditure on Education According to Per Capita GSDP.

The lack of equalization in the SSA grants is not only because of the shortcomings in the design of the grant system but also due to implementation problems. The low-income States have been lagging in fulfilling the conditionalities and availing the grants allocated to them to the full. The positive relationship between the ratio of grants released to allocation shows with per capita GSDP shows that the higher income states are able to implement the scheme better than the less-affluent States. In other words, the low-income States not only are allocated lower per child grants but also they are unable to utilize the grants allocated to them. Inability to utilize the grants by them results in these grants being distributed to those States which fully utilize, thus compounding the inequity. The variations in the utilization rates could be due to their inability to implement the schemes expeditiously, or inability to fulfil the conditions like timely auditing off the accounts, compilation of information on the utilization from the village level or simply, inability to provide matching resources as required in the scheme. This implies that there must be concerted efforts at building capacity to implement the schemes and have to re-examine the reporting requirements.

Considering the importance of the scheme, it may also be useful to think in terms of multi-year implementation plans to avoid losing the grants. As regards matching ratios are concerned, to encourage educationally backward States, the

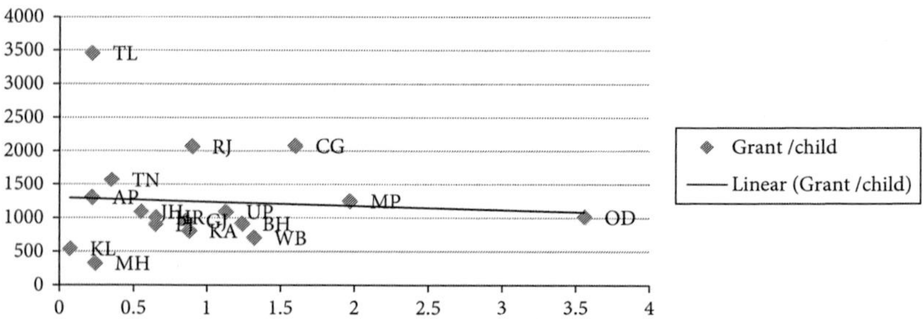

Figure 8.A2.3 Grants/Child According to Dropout Rate 2014–2015.

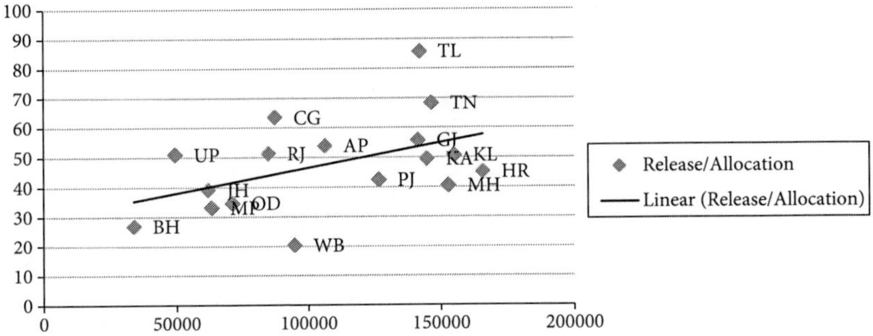

Figure 8.A2.4 Grant Release/Allocation According to Per Capita GSDP.

Central government could introduce varying matching ratio requirements depending on the extent of educational backwardness or the revenue disability. The Special Category States in any case have to make lower matching contributions. Even among the general category States, it may be appropriate to classify them into three categories in terms of educational backwardness/revenue disability and have a matching ratio of 30 per cent, 40 per cent, and 50 per cent for the most backward, middle category, and least backward category States.

After the enactment of RTE, a provision has been made to provide 25 per cent seats in private schools to disadvantaged children on reimbursement of the fees by the government. While this can be a gateway to these children to avail elite education, it can also create some social problems. First only a miniscule minority of the students can get a chance to get admitted in private schools. Second, given that the social background of the disadvantaged students admitted under RTE is very different from the regular students, there can be a feeling of segregation and discrimination. Furthermore, given the varying family backgrounds with the general students having access to parental guidance or paid tuitions after the school, the RTE students may find it hard to compete with the regular students. It is important that the States should work towards improving the standards in government schools by having adequate number of trained teachers, constant upgradation of their skills, enforcing their attendance and regular teaching in schools, and access to teaching materials and aids.

The important issue in SSA should be to reduce educational inequalities among the States so that children are provided with access to education irrespective of the place of their residence and economic and social background. The focus will have to be not on enrolments but on learning. This requires improvements in the design and implementation of the scheme and the capacity and willingness by the States to enforce compliance by the teachers. In particular, there is a need to build capacity in the lagging States. Multiple interventions with minute conditionalities only adds to the problems of implementation and bureaucratic interference. It is necessary to trust the states, handhold them where necessary, help them to build capacity to implement and provide greater flexibility in the use of funds rather than distribute funds across several interventions.

Appendix 8.A3. Analysis of Centrally Sponsored Scheme on Mahatma Gandhi National Rural Employment Guarantee

A3.1. The Scheme

According to the World Bank report, Mahatma Gandhi National Rural Employment Guarantee (MGNREGA) is the world's largest public works programme. This is a programme designed to ensure livelihood security by providing 100 days of guaranteed wage employment in a financial year for an adult member of every household who volunteers to undertake manual work. The programme was introduced by merging and expanding the erstwhile Sampoorna Grameen Rozgar Yojana (SGRY). It was started in 200 districts of the country in 2006 and the coverage was extended to additional 130 districts in 2007 and to the entire country in 2008.

The National Rural Employment Guarantee Act of 2005 provides the framework for the design and implementation of the scheme. The jobseekers are required to obtain the job cards by applying for registration. The job card holders have to be provided with employment within 15 days from the date of application for the job failing which they are entitled to receive unemployment allowance. Contractors are not supposed to execute the works and unskilled wage should constitute 60 per cent of the work plan and the remaining 40 per cent should be incurred for material cost and skilled wages. The entire scheme has to be implemented by the Panchayats and the share of village panchayats should be at least 50 per cent. Priority in the works should be assigned to those involving natural resource regeneration and improving agricultural productivity, drought proofing, and flood protection. Payment to the workers has to be made directly to their bank or post office accounts.

The salient features of the scheme are (i) this is a rights-based scheme for adult members willing to do manual labour; (ii) the employment must be provided to the job card holders within 15 days of their application failing which they are entitled to receive unemployment allowance; (iii) job card holders can receive employment entitlement up to 100 days in a financial year depending upon their demand; (iv) the works chosen must be labour intensive with unskilled wages constituting 60 per cent of the cost; (v) implementation of the scheme is done at decentralized levels with village panchayats required to implement 50 per cent. The entire work plan is supposed to be identified and recommended by the Gram Sabha. The Panchayat Raj Institutions have been given the primacy in planning, implementing, and monitoring the scheme; (vi) the facilities such as crèche, drinking water, first aid, and shade should be provided at the work sites; (vii) women beneficiaries must constitute one-third of the employment provided; (viii) there must be proactive disclosures through social audit, grievance redressal mechanisms to ensure transparency and accountability; and (ix) the States are responsible for implementation and ensure that work as demanded for up to 100 days is ensured.

Under the MGNREGA, the work plan is supposed to be decided on the basis of a participatory planning exercise. The responsibility for preparing the labour budget for the next financial year along with the details of unskilled labour requirement is assigned to the District Programme Coordinator and this task has to be completed by December. The entire exercise leading up to the estimation of the labour budget and identification of the work plans is done in a decentralized planning exercise. The Gram Sabhas are supposed to identify the work plan and the Gram Panchayats wise identification of the shelf of works and estimation of employment demand is aggregated at the block level and thereafter at the district and State levels. These estimates scrutinized by the State Government are submitted to the Empowered Committee chaired by the Secretary, Rural Development of the Central government. After taking account these inputs, the Empowered Committee finalizes the labour budget based on the performance of the State in terms of the employment created during the preceding 4 years, the planning process adopted to finalize the labour budget in the State, an appraisal of the initiatives and strategies of the State to improve delivery mechanism and assessment of the requirement of the State in terms of magnitude and intensity of rural poverty as reflected in the Socio-economic Caste Census, 2011 (SECC) estimates and frequency of the occurrence of natural calamities. The labour budget thus finalized is only indicative and not a ceiling. The States are required to cater to the actual demand for work during implementation.

The funds to the States are released normally in two tranches and there can be more than one instalment in a tranche. The amount in a tranche depends upon the approved labour budget, opening balance, pending liabilities of the previous year, and overall performance. After the approval by the Empowered Committee and adoption in the budget, the State government is required to prepare district-wise, month-wise projections of labour demand. Based on this, the fund requirement is estimated by the NREGA Soft. The first tranche is estimated on the basis of the funds required for first 6 months of the financial year or 50 per cent of the labour budget of the State, whichever is lower. The first tranche is released in April and the amount is calculated on the basis of labour demand projected for the first 3 months, adjustment of unspent balances and pending liability.

The release of the first tranche is subject to the submission of (i) a certificate to the effect that accounts of all the districts of the State for the previous financial have been settled; (ii) a certificate on the settlement of all audit paras under the MGNREGA; (iii) a detailed action taken report on the complaints forwarded to the State; (iv) a certificate indicating satisfactory compliance of Ministry's clarifications/suggestions/guidelines and observations from time to time; (v) a certificate to the effect that there hasn't been any mutualization and misappropriation of funds.

The second tranche is released subject to the fulfilment of the prescribed conditions and on submission of the proposal in the prescribed format by the State. The proposal can be submitted only after the district/State utilizes 60 per cent of the available funds. If the second tranche proposal is submitted after 1 October, it is necessary to submit the audit report of the previous year. The quantum of funds released in the second tranche depends on the performance in the utilization of the funds available.

A3.2. Analysis of the Scheme

Governmental intervention in redistribution is necessary because markets do not bring about the desired state distribution of income and wealth. It is also important that while funding for such redistribution has to come predominantly from the Central government, implementation of anti-poverty intervention has to be at local levels for reasons of comparative advantage (Rao, 2002). There are general questions as to whether such targeted interventions are better or assuring basic minimum levels of income to the targeted groups of population is more desirable. In this report, these issues have not gone into as the objective is to analyse the design and implementation issues in this important specific purpose transfer.

This is undoubtedly an important anti-poverty intervention. The self-selection through manual unskilled work in the scheme makes targeting the benefits of the scheme to the poor automatic. Indeed, there are challenges in implementation and possibilities of misappropriation at the grass-roots level in feudal oligarchic power structure in rural areas. There are also administrative costs and bureaucracy at various stages with potential power to seek rent. These issues of implementation have to be addressed by evolving and strengthening the systems of checks and balances including an effective social audit.

A3.3. Conclusions

The focus of this study is to analyse the design and implementation scheme of this specific purpose transfer for generating wage employment in rural areas to minimize the hardship arising from rural poverty. Although there are multiple objectives in the scheme, the principal focus is to mitigate the distress caused by rural poverty. This would mean that the spending on MGNREGA should spread across the States such that the State with higher concentration of poverty should receive higher amounts. The analysis of spending on MGNREGA across different States shows that in 2014–2015, per rural poor expenditure is negatively correlated (–0.572) with the rural poverty ratio according to the Tendulkar measure (Figure 8.A3.1). This shows shortcomings in the targeting of MGNREGA.

The above finding is reinforced by the pattern of person days of employment generated through MGNREGA in different States relative to their rural poverty ratio (Tendulkar measure) in 2014–2015. Figure 8.A3.2 which presents the analysis shows no particular pattern. It is seen that Tamil Nadu had the highest number of person days employed even though the rural poverty ratio in the state was just 15.8 per cent.

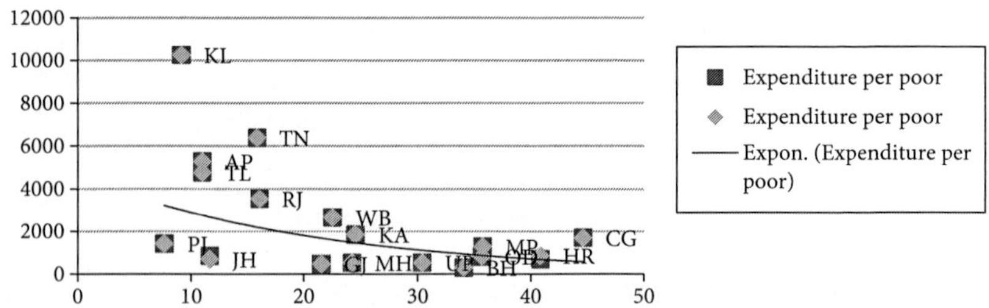

Figure 8.A3.1 Rural Poverty Expenditure per Poor According to Rural Poverty Ratio.

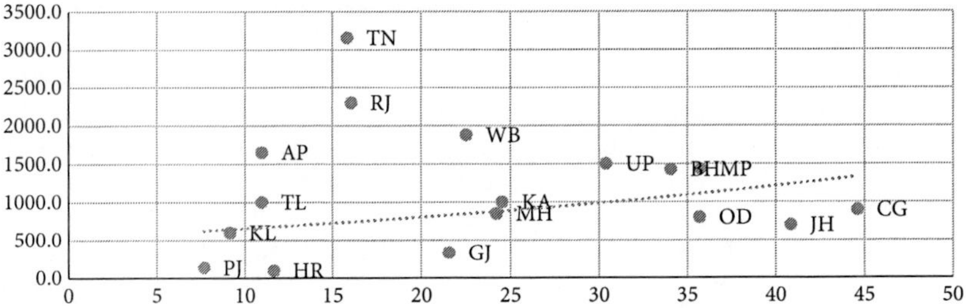

Figure 8.A3.2 Person Days Employed According to Rural Poverty Ratio.

In contrast, Bihar, Chhattisgarh, Jharkhand, and Madhya Pradesh which had the highest rural poverty ratios had much lower person days of employment.

The above result is not surprising as, despite being a demand driven programme, the labour budget is finalized on the basis of factors such as performance of the State in creating employment during the preceding 4 years, the planning process adopted to finalize the labour budget, the initiatives and strategies of the State to improve delivery mechanism, and assessment of the requirement of the State in terms of magnitude and intensity of rural poverty as reflected in the Socio-economic Caste Census (SECC) estimates and frequency of the occurrence of natural calamities. In this list of factors, SECC poverty measure is the only factor that targets the spending on rural poverty. Besides being largely incremental, there is considerable discretion by the Empowered Committee and, consequently, it is not necessarily the States with largest poverty concentration that get the highest MGNREGA grant.

A comparison of originally estimated cost of the programme with the final release of funds under MGNREGA in 2014–2015 shows interesting results. First, although the funding for MGNREGA is claimed to be open ended, the actual release of funds in 2014–2015 for the scheme was lower than the originally estimated expenditures in every State by varying magnitudes (Figure 8.A3.3). This is understandable as the originally estimated cost could include the matching contribution from the States. However, the wide variations in the ratio of original cost estimate to the release shows

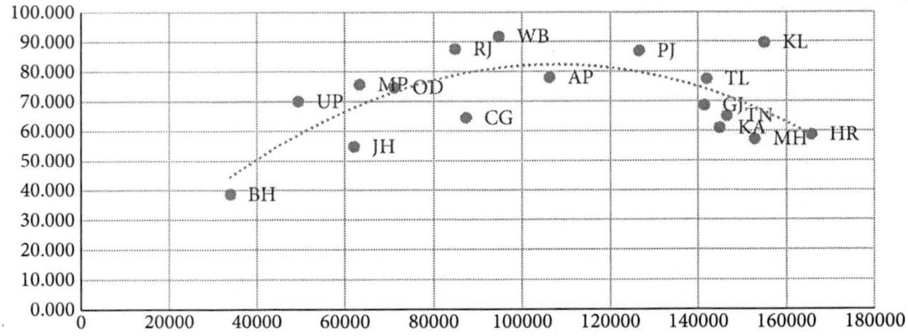

Figure 8.A3.3 Per Cent of Release to Original Cost Estimate.

that there could be a significant difference between originally approved grants and the final grants.

The figure plotting the difference between the original cost estimate and final release of expenditures arranged according to per capita GSDP in the States brings out an interesting pattern (Figure 8.A3.3). The ratio of grant releases by the Centre to the States with very low per capita GSDP is the lowest. The ratio increases as per capita GSDP increases and then declines at very high per capita GSDP levels. The States with low per capita GSDP have the concentration of rural poverty and the programme is much more important to them than more affluent States. At very high income levels where the rural poverty ratio is low, the States themselves may not attach much importance to the programme and utilize the funds.

The important point is that as MGNREGA is a programme of giving wage employment to the poor, it is desirable to design the grant system based on single factor of rural poverty rather than bring in other considerations. If indeed the States do not have the capacity to design the works and implement the programme, the solution lies in developing their capacity through handholding so that the overall objective on providing assured wage employment to the rural poor is met.

One of the reasons for the low ratio of actual release of grants to the original expenditure estimate in the States with low per capita GSDP may be their inability to provide matching contributions. Although MGNREGA is considered as a 'core of the core' programme, the States are required to make a matching contribution of 30 per cent to the Central contribution. The contribution is uniform across the general category States. As suggested in the case of NHM and SSA, it may be desirable to devise a varying system of matching ratios depending on the revenue raising capacities of the States. This would help the States with low per capita GSDP which also are those with high concentration of rural poverty to utilize the grants better.

9

Indian Public Finance in Pandemic Times

The pandemic's mandatory lockdown has set in motion an array of economic, political and global instabilities.

—Dr. Asa Don Brown

9.1. Introduction

The coronavirus pandemic which struck India came as a tragic break to the Indian growth story. Never before in living memory was economic destruction so severe as it was caused by the COVID-19 pandemic. The steady acceleration in economic growth after liberalizing reforms were initiated in 1991 is a well-documented fact. There was a steady acceleration in the growth rate in successive phases from 3.7 per cent during the period 1950–1981 to 7.7 per cent during 2003–2018 (Table 9.1). Achieving double-digit growth was found to be in the feasible realm and exploring the policy paradigm required to achieve this was not found to be unrealistic.[1] The growth, in turn, had a significant impact on reducing poverty as poverty ratios according to the official poverty line declined sharply from 45.7 per cent in 1993–1994 to 22 per cent in 2011–2012 (Panagariya, 2020). Just a few months before the coronavirus pandemic struck, the Prime Minister of India set an aspirational goal of transforming into a five trillion dollar economy target by 2024–2025 from the present level of 2.9 trillion dollars. Of course, the target was too ambitious

[1] Panagariya in his incisive book (2020) devotes as many as eight chapters (out of 13) to discuss specific policy reforms needed to achieve near-double-digit growth trajectory.

Studies in Indian Public Finance. M. Govinda Rao, Oxford University Press. © Oxford University Press 2022.
DOI: 10.1093/oso/9780192849601.003.0009

Table 9.1 Phases of Indian Economic Growth.

Period	Growth in GDP (constant prices)	Growth in per capita GDP (constant prices)
Phase I (1950–1981)	3.7	1.6
Phase II (1981–1988)	4.9	2.8
Phase III (1988–2003)	5.7	3.7
Phase IV (2003–2018)	7.7	6.4

Source: Panagariya (2020).

as it required sustained annual growth of over 9 per cent (or nominal growth at 14 per cent) at the prevailing exchange rate.

In order to achieve the aspirational target, the NITI Aayog had estimated an additional investment of Rs. 108 trillion and 78 per cent of this was supposed to be made by the Union and State governments equally and the remaining 22 per cent was to be from the private sector. This also implied that the capital outlay of the Centre will have to increase from the prevailing 3.5 trillion (2019–2020 RE) to Rs. 10 trillion by 2024–2025 which required significant additional resource mobilization and releasing larger volume of resources for investments by compressing government consumption expenditures, subsidies, and transfers.

Although most observers felt that the target of USD 5 trillion was more aspirational than real, no one had an inkling that even before the ink of these investment projections dried, there would be a catastrophe in the form of COVID-19. The severest lockdown followed when the pandemic struck virtually closed the economy from all business activities and threw the economy into terrible uncertainty. It caused enormous economic destruction and claimed more than 465,000 lives according to official estimates until 18 November 2021. There has been tremendous uncertainty and despite the initiatives taken by the government and the Reserve Bank of India (RBI), the after-effects of the pandemic are likely to manifest in terms of a spate of bankruptcies, loss of employment, increased fragility of the financial system, and tremendous uncertainty for both lives and livelihoods of the people.

By the end of January 2020, it seemed that the pandemic was under control and the economy was well on its way for recovery. The policymakers were self-congratulating for controlling the virus and the Economic Survey declared, 'India has been able to avoid the second wave while ably managing to flatten the epidemiological curve, with its caseload peaking in mid-September'. It went on to state, 'The V-shaped economic recovery is supported by the initiation of a mega vaccination drive with hopes of a robust recovery in the services sector. Together, prospects for robust growth in consumption and investment have been rekindled with the estimated real GDP growth for FY 2021–22 at 11 per cent'. Addressing the World Economic Forum, the Prime Minister had stated, 'Today, India is among countries that have succeeded in saving the maximum lives. The country, which comprises of 18 percent of the world's population, has saved the world from disaster by bringing the situation under control'. Even at the end of March 2020, it was claimed that India is a pharmacy of the world and the Foreign Ministry was working on a plan to supply 160 million doses of COVID-19 vaccines to 60 countries which included 10 million doses in gifts focused on neighbouring countries in the first round.

The economic revival process, well under way until mid-March, was thrown off guard again with the raging second wave of the pandemic. The lethal outbreak of the second wave with its dramatically fast spread put a break on the recovery process. The daily cases in the country jumped from 21,666 on 11 March to 424,443 on 6 May. The outbreak created a dire situation and the lack of medical supplies including oxygen concentrators and ventilators, and limited human resources exposed the underbelly of the poor capacity of the country to deal with the pandemic. It has not taken even a month to see a dramatic change in the mood to one of desperation and despondency. In 2020, we had seen the humanitarian crisis with thousands of migrants with their families walking on in the summer heat from the cities to their villages after the most stringent lockdown for a prolonged period. They were faced with severe uncertainties in the cities without jobs and with hardly any reserves to sustain them. In 2021, there was another type of humanitarian crisis with patients and their family members running from pillar to post in search of hospital beds, ventilators, and oxygen cylinders. Several patients died in constant and unending search for hospital beds and ventilators and gasping for breath for want of oxygen. The situation turned pathetic with scores of dead bodies lined up in ambulances in front of crematoriums and burial grounds and for many, there was no dignity even in death! The unscrupulous took advantage of scarcity situation in misery and death as seen in the large black market for hospital beds, ventilators, oxygen concentrators, and even for the ambulance service and cremation. Even after a year, the complacency reined, and we did not care to create the basic health infrastructure needed because we thought we had won the battle when it was just starting. The sad commentary is that we were always moving from one emergency to another; there was hardly any time to put the healthcare system in the country in place.

The first wave of the pandemic had plunged the economy to almost 7.3 per cent contraction in 2020–2021. But recovery was well under way, and it was hoped that the country would register a double-digit growth in 2021–2022. The official expectation, both from the Government and the RBI, was that the economy will register 10.5 per cent growth in 2021–2022 and the first quarter growth was estimated at 26.2 per cent. However, considering the severity of the second wave, the RBI had to revise the first quarter growth downwards to 18.5 per cent and the overall growth for the year to 9.5 per cent. The CSO has estimated the GDP growth for the first quarter at 20.1 per cent. Most credit rating agencies as well as and multilateral lenders including the IMF and the ADB have made downward revisions in the growth estimate for the year ranging from 9 per cent to 9.5 per cent. Although the new cases have been on the decline since June, the pandemic is still on the rage in some States, and it will take considerable time before some activities like travel and tourism can resume fully.

The adverse economic impact of the pandemic in 2020–2021 was the severest in the living memory. Except agriculture and allied activities, all other sectors suffered contraction by varying degrees. Expectedly, the contraction was the highest in the sector, Trade, Hotels, Transport, Storage and Communication (18.2 per cent) followed by Construction (8.6 per cent), Mining (8.5 per cent) and Manufacturing (7.2 per cent). All the engines of growth have been stuttering. The gross fixed capital formation declined from 34.6 per cent of GDP in the first quarter of 2019–2020 to 24.4 per cent in the first quarter of 2020–2021 and Private final consumer expenditure declined from 56.8 per cent to 55.4 per cent during the same period. The constrained fiscal space did not permit increased government spending on consumption or investment and not surprisingly, public administration and defence and other services showed a negative growth of 4.6 per cent during 2020–2021. With exports too stagnant, there was no engine to lift the growth of the economy.

The pandemic struck at the time when the economy was already slowing down. The estimated GDP growth at 4.2 per cent in 2019–2020 was the lowest in the last 11 years. The quarterly growth trend since 2015–2016 presented in Figure 9.1 shows a steady decline in the growth to reach 3.1 per cent in the fourth quarter of 2019–2020 and this was the lowest in 44 quarters. Even as the economy gradually recovered from the shock of demonetization to record 8 per cent growth in the fourth quarter of 2017–2018, the subsequent periods show a steady decline.

The steady decline in the growth of GDP was the reflection of declining saving and investment in the economy. The aggregate investment as measured by Gross Capital Formation (GCF) as a ratio of GDP (current prices) showed a steady decline from 39 per cent in 2011–2012 to 32.2 per cent in 2018–2019. Of the 6.8 percentage point fall in aggregate GCF, 6.2 points (including valuables) were from households, 1.4 points were from corporates, and 0.3 point was from the public sector (Table 9.2). Thus, the decline was witnessed in all the sectors, though a predominant proportion was by the households. Similarly, over the period 2011–2012 to 2018–2019, the percentage of gross domestic saving to GDP declined by 4.5 percentage points and the entire fall was due to decline in household sector's physical savings.

In fact, in 2019–2020, the ratio of GCF to GDP showed a sharp decline from 32 per cent in the first quarter of 2019–2020 to 28.8 per cent in the last quarter. The private final consumption expenditure was slowing

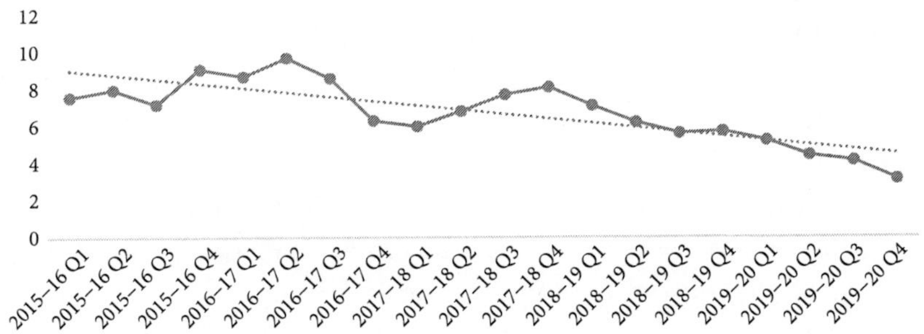

Figure 9.1 Quarterly GDP Growth 2015–2016 to 2018–2020.
Source: Ministry of Statistics and Programme Implementation, Government of India.

Table 9.2 Sectoral Investment Trends (Per cent of GDP at Market Prices).

Year	Households	Valuables	Private corporate	Public	Errors and omissions	Total
2011–2012	15.90	2.90	13.26	7.54	−0.64	38.95
2012–2013	14.73	2.75	13.63	7.23	0.34	38.69
2013–2014	12.61	1.44	12.90	7.08	−0.25	33.78
2014–2015	12.14	1.68	13.36	7.09	−0.74	33.52
2015–2016	9.57	1.48	13.49	7.58	0.00	32.11
2016–2017	10.36	1.09	11.57	7.16	1.78	31.95
2017–2018	11.19	1.28	11.48	6.87	3.39	34.21
2018–2019	11.50	1.06	11.91	7.24	0.50	32.20
2011–2012 minus 2018–2019 (% points)	4.41	1.84	1.35	0.30	−1.14	6.75

Source: Rangarajan and Srivastava (2020).

down, and exports were declining. The only engine of growth that kept the growth rate ticking was the Government consumption expenditure, and with significant contraction in revenues and the reluctance of the government to expand fiscal deficit, even that is likely to be a casualty.

9.2. The Lockdown, Economic Contraction, and Fiscal Impact

The lockdown brought the economy to a grinding halt and the contraction in the economy drained the tax revenues. Even after the relaxations of many restrictions, with continued spread of the pandemic, full-fledged recovery has not been possible because of continued restrictions on many sectors requiring social distancing. The fast spread of the virus has made it imperative to impose restrictions on economic activities by varying degrees by the States. Besides, supply chain disruptions (partly due to restrictions on the imports from China) and unavailability of skilled migrant labour have continued to constrain full-scale recovery. The RBI was quick in announcing a slew of measures immediately when the first wave broke out mainly to ease supply side constraints in terms of ensuring liquidity, regulatory forbearance, and moratorium and initiate some additional measures to advance loans and extend regulatory forbearance during the second wave as well. However, the fiscal stimulus by the government has been tepid, less than 1.5 per cent of GDP in the first phase and less than 1 per cent during the second. The most important measure by the government has been the distribution of free foodgrains to the vulnerable sections and this has avoided starvation deaths. The fiscal measures announced include additional allocation to Mahatma Gandhi National Rural Employment Guarantee Rs. 400 billion, front loading the Kisan Samman Nidhi which was already in the budget and providing 2 per cent of GDP additional borrowing space to the State governments.

While the situation demanded that the Government should have provided substantial demand stimulus by increasing expenditures, the lack of fiscal space limited the expansion. The budget presented by the Finance Minister on 1 February 2021 showed that, in 2020–2021, the shortfall in tax revenue to the Centre in the revised estimate from the budget estimate was Rs. 2.91 trillion and from non-tax revenue, Rs. 1.74 trillion. Of the estimated disinvestment proceeds of Rs. 2.1 trillion, only Rs. 320 billion could be realized. Thus, there was a large shortfall of Rs. 5.43 trillion in revenue and non-debt capital receipts from the budget estimate. On the expenditure side, however, although in the initial months, government adopted an austere approach, after October, public spending had gathered pace. The revised estimate of expenditure presented in the budget for 2020–2021 showed an increase of Rs. 7.64 trillion (28.4 per cent) over the actuals of 2019–2020 and Rs. 4.08 trillion (13.4 per cent) over the budget estimate for the year. While the revenue expenditure was estimated to increase by 28.1 per cent over the previous year, the increase in capital expenditure was estimated at 30.8 per cent. Not surprisingly, the fiscal deficit for the year was estimated at 9.5 per cent and the primary deficit at 5.5 per cent. Although a substantial part of the off-budget liabilities arising from the NSSF loans to the Food Corporation of India have been included in the budget, when the remaining part is added, the fiscal deficit works out to 10.1 per cent.

Looking forward, the Union budget predicates that the economy will register a nominal growth of 14 per cent and the fiscal deficit for 2021–2022 is estimated at 6.8 per cent and revenue receipt is estimated to increase by 15 per cent over the revised estimate of the current year. In addition, the disinvestment proceeds are estimated at Rs. 1.85 trillion. However, aggregate expenditure is budget to increase by less than 1 per cent and the revenue expenditure is budgeted to contract by 2.7 per cent although capital expenditure is budgeted to increase by 26.2 per cent. The fiscal deficit for 2021–2022 is estimated at 6.8 per cent and the primary deficit at 3.1 per cent.

During the first quarter of the current fiscal, the government has been careful and has limited the fiscal deficit at 18.2 per cent of the budgeted mainly due to rebounding revenues and lower expenditures. The impact of the second wave on revenues is likely to be felt in the second quarter and with additional expenditure needed for vaccination, the pressure is likely to build up. Nevertheless, considering the constrained demand situation, it would be prudent for the government to front load capital expenditures even if it may breach the budgeted estimate of deficits to some extent.

In the case of the States, the aggregate deficit will depend on the permission given to them to borrow. Although their FRBM allows them to borrow up to 3 per cent of their respective GSDP, the aggregate fiscal deficit of the States has been around 2.3 to 2.5 per cent of GDP in recent years. In 2020–2021, however, with severe contraction in both their own revenues and tax devolution from the Centre, they are likely to use their entire fiscal space. In addition, as a part of the stimulus, the Centre has allowed them to borrow an additional 2 per cent of GDP. Their borrowing from 3 per cent of GDP to 3.5 per cent is without any conditions. However, additional 1 per cent of GDP borrowing will be permitted only on fulfilling four reform conditions, each giving additional quarter per cent. The reforms to be undertaken are (a) one nation, one ration card which requires linking Aadhaar number into ration cards and installing point of sale machines in all fair price shops; (b) improvement in ease of doing business which requires (i) district level assessment of ease of doing business as Department of Promotion for Industry and Internal Trade norms, (ii) automatic renewal of State industrial, commercial licenses to business, and (iii) making randomized inspections with prior notice and full transparency; (c) power sector reforms which entail reducing aggregate technical and commercial (AT&C) losses, direct benefit transfers to farmers instead of lower tariffs and reducing the gap between average cost and average revenues; and (d) urban local body reforms requiring the States to notify property tax floor rates according to circle property values and notify water and sewer charges. If at least three of the four reform conditions are satisfied, the States can borrow the remaining half a per cent of GDP.

There are questions on whether the Centre should have imposed conditions for borrowing at a time the States are faced with severe fiscal distress. Of course, Article 293 (4) states that 'A consent under clause (3) may be granted subject to such conditions, if any, as the Government of India may think fit to impose'. It must also be admitted that the four reform conditions are important. However, this is for the first time in the history of the country that conditions have been stipulated for market borrowing by the States. In fact, the 15th Finance Commission was asked in its TOR to make recommendation on the conditions that the Government of India may impose on the States while providing consent under Article 293 (3) of the Constitution and the Commission recommended that the conditions can be imposed. Perhaps, instead of imposing conditions when the States are facing a fiscal distress situation, the Government of India could have had discussions with them and found appropriate ways to implement the reforms. In any case, the States do not have much choice, and even if some States avoid undertaking power sector reforms for political reasons, the aggregate borrowing of the States is likely to be about 4.5 per cent of GDP.

The above discussion leads us to make important inferences on the fiscal consequences caused by the COVID-19 crisis. First, the combined fiscal deficit of the Centre and States is likely to be about 14 per cent of GDP and the corresponding debt is likely to be about 90 per cent of GDP. However, household sector saving is expected to be higher due to the precautionary motive and forced demand compression due to the restrictions. Besides, as the commercial lending by the banks has continued to be subdued, there is no immediate fear of financial crowding out of private investments. However, there has been a surge in foreign portfolio investment requiring the RBI to purchase foreign exchange to manage the exchange rate and this has added substantially to the liquidity in the economy. This requires careful monitoring of the price situation.

9.3. Need to Fast-Track Reforms

Crisis is good opportunity to initiate reforms and the Government should not waste this crisis by not undertaking them. Structural reforms are needed not only to revive the economy but also to take it to the trajectory of higher growth. In the short term, the government will have to substantially increase public spending even in the resource-constrained situation prevailing at present. Faced with hard budget constraints, some of the State governments have embarked on an ambitious programme of monetizing residential and commercial land in urban centres and selling of leased land to the lessees to shore up their finances. Hopefully, they will start correcting the historical mistake of not spending adequately on public health, particularly on preventative healthcare by strengthening the wellness centres. A strong system of wellness centres will minimize curative healthcare through hospitalization. The pandemic has clearly brought home the importance of public spending on healthcare.

As mentioned earlier, the sharp decline in revenue collection following the GDP contraction is likely to increase the aggregate fiscal deficit to 14 per cent of GDP. Nevertheless, with the economy estimated to contract by 7.3 per cent in 2020–2021, there was considerable expectation of significant reform signals in the budget not only to revive the economy from the adverse impact of the pandemic but also to address the structural problems responsible for the retrogression in the economy. The Economic Survey has estimated the GDP growth for 2021–2022 at 11 per cent mainly on the back of 7.3 per cent contraction in 2020–2021. The Survey estimates that if the economy grows at 6.5 per cent in 2022–2023, it will still be only about 90 per cent of the trend level of output in 2023–2024. As mentioned earlier, most other agencies that had estimated a double digit growth for 2021–2022 have revised the estimate downwards due to the restrictions on economic activities necessitated by the second wave.

Unfortunately, the past profligacy does not permit the government to undertake countercyclical fiscal policy to any significant extent. The budget presented in 2020–2021 had become unrealistic even before the pandemic as the fiscal deficit projected at the pre-actual estimate compiled by the Controller General of Accounts showed substantial deviation of revenues, expenditures, and deficits from the budget estimate. The severe lockdown following the COVID-19 pandemic from 2020 made it completely irrelevant. The lockdown caused severe contraction in tax revenues and expenditures had to be increased initially to save the lives and livelihoods of the people. The Government was conservative in the initial months and compressed expenditures. Not surprisingly, the estimate of GDP from public administration, defence, and other services showed a contraction of 6.4 per cent in the first half of the year indicating the procyclical stance taken in public spending.

The Fifteenth Finance Commission has recommended the road map for fiscal consolidation to reduce total outstanding liabilities of the Government should reduce the liabilities from 62.9 per cent of GDP to 56.6 per cent and the States are required to marginally reduce the level from 31.1 per cent to 30.5 per cent. To achieve this, the Commission has recommended the road map where the fiscal deficit of the Union government should be reduced from the Commission's estimate of 7.4 per cent in 2020–2021 to 4 per cent in 2025–2026 and the States are required to reduce the fiscal deficit from 4.2 per cent in 2020–2021 to 3 per cent in 2023–2024 and maintain that level thereafter. In its Explanatory Memorandum, the government has stated that it accepts the recommendations relating to the borrowing ceilings of the States and stated that other recommendations (including those relating to the Central roadmap) would be examined separately. In the budget speech, the Finance Minister has also indicated that fiscal deficit will be reduced to 4.5 per cent by 2025–2026 which is in variance with the road map set by the Finance Commission.

The Central government has initiated reforms in a number of areas and that should help to improve the economic environment in the medium and long term. Merging of 24 Central labour laws into four codes is an important reform to impart greater flexibility to the labour market and ending the inspector raj. This has been talked about for long without much progress. The Industrial Relations Code allows the manufacturing units up to 300 workers to hire and fire without the Government's approval and for those with more than 300 workers, approval is needed but if the labour department does not respond within the time frame, the approval is deemed to have been received. The three new legislations enacted in the farm sector was supposed to provide flexibility to the farmers to sell their products anywhere. The amended Essential Commodities Act deregulates production, storage, supply, and distribution of cereals, pulses, potato, onion, and oilseeds and enables the private sector to play an important role in these activities. The Farmers' (empowerment and protection) Agreement of Price Assurance and Farm Services Act allows the small farmers to enter into agreement with corporates for contract farming. However, under pressure from farmers' unions and due to electoral compulsion, the Prime Minister has announced that the reform will be reversed and the three acts will be repealed.

Two recent books painted a grim picture of the Indian banking system and chinks in its regulation (Acharya, 2020; Patel, 2020). The problems confronting the financial system in general and banks in particular are systemic. Acharya (2020) has persuasively argued that fiscal dominance has adversely impacted financial stability in a variety of ways and Patel (2020) has alluded to the constraints in regulation due to government's ownership of banks. The balance sheets of the banks continue to be stressed. In addition, the fear of investigation agencies on lending decisions had turned the public sector bankers to be risk averse. The Non-banking financial company (NBFC) crisis beginning with the failure of IL&FS and followed by DHFL, Reliance Capital, and Altico deepened the malice. These developments have adversely impacted on corporates, infrastructure financing, and liquidity availability for the small and medium enterprises. The NBFCs crisis worsened the stressed balance sheets of the banks further.

The most important factor the government must address is the issue of governance in public sector banks. Although the Financial Stability Report shows easing of the NPA situation and many of the public sector banks have turned around in terms of their profitability, the commercial lending is still tepid. We have a peculiar situation where the corporates are deleveraging and moving on a slow lane in borrowing and the banks are unwilling to lend. This shows that new investments are not taking place at the level required. The decision to privatize two public sector banks is important and it is hoped that this will change the culture of banking, but it is important to initiate reforms in the governance in public sector banks on the lines recommended by the P. J. Nayak committee.

The Insolvency and Bankruptcy Code (IBC) has been hailed as a landmark reform, but there have been problems in implementation. The two important problems plaguing the system are the enormous delays in resolution and huge haircuts the lenders take. It is important to ensure that the insolvency resolution process is timely, effective, and reasonable. The delays are caused by the promoters succeeding in gaming the system and acute capacity constraint of the resolution professionals to manage the National Company Law Tribunals. There have been enormous delays in the admission of the application under the resolution process itself. The immediate need is to strengthen the information utility (IU) system under the IBC which in fact was conceptualized to ensure faster admission. The delays have also resulted in low recoveries and the lenders taking very high losses.

Another important reform in the budget is the ambitious programme of privatization and strategic disinvestment. The budget has promised to privatize a number of public sector companies including Air India, Container Corporation of India, Shipping Corporation of India, Bharat Earth Movers Limited, Bharat Petroleum and Chemicals Corporation, and the IDBI Bank. It has also stated that two more public sector banks will be privatized. In respect of other public sector companies, NITI Aayog has been asked to work out more companies for strategic disinvestment. Privatization of Air India is perhaps, the most important decision and this provides a clear signal in the intent of the government. The press reports indicate that the disinvestment of LIC and privatization fo two commercial banks could be done during this fiscal year. It remains to be seen how these will be implemented to free the government from the shackles of activities which are truly in the domain of the private sector and the interventions.

Since 2017, the government has slipped into the protectionist mode although the history of this country clearly shows that this would be self-defeating. The 'Atmanirbhar Bharat' will not help the country to achieve competitiveness but will only add to the protectionist stance. The announcement of reducing the list of exemptions in tariff list in October will only add to protectionism. Myopic view of giving protection and subsidizing some sectors through PLIs is like creating scaffolding rather than building walls and it is important to shun such an approach and having seen its devastating impact on competitiveness and economic growth.

9.4. Concluding Remarks

The government has initiated a number of reforms in earnest, particularly to infuse flexibility to land and labour markets, regulatory systems in education and healthcare, and has made additional borrowing to the States conditional on undertaking power sector reforms and property tax reforms and improving the ease of doing business. A notable development is the decision of the government to do away with retrospective taxation and the willingness to settle the past disputes invoking the provision. This will provide predictability to the tax system and also signal that the government intends to attract foreign investment in the country. However, implementation of these reforms holds the key for their effectiveness. There is considerable urgency in the reform of the banking sector to ensure smoother credit flow to productive sectors. The moratorium and restructuring done during the pandemic is likely to subject the banks to severe stress as revealed by the stress test conducted by the RBI in its financial stability report. It is important to fast-track the privatization programme and use the proceeds to provide the much needed investment in infrastructure. Also, reforms in sectors like police and judiciary are overdue for the basic incentive for investment decisions is to protect the life and property of people and enforce contracts to improve the ease of doing business in the country.

One of the areas which requires immediate action is to reverse the protectionist stance the government has increasingly been adopting during the last 4 years. There have been across the board increases in important duties and non-tariff barriers. The decision not to join the Regional Comprehensive Economic Partnership (RCEP), a 15-member free-trade block of ASEAN countries along with China, Australia, and New Zealand, is retrograde. There are signs of the country going back to the import-substitution regime that existed prior to 1991 despite bipartisan efforts to dismantle protection since then. Experience has shown that the policy of important substation hurts the competitive strength of the country.

The most important reform needed in the country today is judicial reforms to ensure that the basic duty of the State of ensuring property rights and enforcing contracts effectively in a timely manner is accomplished and that is the most important factor in the ease of doing business. The last 3 years have seen a steady creeping of protectionist stance in the government and the pandemic and the stand-off with China has raised the pitch for more protection. This is self-defeating as the history in this country has shown. Denying the benefit of goods at international prices to the consumers to protect the producers has only helped them not to be competitive and ask for more protection. Hope the government will reverse the trend quickly and make the economy export oriented.

The time is opportune to initiate structural reforms in a number of areas which would help the economy to move towards higher growth potential. The Insolvency and Bankruptcy Code enacted is a great reform, but the implementation is stuck for several reasons and they need to be removed to hasten the resolution process. It is also important to reverse the protectionist tendency that has crept into the policy regime in the last 3 years to impart greater competitiveness. There are still large infrastructure gaps that need to be bridged and substantial investments are required to be made. One of the most important and urgent call should be on judicial reforms. Protecting life and property of the people and enforcement of contracts is the basic public good that the government must provide. Long judicial delays result in most people being denied justice and the powerful sections resorting to informal and illegal means to secure justice. Incentive to invest and grow depends on ensuring speedy and efficient resolution of the disputes.

References

Acharya, Viral. (2020), *A Quest for Restoring Financial Stability*, New Delhi: Sage Publications.

Acharya, Viral and Raghuram Rajan. (2020), 'Indian Banks: A Time to Reform?' (Mimeographed). http://pages.stern.nyu.edu/~sternfin/vacharya/public_html/pdfs/indian-banks-reform.pdf.

Acosta-Ormaechea, Santiago and Atsuyoshi Morozumi. (2019), 'The Value Added Tax and Growth: Design Matters', IMF Working Paper No. 19/196, Washington, DC: International Monetary Fund.

Adhia, Hasmukh. (2019), 'How the States Are Doing Post GST?', *Business Standard*, September 6. https://www.business-standard.com/article/opinion/how-the-states-are-doing-post-gst-119090501480_1.html.

Ahmad, Ehtisham. (1997), 'Intergovernmental Transfers: An International Perspective', in Ehtisham Ahmad (Ed), *Financing Decentralized Expenditures*, Cheltenham, UK: Edward Elgar, pp. 1–17.

Ahmad, Ehrisham and Nicholas Stern. (2011), 'Effective Carbon Taxes and Public Policy Options', in M. Govinda Rao and Mihir Rakshit (Eds), *Public Economics: Theory and Policy*, New Delhi: Sage Publications, pp. 163–79.

Alesina, A. and G. Tabelini. (1990), 'A Positive Theory of Fiscal Deficits and Government Debt', *Review of Economic Studies*, vol. 57, pp. 403–14.

Arora, B. and D. Verney. (1995), *Multiple Identities in a Single State: Indian Federalism in Comparative Perspective*, New Delhi: Konarak Publishers.

Auerbach, Alan J. (2008), 'The Choice between Income and Consumption Taxes: A Primer', in Alan J. Auerbach and A. D. Shaviro (Eds), *Institutional Foundations of Public Finance: Economic and Legal Perspectives*, Cambridge, MA: Harvard University Press, pp. 13–46.

Auerbach, Alan J., Michale P. Devereux, and Helen Simpson. (2010), 'Taxing Corporate Income', National Bureau of Economic Research; Working Paper 14494. http://www.nber.org/papers/w14494.

Bagchi, Amaresh. (2000), 'Rethinking Federalism', *Economic and Political Weekly*, vol. XXXV, No. 17 (August 19), pp. 3025–35.

Bagchi, Amaresh, Richard M. Bird, and Arindam Das-Gupta. (1995), *An Economic Approach to Tax Administration Reform*, Toronto, Canada: University of Toronto, International Centre for Tax Studies.

Bagchi, Amaresh and Pulin Nayak, (1994), 'A Survey of Public Finance and the Planning Process', in Amaresh Bagchi and Nicholas Stern (Eds), *Tax Policy and Planning in Developing Countries*, New Delhi: Oxford University Press.

Bahl, Roy W. (2002), 'Implementation Rules for Fiscal Decentralization', in M. Govinda Rao (Ed), *Development, Poverty and Fiscal Policy*, New Delhi: Oxford University Press, pp. 253–77.

Bardhan, Pranab and Dilip Mookherjee. (2000), 'Relative Capture of Government at National and Local Level', *American Economic Review*, vol. 90, No. 2, pp. 135–39.

Besley, T. and S. Coate. (2003), 'Centralized versus Decentralized Provision of Public Goods: A Political Economy Approach', *Journal of Public Economics*, vol. 87, pp. 2611–37.

Bhaskar, V. (2019), 'GST Revenue Conceals More Than It Reveals', *Business Standard*, March 6. https://www.business-standard.com/article/opinion/gst-revenue-conceals-more-than-it-reveals-119030600040_1.html.

Bird, Richard M. (2000), 'Fiscal Decentralization and Competitive Governments', in Gianluigi Galeotti, Pierre Salmon, and Ronald Wintrobe (Eds), *Competition and Structure: The Political Economy of Collective Decisions* (Essays in Honor of Albert Breton), Cambridge, UK: Cambridge University Press, pp. 129–48.

Bird, Richard M. (2004), 'Administrative Dimensions of Tax Reform', *Asia-Pacific Tax Bulletin*, vol. 10, No. 3, pp. 134–50.

Bird, Richard. (2012), 'The GST/HST: Creating an Integrated Sales Tax in a Federal Country', *The School of Public Policy Research Papers*, vol. 5, No. 2 (March), pp. 1–35.

Bird, Richard and Enid Slack. (2007), 'An Approach to Metropolitan Governance and Finance', *Environment and Planning C: Government and Policy*, vol. 29, pp. 729–55.

Bird, Richard M. and Eric Zolt. (2005), 'Redistribution via Taxation: The Limited Role of the Personal Income Tax in Developing Countries', *UCLA Law Review*, vol. 52, No. 6, pp. 1627–95.

Bird, Richard M. and Eric Zolt. (2008), 'Tax Policy in Emerging Countries', *Environment and Planning C: Government and Policy*, vol. 26, No. 1, pp. 73–86.

Bird, Richard M. and François Vaillancourt. (1998), 'Fiscal decentralization in Developing Countries: An Overview', in Richard M. Bird and François Vaillancourt (Eds), *Fiscal Decentralization in Developing Countries*, Cambridge: Cambridge University Press, pp. 1–48.

Bird, Richard and Michael Smart. (2009), 'Assigning State Taxes in a Federal Country: The Case of Australia'. https://papers.ssrn.com/sol3/papers.cfm?abstract_id=1435520.

Bird, Richard M. and Pierre-Pascal Gendron. (2007), *The VAT in Developing and Transitional Countries*, Cambridge, UK: Cambridge University Press.

Boadway, R. W. and Frank Flatters. (1982), *Equalization in a Federal State: An Economic Analysis*, Economic Council of Canada, Ottawa: Canadian Government Publishing Centre.

Bradford, David F. and Wallace E. Oates. (1974), 'Suburban Exploitation of Central Cities and Government Structure', in Harold Hochman and George Peterson (Eds), *Redistribution through Public Choice*, New York: Columbia University Press, pp. 43–90.

Brennan, Geoffrey and James Buchanan. (1980), *The Power to Tax: Analytical Foundations of a Fiscal Constitution*, Cambridge, UK: Cambridge University Press.

Breton, Albert. (1965), 'A Theory of Government Grants', *Canadian Journal of Economics and Political Science*, vol. 31, No. 2, pp. 175–87.

Breton, Albert. (1981), 'Federalism versus Centralism in Regional Growth', in *Public Finance and Economic Growth: Proceedings of the 37th Congress of the International*

Institute of Public Finance, Tokyo, Detroit, Michigan: Wayne State University Press, pp. 252–63.

Breton, Albert. (1987), 'Towards a Theory of Competitive Federalism', *European Journal of Political Economy*, vol. 2, Nos. 1–2, pp. 263–329.

Breton, Albert. (1996), *Competitive Governments*, Cambridge, UK: Cambridge University Press.

Breton, Albert. (2000), '"Federalism and Decentralization": Ownership Rights and the Superiority of Federalism', *Publius: The Journal of Federalism*, vol. 30, No. 2, pp. 1–15.

Breton, Albert. (2002), 'An Introduction to Decentralization Failure', in Ehtisham Ahamad and Georgio Brosio (Eds), *Managing Fiscal Decentralization*, New York and London: Routledge, pp. 31–45.

Breton, Albert. (2006), 'Modeling Vertical Competition', in Ehtisham Ahmad and Georgio Brosio (Eds), *Handbook in Fiscal Federalism*, Cheltenham, UK: Edward Elgar, pp. 86–105.

Buchanan, J. M. (1950), 'Federalism and Fiscal Equity', *American Economic Review*, vol. 40, No. 4 (September), pp. 421–32.

Buchanan, James. (1958), *Public Principles of Public Debt*, Homewood, IL: Richard D. Irwin.

Buchanan, James M. and Richard A. Musgrave. (1999), *Public Finance and Public Choice: Two Contrasting Views of the State*, Cambridge, MA: MIT Press.

Buiter, Willem and Urjit Patel. (1994), 'Debt, Deficits and Inflation: An Application to the Public Finance in India', in Amaresh Bagchi and Nichalas Stern (Eds), *Tax Policy and Planning in Developing Countries*, New Delhi: Oxford University Press.

Buiter, Willem and Urjit Patel. (2006), 'Deficits, the Financial Sector, and Growth', *India Policy Forum*, pp. 1–55.

Chakraborty, Pinaki and Manish Gupta. (2016), 'Evolving Centre-State Relations: Role of the New Framework for Grants', *Economic and Political Weekly*, vol. 51, No. 16, pp. 43–6.

Chelliah, Raja. (1991), 'Towards a Decentralized Polity', L. K. Jha Memorial Lecture, New Delhi: Fiscal Research Foundation.

Chelliah, Raja J. and Ram N. Lal. (1978), *Incidence of Indirect Taxation in India*, New Delhi: National Institute of Public Finance and Policy.

Choi, K. (1990), 'Value-Added Taxation: Experiences and Lessons of Korea', in R. M. Bird and O. Oldman (Eds), *Taxation in Developing Countries*, Baltimore: Johns Hopkins University Press, pp. 269–87.

Cnossen, Sijbern. (2010), 'VAT Coordination in Common Markets and Federations: Lessons from the European Experience', *Tax Law Review*, vol. 63, pp. 584–603.

Coase, Ronald. (1960), 'The Problem of Social Cost', *Journal of Law and Economics*, vol. 3, pp. 1–44.

Cyan, Musharraf, Jorge Martinez-Vazquez, and Violeta Vulovicr. (2013), 'Measuring Tax Effort: Does the Estimation Approach Matter and Should Effort Be Linked to Expenditure Goals?', International Center for Public Policy Working Paper Series 39. https://scholarworks.gsu.edu/icepp/39/.

Das-Gupta, Arindam and Dilip Mookherjee. (1998), *Incentives and Institutional Reform in Tax Enforcement*, New Delhi: Oxford University Press.

Domar, Evsey D. (1944). 'The Burden of Debt and National Income', *American Economic Review*, vol. 34, No. 4, pp. 798–827.

Elster, J. (1994), 'The Impact oof Constitutions on Economic Performance', *World Bank Economic Review*, vol. 8, Issue Supplement 1, pp. 209–26.

Emran, M. Shahe and Joseph E. Stiglitz. (2005), 'On Selective Indirect Reform in Developing Countries', *Journal of Public Economics*, vol. 89, No. 4, pp. 599–623.

Engel, Eduardo M. R. A., Alexander Galetovic, and Claudio E. Raddatz. (1999), 'Taxes and Income Distribution in Chile: Dome Unpleasant Redistributive Arithmetic', *Journal of Development Studies*, vol. 59, No. 1, pp. 155–92.

Feldstein, Martin S. (1975), 'Wealth Neutrality and Local Choice in Public Education', *American Economic Review*, vol. 65, pp. 75–89.

Feldstein, Martin. (1995), 'The Effect of Marginal Tax Rates on Taxable Income: A Panel Study of the 1986 Tax Reform Act', *Journal of Political Economy*, vol. 103, No. 3, pp. 551–72.

Feldstein, Martin. (2004), 'Budget Deficits and National Debt', L. K. Jha Memorial Lecture, Mumbai: Reserve Bank of India.

Gordon, Roger. (2011), 'Commentary on Tax Design: The Mirrlees Review', *Fiscal Studies*, vol. 32, No. 3, pp. 395–414.

Gramlich, Edward. (1977), 'Intergovernmental Grants: A Review of Empirical Literature', in Wallace E. Oates (Ed), *The Political Economy of Fiscal Federalism*, Lexington, MA: Heath–Lexington Books, pp. 219–39.

Hagemann, Robert. (2011), 'How Can Fiscal Councils Strengthen Fiscal Performance?', *OECD Journal: Economic Studies*, vol. 1, pp. 75–98.

Hahn, Frank. (1973), 'On Optimum Taxation', *Journal of Economic Theory*, vol. 6, No. 1, pp. 96–106.

Harberger, Arnold C. (1962), 'Incidence of Corporation Tax', *Journal of Political Economy*, vol. LXX, No. 3, pp. 215–40.

Harberger Arnold C. (1990), 'Principles of Taxation Applied to Developing Countries: What Have We Learned?', in Michael Boskin and Charles E. McLure, Jr. (Eds), *World Tax Reform: Case Studies of Developed and Developing Countries*, San Francisco, CA: ICS Press, pp. 25–46.

Harberger, Arnold C. (2003), 'Reflections on Distributional Considerations and the Public Finances', Paper prepared for a course on 'Practical Issues of Tax Policy in Developing Countries, The World Bank'. http://www.econ.ucla.edu/harberger/ah-reflections.pdf.

Hayek, F. A. ([1944] 2007), *The Road to Serfdom, The Definitive Edition*, Bruce Caldwell (Ed), Chicago: The University of Chicago Press.

IMF. (2011), 'Revenue Mobilization in Developing Countries', Fiscal Affairs Department, International Monetary Fund Policy Paper. https://www.imf.org/external/np/pp/eng/2011/030811.pdf.

IMF. (2013), 'The Functions and Impact of Fiscal Councils', Washington, DC: International Monetary Fund. https://www.imf.org/external/np/pp/eng/2013/071613.pdf.

Independent Commission for the Reform of International Corporate Taxation. (2018), 'A Roadmap to Improve Rules for Taxing Multinationals: A Fairer Future Global Taxation', High Level Declaration of Independent Commission for the Reform of International Corporate Taxation. http://www.dbriefsap.com/bytes/

Feb2018_3.IndependentCommissionforReformofInternationalCorporateTaxreport.pdf.

India. (1966), 'Report of the National Education Commission' (Chairman: D. S. Kothari), Government of India.

India. (1968), 'Report of the Administrate Reforms Commission', Government of India.

India. (1997), 'Report of the Committee of State Education Ministers on Implications of the Proposal to Make Elementary Education a Fundamental Right' (Chairman: Muhi Ram Saikia), New Delhi: Ministry of Human Resource Development.

India. (2001), 'Report of the Expert Group on Taxation of Services' (Chairman: M. Govinda Rao), Ministry of Finance, Government of India.

India. (2003), 'Report of the Task Force on Indirect Taxes' (Chairman: Vijay Kelkar), Ministry of Finance, Government of India.

India. (2009), 'Report of the 13th Finance Commission', Ministry of Finance, Government of India.

India. (2011a), Report of the High Level Expert Group Report on Universal Health Coverage in India', (Chairman: Srinath Reddy), Planning Commission, Government of India.

India. (2011b), 'Report of the High Level Committee on Efficient Management of Public Expenditures', Planning Commission, Government of India.

India. (2014), 'Tax Administration Reform in India Spirit, Purpose and Empowerment', First Report of the Tax Administration Reforms Commission. http://www.nadt.gov.in/writereaddata/MenuContentImages/First_report_TARC635480254365343004.pdf.

India. (2015a), 'Report on the Revenue Neutral Rate and Structure of Rates for the Goods and Services Tax (GST)' (Chairman: Arvind Subramanian). Ministry of Finance, Government of India.

India. (2015b), 'Report of the Tax Administration Reforms Commission'. Ministry of Finance, Government of India.

India. (2017), 'Report of the Comptroller and Auditor General of India for the Year Ended March 2017'. https://cag.gov.in/sites/default/files/audit_report_files/Report_No.40_of_2017_-_Compliance_Audit_on_Department_of_Revenue_%E2%80%93_Direct_Taxes_Union_Government.pdf.

India. (2019), 'Report No. 11 of 2019: Compliance Audit—Department of Revenue: Goods and Services Tax, Comptroller and Auditor General', Government of India. file:///C:/Users/mgrao/OneDrive/GST/Report_No_11_of_2019_Compliance_Audit_of_Union_Government_Department_of_Revenue_Indirect_Taxes_Goods_and_Services_Tax.pdf.

Inman, Robert P. (1988), 'Fiscal Assistance Local services in the United States: The Evolution of a New Federalist Fiscal Order', in H. Rosen (Ed), *Fiscal Federalism*, Chicago: University of Chicago Press, pp. 33–74.

Inman, Robert P. and Daniel Rubinfeld. (1997a), 'Rethinking Federalism', *Journal of Economic Perspectives*, vol. 11, pp. 43–64.

Inman, Robert P. and D. Rubinfeld. (1997b), 'Political Economy of Federalism', in Dennis Mueller (Ed), *Perspectives in Public Choice: A Handbook*, Cambridge, UK: Cambridge University Press, pp. 73–105.

Jenkins, Glenn P., Hatice P. Jenkins, and Chun Yan Kuo. (2006), *Is the VAT Naturally Progressive?*, Kingston: Queen's Economics Department Working Paper No. 1059, Queen's University. https://ideas.repec.org/p/qed/wpaper/1059.html.

Johnson, Paul and Gareth Myles. (2011), 'The Mirrlees Review', *The Journal of Applied Public Economics*, vol. 32, No. 3, pp. 319–29.

Keen, Michael. (2007), 'VAT Attacks', *International Tax and Public Finance*, vol. 14, No. 4, pp. 365–81.

Keen, Michael. (2009), 'What Do (and Don't) We Know About the Value Added Tax?', *Journal of Economic Literature*, vol. 47, No. 1, pp. 157–70.

Keen, Michael. (2013), 'Targeting, Cascading and Indirect Tax Design', IMF Staff Paper: 13/57, Washington, DC: International Monetary Fund.

Keen, Michael and Ben Lockwood. (2010), 'The Value Added Tax: Its Causes and Consequences', *Journal of Development Economics*, vol. 92, pp. 138–51.

Keen, Michael and Jenny E. Lingthart. (2002), 'Coordinating Tariff Reduction and Domestic Tax Reform Under Imperfect Competition', *Journal of International Economics*, vol. 13, No. 2, pp. 385–90.

Keen, Michael and Jack Mintz. (2004), 'The Optimal Threshold for a Value-Added Tax', *Journal of Public Economics*, vol. 88, No. 3/4, pp. 559–76.

Keynes, John Maynard. (1936), *The General Theory of Employment, Interest and Money*, London: Palgrave Macmillan.

Kingdom, Geeta Gandhi and Arvind Panagariya. (2020), 'Heart of the problem: NEP 2020 Charts New Roadmap, but Fails to Make Public School Teachers Accountable'. https://timesofindia.indiatimes.com/blogs/toi-edit-page/heart-of-the-problem-nep-2020-charts-new-road-map-but-fails-to-make-public-schoolteachers-accountable/.

Kopitz, George. (2011), 'Independent Fiscal Institutions: Developing Good Practices', *OECD Journal of Budgeting*, vol. 2011/3.

Krever, Richard. (2014), 'Combating VAT Fraud: Lessons from Korea?' *British Tax Review*, vol. 2014. No. 3, pp. 303–15.

Kumar, M. S. and Teresa Ter-Minassian. (2007), *Promoting Fiscal Discipline*, Washington, DC: International Monetary Fund.

Langford, Ben and Tim Oldenburg. (2016), 'Tax Revenue Potential and Effort: An Empirical Investigation', Working Paper S-43202-UGA-I, London: International Growth Centre.

Le, Tuan Minh, Moreno-Dodson, Blanca, and Bayraktar, Nihal. (2012), 'Taxable Capacity and Tax Effort: Extended Cross-Country Analysis for 1994 to 2009', Policy Research Working Paper, No. 6252, Washington, DC: World Bank.

Levaggi, R. (2002), 'Decentralized Budgeting Procedures for Public Expenditures', *Public Finance Review*, vol. 30, pp. 273–95.

Lerner, Abba P. (1948), 'The Burden of the National Debt,' in Lloyd A. Metzler et al. (Eds), *Income, Employment and Public Policy*, New York: W. W. Norton and Company, pp. 255–75.

Little, I. M. D. and Vijay Joshi. (1996), *India's Economic Reforms 1991–2001*, Delhi: Oxford University Press.

McKinnon, Ronald L. (1997), 'Market Preserving Fiscal Federalism in the American Monetary Union', in Mario Blejer and Teresa Ter-Minassian (Eds), *Macroeconomic*

Dimensions of Public Finance: Essays in Honor of Vito Tanzi, London and New York: Routledge, pp. 73–93.

Milgrom, Paul and John Roberts. (1988), 'An Economic Approach to Influence Activities in Organizations', *American Journal of Sociology*, vol. 94 (Supplement), pp. S154–79.

Milka Casanegra de Jantscher. (1990), 'Administering a VAT', in M. Gillis, C. S. Shoup and G. P. Sikat (Eds), *Value Added Taxation in Developing Countries*, Washington DC: The World Bank, pp. 179–90.

Mirrlees6, James. (1971), 'An Exploration in the Theory of Optimal Income Taxation', *The Review of Economic Studies*, vol. 38, No. 2, pp. 175–208.

Musgrave, Richard M. (1959), *The Theory of Public Finance*, New York: McGraw-Hill.

Newbery, David (1987), 'Taxation and Development', in David Newbery and Nicholas Stern (Eds), *The Theory of Taxation for Developing Countries*, Oxford: Oxford University Press, pp. 163–204.

NIPFP. (1993), *The Ninth Finance Commission: Issues and Recommendations*, New Delhi: National Institute of Public Finance and Policy.

NIPFP. (1994), *Reform of Domestic Trade Taxes in India*, New Delhi: National Institute of Public Finance and Policy.

Oates, W. E. (1968), 'The Theory of Public Finance in Federal System', *Canadian Journal of Economics*, vol. 1, No. 1, pp. 37–54.

Oates, W. E. (1969), 'Effect of Property Taxes and Local Public Spending on Property Value: An Empirical Study of Tax capitalization and Tiebout Hypothesis', *Journal of Political Economy*, vol. 77, pp. 957–71.

Oates, W. E. (1972), *Fiscal Federalism*, New York: Harcourt, Brace and Jovanovich.

Oates, W. E. (1977), 'An Economist's Perspective on Fiscal Federalism', in W. Pates (Eds), *The Political Economy of Fiscal Federalism*, Lexington, MA: Lexington Books, pp. 3–20.

Oates, W. E. (1999), 'An Essay on Fiscal Federalism', *Journal of Economic Literature*, vol. XXXVII (September), pp. 1120–49.

Oates, W. E. (2005), 'Toward a Second-Generation Theory of Fiscal Federalism', *International Tax and Public Finance*, vol. 12, pp. 349–73.

OECD. (2013), 'OECD Principles for Independent Fiscal Institutions', Public Governance Committee; Public Governance and Territorial Development Directorate, Paris: OECD.

Olson, Mancur. (1965), *The Logic of Collective Action: Public Goods and the Theory of Group*, New Haven: Yale University Press.

Olson, Mancur. (1993), 'Dictatorship, Democracy and Development', *The American Political Science Review*, vol. 87, No. 3, pp. 567–76.

Ostrom, E. (1985), 'Are Successful Efforts to Manage Common-Pool Resources a Challenge to the Theories of Garrett Hardin and Mancur Olson?', Working paper W85-31, Workshop in Political Theory and Policy Analysis, Indiana University.

Panagariya, Arvind. (2020), *India Unlimited: Reclaiming the Lost Glory*, New Delhi: Harper Collins Publishers.

Panagariya, Arvind, Pinaki Chakroborty, and M. Govinda Rao. (2014), *State Level Reforms: Growth and Development in Indian States*, New York: Oxford University Press.

Patel, Urjit. (2020), *Overdraft—Saving the Indian Saver*, Noida: Harper Business.

Patnaik, Ila and Ajay Shah. (2011), *Do Multinationals Pay Lower Taxes?* (mimeo), New Delhi: National Institute of Public Finance and Policy.

Peacock, Alan and Jack Wiseman. (1961), *The Growth of Public Expenditure in the United Kingdom*, Princeton: Princeton University Press.

Pechman, Joseph A. (1985), *Who Bears the Tax Burden?* Washington, DC: The Brookings Institution.

Petr, Janský and Alex Prats. (2013), 'Multinational Corporations and the Profit Shifting Lure of Tax Havens', Christian Aid Occasional Paper No. 9. (March). https://www.christianaid.org.uk/sites/default/files/2017-08/multinational-corporations-profit-sharing-lure-tax-havens-march-2013.pdf.

Piggott, Johen and John Whalley. (2001), 'VAT Base Broadening, Self Supply and the Informal Sector', *American Economic Review*, vol. 91, pp. 1084–94.

Prud'homme, Rémy. (1995), 'The Dangers of Decentralization', *World Bank Research Observer*, vol. 10, pp. 201–20.

Ramsey, Frank P. (1927), 'A Contribution to the Theory of Taxation', *The Economic Journal*, vol. 37, No. 1, pp. 47–61.

Rangarajan, C. and D. K. Srivastava. (2020), 'India's Growth Prospects and Policy Options Emerging from the Pandemic's Shadow', *Indian Public Policy Review*, vol. I, No. 1, pp. 1–18.

Rao, M. Govinda. (1997), 'Invisible Transfers in Indian Federalism', *Public Finance/Finances Publiques*, vol. 52, Nos. 3–4, pp. 429–48.

Rao, M. Govinda. (2000), 'Tax Reforms in India: Achievements and Challenges', *Asia-Pacific Development Journal*, vol. 7, No. 2, December 2000, pp. 59–74.

Rao, M. Govinda. (2002), 'Poverty Alleviation Under Fiscal decentralization', in M. Govinda Rao (Ed), *Development, Poverty and Fiscal Policy*, New Delhi: Oxford University Press, pp. 278–98.

Rao, M. Govinda. (2006), 'Fiscal Federalism in Planned Economies', in Ehtisham Ahmad and Georgio Brosio (Eds), *Handbook of Fiscal Federalism*, Cheltenham, UK: Edward Elgar Publishers, pp. 224–39.

Rao, M. Govinda. (2011), 'Goods and Services Tax: Is It a Gorilla, Chimpanzee or a Genus Like Primate?', *Economic and Political Weekly*, vol. XlVI, No. 7 (February 12), pp. 43–8.

Rao, M. Govinda. (2014), 'Public Finance: Development, Equity and Political Economy', in Bimal Jalan and Pulapre Balakrishnan (Eds), *Politics Trumps Economics*, New Delhi: Rupa Publications India Private Ltd, pp. 170–86.

Rao, M. Govinda. (2015–2016), 'Tyranny of Status Quo: Challenges of Reforming the Indian Tax System', *India Policy Forum*, vol. 12. pp. 47–103.

Rao, M. Govinda. (2018), 'Public Finance in India: Some Reflections', *Decision*, vol. 45, No. 2, pp. 113–27.

Rao, M. Govinda. (2020), 'Evolving Landscape of Indian Fiscal Federalism and Institutional Challenges: Reinventing the Role of the Finance Commission', in Sudha Pai (Ed), *Constitutional and Democratic Institutions in India* (Chapter 16), Hyderabad: Orient Blackswan, pp. 400–20.

Rao, M. Govinda. (2020), 'India Does Need a Fiscal Council', *The Hindu*, August 25. https://www.thehindu.com/opinion/lead/india-does-need-a-fiscal-council/article32432565.ece.

Rao, M. Govinda and Mita Chaudhury. (2012), 'Healthcare Financing Reform in India's Decentralized Healthcare System', in Benedict Clements, David Cody and Sanjeev Gupta (Eds), *The Economics of Public Health Care Reform in Advanced and Emerging Economies*, International Monetary Fund, pp. 283–306.

Rao, M. Govinda and Chelliah Raja J. (1996), *Fiscal Federalism in India*, Research in Economics Monograph 8, New Delhi: Indian Council of Social Science Research.

Rao, M. Govinda and R. Kavita Rao. (2005), 'Trends and Issues in Tax Policy and Reforms in India', *India Policy Forum*, vol. 2, pp. 55–123.

Rao, M. Govinda and Kavita Rao. (2010), 'Tax System Reform in India', in Roger Gordon (Ed), *Taxation in Developing Countries*, New York: Columbia University Press, pp. 109–52.

Rao, M. Govinda and U.A. Vasanth Rao. (2008), 'Expanding the Resource Base of Panchayats: Augmenting Own Revenues', *Economic and Political Weekly*, vol. 45, No. 4.

Rao, M. Govinda and Nirvikar Singh. (2005), *Political Economy of Federalism in India*, New Delhi: Oxford University Press.

Rao, M. Govinda and Subrata Mandal. (2009), 'Resource Endowment, Fiscal Flows, and Regional Equity in Indian Federalism', in Rao M. Govinda and Anwar Shah (Eds), *States' Fiscal Management and Regional Equity*, New Delhi: Oxford University Press, pp. 171–86.

Rao, M. Govinda and Sudhanshu Kumar. (2018), 'Envisioning Tax Policy for Accelerated Development of India', *Asia Pacific Journal of Sustainable Development*, vol. 2018, No. 1, pp. 85–107.

Rao, M. Govinda and Tapas K. Sen. (1996), *Fiscal Federalism in India—Theory and Practice*, New Delhi: Macmillan India.

Rao, Kavita and Sengupta, D. P. (2014), 'Action Plan on Base Erosion and Profit Shifting: An Indian Perspective', NIPFP Working Paper 2014-133. http://www.nipfp.org.in/publications/one-pagers/action-plan-base-erosion-and-profit-shifting-indian-perspective/.

Reddy, Y. V. and G. R. Reddy. (2019), *Indian Fiscal Federalism*, New Delhi: Oxford University Press.

Reserve Bank of India. (2016), *State Finances: A Study of Budgets 2015–16*, Mumbai, India: Reserve Bank of India.

Riker, W. (1964), *Federalism: Origins, Operation, Significance*, Boston: Little, Brown.

Rodden, Jonathan, Gunner Eskeland and Jennie Litvack. (2003), *Decentralization and Hard Budget Constraints*, Cambridge, MA: MIT Press.

Salmon, Pierre. (2006), 'Horizontal Competition among Governments', in Ehtisham Ahmad and Georgio Brosio (Eds), *Handbook of Fiscal Federalism*, Cheltenham, UK: Edward Elgar, pp. 61–85.

Scott, A. (1950), 'A Note on Grants in Federal Countries', *Economica*, vol. 17, pp. 416–22.

Scott, A. (1964), 'Economic Goals of Federal Finance', *Public Finance/Finances Publiques*, vol. 13, No. 3, pp. 241–88.

Seabright, P. (1996), 'Accountability and Decentralization in Government: An Incomplete Contracts Model', *European Economic Review*, vol. 40, pp. 61–89.

Slemrod, Joel and Christian Gillitzer. (2014), *Tax Systems*, Boston, MA: MIT Press.

Tamil Nadu. (1971), 'Centre-State Relations Enquiry Committee' (Chairman: P. V. Rajamannar), Madras: Government of Tamil Nadu.

Tanzi, Vito. (2001), 'Pitfalls on the Road to Fiscal Decentralization', in Ehtisham Ahmad and Vito Tanzi (Eds), *Managing Fiscal Decentralization*, London and New York: Routledge, pp. 17–30.

Tiebout, Charles M. (1956), 'A Pure Theory of Local Expenditures', *Journal of Political Economy*, vol. 64, pp. 416–24.

Tommasi, M. (2003), 'Centralization versus Decentralization: A Principal Agent Analysis', *Journal of Public Economic Theory*, vol. 9, No. 2, pp. 369–89.

Varsano, Ricardo. (2000), 'Subnational Taxation and Treatment of Interstate Trade in Brazil: Problems and a Proposed Solution', in Javed Burki and Guillermo Perry (Eds), *Decentralization and Accountability of the Public Sector*, Washington, DC: The World Bank, pp. 339–55.

Von Hagen, J. (2010), 'The Scope and Limits of Fiscal Councils', Paper presented at the Conference on Independent Fiscal Councils, Budapest, March 18–19.

Watts, Ronald. (1996), *Comparing Federal Systems in the 1990s*, Kingston: Institute of Intergovernmental Relations, Queen's University.

Weingast, Barry R. (2009), 'Second Generation Fiscal Federalism: The Implications of Fiscal Incentives', *Journal of Urban Economics*, vol. 65, pp. 279–93.

Wheare, Kenneth. (1964), *Federal Government* (Fourth Edition), London: Oxford University Press.

Index

9 780192 849601